Bib
1

EVALUATING THE CHURCH GROWTH MOVEMENT

Books in the Counterpoints Series

Church Life

Exploring Theology

EVALUATING THE CHURCH GROWTH MOVEMENT

5 VIEWS

- Elmer Towns
- Craig Van Gelder
- Charles Van Engen
- Gailyn Van Rheenen
- Howard Snyder

- **Paul E. Engle** *series editor*
- **Gary L. McIntosh** *general editor*

ZONDERVAN.com/
AUTHORTRACKER
follow your favorite authors

▌ZONDERVAN®

Evaluating the Church Growth Movement
Copyright © 2004 by Gary L. McIntosh

Requests for information should be addressed to:
Zondervan, *Grand Rapids, Michigan 49530*

Library of Congress Cataloging-in-Publication Data

Evaluating the church growth movement : five views / contributors,
    Elmer Towns ... [et al.] ; Gary L. McIntosh, general editor.
       p. cm. — (Counterpoints)
    Includes bibliographical references and index.
    ISBN 0-310-24110-3
    1. Church growth. I. Towns, Elmer L. II. McIntosh, Gary, 1947–
III. Counterpoints (Grand Rapids, Mich.)
BV652.25.E93 2004
254'.5—dc22

2004008616

Printed in the United States of America

CONTENTS

WHY CHURCH GROWTH CAN'T BE IGNORED

Gary L. McIntosh

When you hear the term *church growth*, what words or phrases come to mind? You may think of megachurches, small groups, numbers, contemporary worship, marketing, or a host of other concepts that have occasionally been promoted as popular church-growth theory.

In contrast, you may identify the term *church growth* with effective evangelism, church planting, church extension, making disciples, church multiplication, or other aspects of outreach that seek to win people to Christ and enlist them as responsible members of his church.

These differing perceptions of the term *church growth*, and the emotions that arise from them, clearly point to misunderstanding and disagreement regarding the term, as well as the movement. Church growth is one of those ideas that cause us to draw lines in the sand. We are either for an emphasis on church growth or against it. There seems to be little neutral ground. Donald McGavran, the father of the modern Church Growth movement, recognized early on the divisive nature of Church Growth thought in a letter to his wife, written from Costa Rica on September 8, 1961: "It is clear that emphasizing the growth of the churches divides the camp. It is really a divisive topic. How strange when all are presumably disciples of the Lord Jesus Christ."[1] Dr. McGavran's words still ring true today. Church Growth continues to divide the camp, as the five viewpoints expressed in this book will demonstrate.

SIGNIFICANT CONTRIBUTIONS

There is agreement, however, among Church Growth critics and adherents alike that the Church Growth movement has made significant contributions to the mission of the church, contributions that cannot be ignored. For instance, one early critic of the movement believes its major contribution is in "clarifying of the mission of the church and focusing mission activity on the responsive."[2] Other critics add that the movement has provided a "strategy and a set of priorities for mission";[3] "a militant, optimistic, and forward-looking approach to the missionary enterprise";[4] and a way to "make us all aware of peoplehood and its human diversity as a tool in world evangelization."[5] Another critic suggests two major theological contributions of the Church Growth movement: "The first contribution is the theological clarification that the growth of the Church is not something that should be simply an overflow of the life of the Church. Rather, growth must be something that is *intentional* and embraced at the *purpose level* of the Church. [The] second contribution is the clarification and development of the Church's understanding of the leadership qualities and characteristics necessary to catalyze and mobilize a group of Christians."[6]

Advocates of Church Growth thought suggest that the movement has contributed even more to the advancement of Christ's mission in the world. One Church Growth advocate writes, "The Church Growth Movement emerged in the service of a powerful theological vision: to fulfill the ancient promise to Abraham, and to fulfill Christ's Great Commission, by reaching the lost people, and peoples, of the earth."[7] He then lists twenty specific contributions from the Church Growth school that have impacted church ministry, particularly evangelism. For example, the first five major contributions can be described as networks, receptivity, indigenous forms, new units, and people groups. Church Growth has taught us:

1. The gospel spreads most contagiously, not between strangers, nor by mass evangelism, nor through mass media, but along the lines of the kinship and friendship *networks* of credible Christians, especially new Christians.
2. The gospel spreads more easily to persons and peoples who are in a *receptive* season of their lives, and Church

Growth research has discovered many indicators of likely receptive people.
3. The gospel spreads more naturally among a people through their language, and the *indigenous* forms of their culture, than through alien languages or cultural forms.
4. "First generation" groups, classes, choirs, congregations, churches, and ministries, and other *new units*, are more reproductive than old established units.
5. Apostolic ministry is more effective when we target *people groups* than when we target political units or geographical areas.[8]

While critics and adherents will no doubt continue to debate the specific contributions of the Church Growth movement, most would agree that the "church-growth movement is extraordinarily influential and significant within American churches today. At its best, it should be applauded. Where it is not at its best, it requires criticism so that it might be."[9]

A simple way to summarize the current views on Church Growth is as follows: Some people love it. Others dislike it. Many simply misunderstand it. Understanding Church Growth, of course, is more complex than such a simplistic summary, which is why this book has been written. To make certain we all begin on the same page, it will be helpful to look at a brief historical sketch of the Church Growth movement, particularly as it has developed in North America.

BRIEF HISTORY

Church growth has occurred throughout the Christian era, of course, and is not really new or modern. Even contemporary Church Growth thought had a precursor, in the thought of the Dutch missiologist Gisbertus Voetius (1589–1676). Voetius believed that the "first goal of mission is the conversion of the heathen; the second, the planting of churches; and the highest, the glory of God."[10] These three goals comprise a condensed version of today's Church Growth movement. The particular expression of Church Growth theory and theology under discussion in this book, however, first crystallized in the mind of Donald A. McGavran, during the years 1930 to 1955.

EARLY INFLUENCES IN INDIA

Donald Anderson McGavran was born in Damoh, India, on December 15, 1897. MacGavran was a third-generation missionary; by 1954, his family had served a total of 279 years in India.[11] He attended Butler University (B.A., 1920), Yale Divinity School (B.D., 1922), the former College of Mission in Indianapolis (M.A., 1923), and following two terms in India, Columbia University (Ph.D., 1936).[12]

When Donald McGavran went to India as a missionary in 1923, he worked primarily as an educator under appointment of the United Christian Missionary Society of the Christian Church (Disciples of Christ). In 1929, he became director of religious education for his mission before returning to the United States to work on his Ph.D. at Columbia University. After his return to India, he was elected field secretary in 1932 and was placed in charge of administering the denomination's entire India mission.

During the late 1920s and early 1930s, the stirrings of what would eventually become Church Growth thought began to develop in McGavran's mind. Several forerunners contributed to McGavran's developing insights, such as William Carey, Roland Allen, and Kenneth Scott Latourette. The most direct influence, however, was J. Waskom Pickett, of whom McGavran was fond of saying, "I lit my candle at Pickett's fire."[13]

Pickett and McGavran were both influenced by the ministry of John R. Mott and the student volunteer movement. In 1886, Dwight L. Moody led a missionary awakening at Mount Hermon, Massachusetts, which resulted in one hundred students dedicating themselves to missionary service and the founding of the student volunteer movement. The slogan "The evangelization of the world in this generation" became a watchword for missions during the first two decades of the twentieth century. As a senior at Butler University, McGavran attended the student volunteer convention at Des Moines, Iowa, during the Christmas season of 1919. Describing that event, he wrote, "There it became clear to me that God was calling me to be a missionary, that he was commanding me to carry out the Great Commission. Doing just that has ever since been the ruling purpose of my life. True, I have from time to time swerved from that purpose but never for long. That decision lies at the root of the church-growth movement."[14]

Pickett served in India for forty-six years as pastor, editor, publisher, secretary of Christian councils, and bishop in the Methodist Church. Reflecting how John R. Mott influenced him to look for results, he writes, "Acting on advice given to me by the great missionary statesman, John R. Mott, I had determined to challenge every assumption that I could recognize as underlying the work of my Church in India, not to prove any of them wrong, but to find out, if I could, whether they seemed to be right or wrong as indicated by their results."[15]

In 1928, Pickett was asked by the National Christian Council of India, Burma, and Ceylon to make an extensive study of Christian mass movements in India. The study required the development of research instruments, testing, and study of ten representative areas. The results were published in *Christian Mass Movements in India*.[16]

McGavran read Pickett's book, enthusiastically endorsed it, and recommended to his mission headquarters in Indianapolis, Indiana, that they employ the services of Pickett to study why similar mass movements to Christ were not happening in their ministry area of mid-India. As supervisor of eighty missionaries, five hospitals, several high schools and primary schools, evangelistic efforts, and a leprosy home, McGavran had become deeply concerned that after several decades of work, his mission had only about thirty small churches, all of which were experiencing little growth. At the same time, he saw "people movements" taking place in scattered areas of India, in which thousands of people in groups, rather than as individuals, were coming to Christ. He wondered why his denomination's churches were growing at the rate of only 1 percent a year, while other churches were seeing much higher rates of conversions to Christ. Pickett was appointed to do the study; McGavran assisted him and became the chief architect of the study in Madhya Pradesh. The results of the study were published under the title *Christian Missions in Mid-India*, which was later revised to *Church Growth and Group Conversion*.[17]

Through this study, McGavran discovered that of the 145 areas where mission activity was taking place, 134 areas had grown only 11 percent between 1921 and 1931. The churches in those areas were not even conserving their own children in the faith. Yet in the other 11 areas, the church was growing by 100 percent, 150 percent, and even 200 percent a decade. A curiosity arose within McGavran that was to occupy his life and ministry until his death. He wondered why some churches were growing, while others, often just a few miles away, were not. He eventually identified four major questions that were to drive the Church Growth movement:

1. What are the *causes* of church growth?
2. What are the *barriers* to church growth?
3. What are the factors that can make the Christian faith a *movement* among some populations?
4. What *principles* of church growth are reproducible?[18]

During this same time period, McGavran was quietly changing his view of mission and theology. In the formative years of his childhood, mission was held to be carrying out the Great Commission, winning the world for Christ, and saving lost humanity. This was the view McGavran held when he returned to the United States for his higher education. While attending Yale Divinity School, McGavran was introduced to the teachings of the influential Christian professor H. Richard Niebuhr. According to McGavran, Niebuhr "used to say that mission was everything the church does outside its four walls. It was philanthropy, education, medicine, famine relief, evangelism, and world friendship."[19] McGavran espoused this liberal view of mission when he went to the mission field in 1923. As he became involved in education, social work, and evangelism in the real world of India, however, he gradually reverted to the classical view that mission was making disciples of Jesus Christ. Commenting on this change, he wrote, "As my convictions about mission and church growth were being molded in the 1930s and 40s they ran headlong into the thrust that mission is doing many good things in addition to evangelism. I could not accept this way of thinking about missions. These good deeds must, of course, be done, and Christians will do them. I myself was doing many of them. But they must never replace the essential task of mission, discipling the peoples of earth."[20]

As McGavran's theological views turned more conservative, and his studies of church growth increased, he began to fervently encourage his mission and fellow workers to engage in direct evangelism. When his three-year term as mission secretary was up in 1936, he was not reelected. According to McGavran, in effect the mission said to him, "Since you are talking so much about evangelism and church growth, we are going to locate you in a district where you can practice what you preach."[21] It was clearly a demotion, as evangelists worked with the poorly educated and illiterate people. Believing that it was God's leading, however, McGavran accepted his new appointment and spent the next seventeen years trying to start a people movement to Christ among the Satnamis caste. He felt his work was somewhat successful, but no people movement resulted. About one thousand people were won to Christ, fifteen small, village churches were planted, and the Gospels were translated into Chattisgarhee. These years brought about the formation of his Church Growth theory out of the hard realities of missionary service. He was no ivory-tower theoretician!

FOUNDING A MOVEMENT

With his work among the Satnamis coming to a close, McGavran took a vacation in 1951 in the hills north of Takhatpur to begin writing a manuscript titled "How Peoples Become Christian." McGavran hunted for one hour each morning and evening and spent the time in between working on his manuscript. In addition to his own ministry among the Satnamis, McGavran had done on-the-spot studies of growing churches and people movements in several provinces of India for several denominations, and he was eager to share his discoveries with others. The rough draft was completed in 1953, but McGavran thought it was too strictly Indian. During the summer of 1954, the McGavran family went to the United States on furlough. His mission granted a request to route his travel home through Africa so that he could study people movements on that continent. In seven nations, he saw twenty missions and hundreds of churches. As a result, he rewrote sections of his book, and it was eventually published in 1955 under the title *The Bridges of God*.[22] This book has been labeled the Magna Carta of the Church Growth movement. It became the most widely read book on mission theory in 1956 and has played a determinative role in Church Growth thinking ever since.

After arriving in the United States for his furlough, McGavran went directly to Yale University, where he had been granted a research fellowship. He used the time to continue his research and to begin writing a new book. Following the furlough, McGavran intended to return to India, but his mission board was intrigued by his discoveries about church growth and sent him to various parts of the world to research the growth of churches in other countries. This research added considerably to his understanding, and in 1959 he published *How Churches Grow*.[23]

A number of key elements then began to bring the Church Growth movement into prominence. In 1958, McGavran resigned from his mission society to found an institution through which he could teach his newly discovered Church Growth theories. Since he was sixty years old, it was a risky move, but one he believed God desired him to take. Three seminaries turned down his proposals for a Church Growth institute, but eventually an offer came from an undergraduate college in Eugene, Oregon. The northwest corner of the United States was not the most promising place to begin an interdenominational institute of Church Growth, but he seized the opportunity with both hands, particularly since it was the only offer. On January 2, 1961, the Institute of Church Growth at Northwest Christian College opened with one lone student. Over the next four years, fifty-seven missionaries studied at the institute while on furlough. God was at work behind the scenes, preparing McGavran for even larger influence around the world. The years at Northwest Christian College gave him the opportunity to develop case studies of growing churches, refine lectures, develop reading lists, and lead Church Growth conferences. The years in Eugene provided sort of an experimental workshop that enabled McGavran and his students to refine research methodology and clarify basic terminology, as well as publish early Church Growth studies from around the world.

In 1961, the Evangelical Foreign Missions Association invited McGavran to speak at its September meeting in Winona Lake, Indiana. This meeting developed into an annual conference that touched over a thousand missionaries and had a pronounced effect on Church Growth thinking throughout the world. Other seminars on church growth were held on the campus of the Alliance School of Missions in Nyack, New York, and on the campus of Biola College in La Mirada, California. Along with the seminars and conferences came the publication of the *Church Growth Bulletin* (first circulated in 1964), a sixteen-page bimonthly periodical published by Overseas Crusades, Inc.

The next key event occurred when David Hubbard, president of Fuller Theological Seminary, invited McGavran to become the founding dean of a third graduate school—the School of World Mission—in September 1965. McGavran accepted the invitation and emerged from semiretirement at age sixty-seven to begin a second career. The school opened with fifteen graduate students but grew over the years to become one of the most influential schools of missiology in the world. In his role as dean, McGavran's understanding of church growth continued to expand as he collaborated with colleagues like Alan Tippett, J. Edwin Orr, Charles H. Kraft, Ralph Winter, Peter Wagner, and Arthur Glasser. Along with these leaders, a significant vehicle for communicating Church Growth thinking was the William Carey Library, a publishing house devoted to producing books about Great Commission missions. McGavran's continued travels and research eventually resulted in the publication of *Understanding Church Growth* in 1970, which is considered as his magnum opus.[24] It also played a major role in preparing the United States for the burgeoning Church Growth movement.

As McGavran saw it, "Christian mission is bringing people to repent of their sins, accept Jesus Christ as Savior, belong to His Body the Church, do as He commands, go out and spread the Good News, and multiply churches."[25] He believed that evangelism had been confused with numerous good things, such as education, catechism classes, medical relief, and social programs. McGavran felt that while all good works are necessary and helpful, they are not evangelism. Evangelism, he said, was an *input term* meaning that the lost should be won to Christ and then baptized and brought into the church. The result was an *output term:* Church Growth! As coined by McGavran, Church Growth is simply the expected result of being obedient to the Great Commission. Church Growth was, and is, effective evangelism.

THE CORE OF CHURCH GROWTH PRINCIPLES

The essential Church Growth principles, as developed by Donald McGavran, can be summarized in three statements. The first essential principle is to realize that God wants his lost children found and enfolded. Church growth explodes from the life-giving nature of the eternal God. Jesus Christ gave his disciples the Great Commission, and the entire New Testament assumes that Christians will proclaim Jesus Christ as God and Savior and encourage men and women to become his disciples and responsible members of his church.

Discovering the facts of church growth is the second essential principle of Church Growth thinking. Responsible research into the causes and barriers to church growth must be conducted. God has given us the Great Commission, and we dare not assume that all is going well or that we are doing the best that can be done. The Lord of the harvest wants his lost sheep found, and we must be accountable to his command. Discovering the degree of growth or decline and stating such facts meaningfully is crucial to faithful ministry.

The third essential principle is developing specific plans based on the facts that are discovered. Taking the initiative to set goals and develop bold strategies to win people to Christ and to plant new churches must be the practical results of meaningful conviction and research. These three essential principles form the core of Church Growth thought, although several other principles were developed in conjunction with these three essentials.[26]

CHURCH GROWTH IN THE UNITED STATES

When McGavran became dean of the Fuller School of World Mission, he set up entrance requirements that excluded pastors from North America. As a career missionary, his primary concern was international missions, and he desired to share his insights with those who would take the gospel to people who had never heard of Jesus Christ. Thus, the entrance requirements of the School of World Mission included three years of cross-cultural experience, validated by fluency in a second language, which effectively excluded most church leaders in North America.

Pastors in North America, however, began to hear about the fresh insights coming from the new Church Growth school and encouraged Peter Wagner, who taught at Fuller, to apply Church Growth ideas to the American church. Wagner had already considered developing such a class after coming to Fuller full-time in 1971, and in 1972, he and McGavran taught a pilot class in Church Growth for pastors and denominational leaders from

North America. The class became the springboard for the American Church Growth movement.

One student, Win Arn, resigned his executive position with the Evangelical Covenant Church to found the Institute for American Church Growth (now Church Growth, Inc.) in 1972, with McGavran as chairman of the board. One of the pioneers of the Church Growth movement in the United States, Arn is the producer of numerous films, videos, and self-study kits and the author or coauthor of fourteen books. His institute promoted Church Growth through seminars, workshops, pastor's conferences, films, and the first magazine devoted to American Church Growth, *Church Growth, America* (later titled the *Win Arn Growth Report*). In 1973, McGavran and Arn coauthored *How to Grow a Church*, a pioneering book in applying Church Growth insights to North American churches.[27]

A few years later, Peter Wagner wrote *Your Church Can Grow*, which became one of the most influential books in spreading Church Growth thought in North America.[28] Wagner, who was chief executive officer of the Fuller Evangelistic Association, asked John Wimber to pioneer the Charles E. Fuller Institute for Evangelism and Church Growth. Wimber organized the Fuller Institute as a Church Growth consulting firm and then left in 1978 to plant a church in Yorba Linda, California. Carl George, who has become well known for the metachurch concept of church ministry, led the Fuller Institute from 1978 until its closure in 1995.

Two other developments helped Church Growth thought spread rapidly in North America: the Fuller doctor of ministry program and the American Society for Church Growth. Fuller's School of Theology started offering the doctor of ministry program in 1975. Peter Wagner was chosen from the School of World Mission faculty to contribute courses to the program. Quite naturally, Wagner offered courses on Church Growth. As the word spread that a degree in Church Growth studies was available to church leaders within North America, Wagner's courses became the major draw for students applying for the program. Over the years, several leaders earned doctor of ministry degrees in Church Growth from Fuller Seminary and went on to found ministry organizations to disseminate Church Growth training, consulting, and materials. Among those who received doctor of ministry degrees from Fuller Seminary and became leaders in the Church Growth movement are Elmer

Towns, Kent Hunter, John Vaughan, John Maxwell, Rick Warren, Bob Logan, Bill Sullivan, Leith Anderson, Paul Ford, and Eddie Gibbs. By 1985, over 1,150 American clergy had been trained in Church Growth through the Fuller doctor of ministry program.[29]

The last element that brought Church Growth to prominence in North America was the establishment of academic credibility and permanence. This was achieved through two actions. The red-letter day for the Church Growth movement was November 4, 1984, when Peter Wagner was installed as the first incumbent of the Donald A. McGavran Chair of Church Growth at Fuller Seminary's School of World Mission. An endowed Chair of Church Growth signaled the academic validity of the movement as a member of the academy. The following year saw the establishment of the American Society for Church Growth as an academic society networking professors, pastors, consultants, and denominational executives for study and promotion of Church Growth. The rotating presidency of the American Society for Church Growth has included prominent Church Growth leaders such as George Hunter III, Charles Van Engen, Charles Arn, and several of the Church Growth leaders mentioned previously. The society publishes the *Journal of the American Society for Church Growth* three times a year and hosts a yearly conference each November.[30]

By 1985, the classical Church Growth movement, with direct roots to McGavran, was represented by two major prongs (see figure 1). One prong focused on international missiology as designed and taught by McGavran and his contemporaries at the Institute for Church Growth at Northwest Christian College in Eugene, Oregon, the School of World Mission at Fuller Seminary, and the schools of missiology that developed from them. Two significant organizations that flow directly from the international stream of Church Growth are the U.S. Center for World Mission and Discipling a Whole Nation (DAWN). Ralph Winter built on the people movement principle to found the U.S. Center for World Mission to help reach "hidden" or "unreached" peoples of the world, and Jim Montgomery founded DAWN with an emphasis on reaching the receptive peoples of the world.

The second prong focused on North American missiology, as best represented by the Institute for American Church Growth (Win Arn), the Charles E. Fuller Institute for Evangelism and

Church Growth (Wagner, Wimber, and George), and the Fuller Seminary doctor of ministry program (and the numerous centers and institutes of Church Growth founded by graduates of these programs).

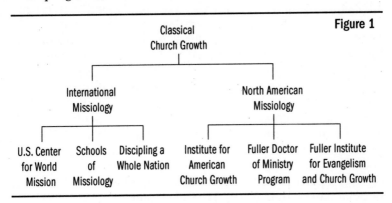

Figure 1

Classical Church Growth
- International Missiology
  - U.S. Center for World Mission
  - Schools of Missiology
  - Discipling a Whole Nation
- North American Missiology
  - Institute for American Church Growth
  - Fuller Doctor of Ministry Program
  - Fuller Institute for Evangelism and Church Growth

At the same time that classical Church Growth in the McGavran form was growing, a parallel popular Church Growth prong was also forming (see figure 2).

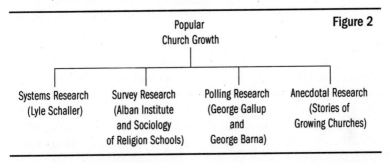

Figure 2

Popular Church Growth
- Systems Research (Lyle Schaller)
- Survey Research (Alban Institute and Sociology of Religion Schools)
- Polling Research (George Gallup and George Barna)
- Anecdotal Research (Stories of Growing Churches)

The decline of churches in the 1960s, primarily mainline churches, sparked a renewed interest in research to help turn around struggling churches. Much of this research, though helpful, did not flow directly from the Church Growth school as developed by McGavran, but it was often labeled as Church Growth in a popular sense since the research sought to help churches grow. As a trained city planner, Lyle Schaller uses his skills to study church systems. George Gallup and George Barna use their training to poll the attitudes and practices of churches and people within the United States. The Alban Institute, as well as several Sociology of Religion Schools in secular universities, conducts various surveys each year. Pastors of growing churches write books sharing their anecdotal success stories with others. All of these streams of research have come together to form a popular form of Church Growth lore that is not technically Church Growth thought as devised by McGavran and his followers. Unfortunately, while all of this research is helpful to some degree in growing churches, it has created confusion regarding the true nature of Church Growth. For example, since the publication of George Barna's book *Marketing the Church* in 1988, it has been popular to identify Church Growth as simply a methodology for marketing churches.[31] While classical McGavran Church Growth thought allows for marketing the church as one response to evangelizing responsive people groups, church marketing is actually more directly related to the popular stream than to the classical stream.

CHURCH GROWTH TODAY

The 1990s found the Church Growth movement going through a number of transitions that seemed to undermine the technical understanding of church growth as developed by McGavran. For most of the first forty years of the Church Growth movement, the key spokesperson was Donald McGavran. He was the soul of the movement; he personified its values, epitomized its strength, and motivated its followers. Upon McGavran's death in 1990, the task of promoting the Church Growth movement fell to Peter Wagner, who began to steer the movement toward spiritual factors, notably prayer and spiritual warfare. Since Wagner's retirement from the McGavran Chair of Church Growth in 1999, the movement has been without a clear spokesperson within the United States. A number of individuals have taken up the Church Growth banner in different denominations and associations, but none has found the platform that McGavran or Wagner enjoyed. Without a clear, focused, singular voice for the Church Growth movement, a number of voices have been heard that are driven more by popular notions of Church Growth than by a root understanding of the Church Growth movement.

The downsizing of Win Arn's Church Growth, Inc. (formerly the Institute for American Church Growth), and the closure of the Fuller Institute for Evangelism and Church Growth in 1995 left the Church Growth movement without its two primary communicators of Church Growth training, materials, and conferences in the United States. A number of smaller ministries and organizations still promote Church Growth in its classical form, but none has the visibility and reach these two ministries had in the 1970s and 1980s. Along with this has been the willingness of publishers to promote as Church Growth just about any book or product that speaks vaguely of growing a church. Many "Church Growth" promotions are offering "Church Growth" books, training, and programs without knowing the true nature of the Church Growth movement.

The diversification of Church Growth into specializations and subspecializations has led to quite a variety of ministries promoted under the label of Church Growth. For example, church planting, cell groups, prayer, spiritual warfare, generational studies, conflict management, change agency, long-range planning, leadership, fund raising, and other ministries have contributed to a misunderstanding of Church Growth. Related to this diversification is the number of organizations identified as part of the Church Growth movement. For example, one survey discovered that the following ministries were mentioned as Church Growth organizations: Campus Crusade for Christ, Renewal Magazine, Dallas Theological Seminary, Leadership Network, and Son Life.[32] Each of these ministries is certainly helpful in the cause of Christ, but they are not directly part of the Church Growth movement.

The conceptual broadening of the term *church growth* to embrace more and more subspecializations of ministry and more and more ministry organizations has created, to a large extent, a popular misunderstanding and wrongful criticism of the Church Growth movement. One critic writes, "Many people identify the church-growth movement narrowly with its specific architects and advocates—most famously, McGavran, Wagner, and the Charles E. Fuller Institute of Evangelism and Church Growth School.... But as I use the term *church growth*, these individuals and churches are part of a much wider and more important movement."[33] The criticisms presented by this individual are based in part on a broader definition of Church Growth than is warranted. Technically, Church Growth is a movement that is rooted in Donald McGavran. He forever established a paradigm, and anyone or any organization that does not accept the McGavran paradigm is not a Church Growth person or organization. As Peter Wagner noted, "Certainly, there is room for variation. No one is forced to agree with everything McGavran ever said or wrote. But if you don't accept his way of looking at the church ..., then you should use some other name because you're not part of the Church Growth Movement."[34]

As the Church Growth movement has entered the twenty-first century, McGavran's Church Growth principles have been grafted into the thinking of most North American Protestant denominations and church bodies. Church Growth principles are valued, respected, and widely taught in pastoral theology and missiology courses. Unfortunately, confusion continues to surround Church Growth, as illustrated in a best-selling book of 1997, *Fresh Wind, Fresh Fire,* by Jim Cymbala.[35] Cymbala makes critical comments in his book regarding Church Growth, but readers will discover that he is actually following many Church Growth principles, such as prayer, passionate spirituality, commitment to the authority of Scripture, and cultural relevance, in his church without even recognizing them as Church Growth principles.

Another interesting case is the recent use of the term *church health* rather than *church growth.* People in some circles have moved toward acceptance of the new terminology, and the new paradigm, of church health. The most popular church-health book is *Natural Church Development* by Christian Schwartz.[36] The author positions his book as anti–Church Growth but then goes on to present findings from what is reported to be the largest study of churches ever completed. To readers versed in Church Growth literature, Schwartz's eight essential qualities of healthy churches are simply affirmations of previous Church Growth findings presented in the 1970s and 1980s. One reviewer writes, "In my opinion, if church leaders embrace natural church development, they've adopted the heart of Donald McGavran's church growth thinking."[37] Oddly, most pastors and denominational leaders who have embraced Natural Church Development feel they have rejected Church Growth thinking and adopted church-health thinking. Church Growth principles have become so deeply imbedded that leaders do not realize they are actually using Church Growth insights!

Given the changes just described in the 1990s and early 2000s, one might rightfully ask, Is anyone interested in the Church Growth movement now that we have entered the twenty-first century? The answer is yes; there continues to be great interest in the movement. Church Growth books continue to be written and published each year, seminaries continue to teach Church Growth principles at both the master's and doctorate levels, and practitioners continue to espouse insights and principles of Church Growth throughout the United States and in most foreign countries.[38]

AN OVERVIEW OF THE FIVE VIEWPOINTS

Criticism of Church Growth is nothing new. Since the founding of the Church Growth movement, debate over the theology, theory, and principles of the movement has come and gone almost yearly. In the 1970s, the debate was over issues such as numerical growth, the validity of people movements, and the use of strategy. In the 1980s, the conversation focused on issues such as the hermeneutic of church growth, the use of communication theory and business practices, and proclamation versus persuasion. In the 1990s, the discussion was around seeker sensitivity, meeting felt needs, and marketing the church. One thing is certain: the Church Growth movement is alive and well. The debate continues.

As the Church Growth movement reaches its fiftieth year in 2005, interest and debate about the movement remains high. Like any middle-aged movement, it has its share of enthusiasts and detractors. It is time to reflect deeply on the Church Growth movement. What exactly are the major viewpoints on the Church Growth movement in the twenty-first century? What are the strengths and weaknesses of the movement? What is the direction of the movement? What will be the issues of debate in the future?

These questions will be addressed in *Evaluating the Church Growth Movement*. This book brings together five national church leaders in a major discussion and reflection on the Church Growth movement in the United States. The focus of the discussion will be the classical Church Growth perspective as developed by Donald A. McGavran and his followers. For nearly half a century, proponents and detractors of Church Growth thought have presented their viewpoints in various forums, but this is the first time both have been brought together in one book. Research has determined there are five main positions on Church Growth today: the Reformist view, the Gospel and Our Culture view, the Renewal view, the Centrist view, and the Effective Evangelism view.

The Effective Evangelism view holds that the Church Growth movement effectively confronts and penetrates the culture with the gospel. Dr. Elmer Towns is the spokesperson for this position. Elmer has written over seventy books on the subjects of church growth, evangelism, and church ministry. He is widely recognized as the author of the first Church Growth book aimed at North American churches, *The Ten Largest Sunday Schools and What Makes Them Grow*, which he followed up with *America's Fastest Growing Churches*.[39]

The Gospel and Our Culture view holds that the Church Growth movement lacks a sufficient ecclesiology, which hinders it from being able to effectively engage the culture. Dr. Craig Van Gelder is the spokesperson for this viewpoint. Craig is professor of congregational mission at Luther Seminary in St. Paul, Minnesota. He previously taught at Calvin Theological Seminary as professor of domestic missiology. He is the general editor of the Gospel and Our Culture series, published by Eerdmans, and is the editor of *Confident Witness—Changing World*.[40] He has recently written *The Essence of the Church: A Community Created by the Spirit*.[41]

The Centrist view holds that the Church Growth movement is based on an evangelistically focused and a missiologically applied theory. Dr. Charles Van Engen is the spokesperson for this viewpoint. Charles is the Arthur F. Glasser Professor of Biblical Theology of Mission in the School of Intercultural Studies at Fuller Theological Seminary. His doctoral dissertation, done at the Free University of Amsterdam, was on the ecclesiology of the Church Growth movement and was titled "The Growth of the True Church." Chuck has written numerous books, among which are *God's Missionary People: Rethinking the Purpose of the Local Church* and *Mission on the Way: Issues in Mission Theology*.[42] As a missionary, he worked in Theological Education by Extension, for pastors in Mexico.

The Reformist view holds that the Church Growth movement assumes theology but ineffectively employs it to analyze culture, determine strategy, and perceive history. Dr. Gailyn Van Rheenen is the spokesperson for this viewpoint. Gailyn served for fourteen years as a missionary in East Africa and is fluent in two African languages. He is the professor of missions at Abilene Christian University and the author of *Biblically Anchored Missions* and *Missions: Biblical Foundations and Contemporary Strategies*.[43]

The Renewal view holds that the Church Growth movement must be based on a biblical vision of the church as the vital community of the kingdom of God in order to be effective. Dr. Howard Snyder is the spokesperson for this viewpoint. Howard is professor of the History and Theology of Mission at Asbury Theological Seminary and the author of numerous books, including *The Problem of Wineskins: Church Structure in a Technological Age* and *Decoding the Church: Mapping the DNA of Christ's Body*.[44]

Each of the contributors was selected because he represents one of the key voices for his particular point of view, but also because of his personal involvement with Church Growth as a practical discipline. As with previous Counterpoints books, each writer wrote a position paper, and then the papers were circulated among the writers so each could critique the others. Except for minor editing, the chapters were not changed following the writing of the original drafts. Since this book deals with Church Growth, it was felt that having practicing pastors review the chapters and responses would provide an interesting balance to what is somewhat of an academic discussion. Thus, the following pastors also read the final manuscript and provided short reflections on the entire discussion: David Fisher has served as a pastor for thirty-four years, most recently as senior pastor of the Colonial Church in Edina, Minnesota. Roberta Hestenes serves as an international minister with World Vision. She recently pastored Solana Beach Presbyterian Church in Southern California. Douglas Webster is pastor of the first Presbyterian Church in San Diego, California.

While there were, and continue to be, significant differences of viewpoint among the writers, one point of agreement is that God wants his church to grow. Thus, this book is presented with the hope that the discussion herein will provide a balanced understanding of Church Growth and be a helpful resource for pastors and church leaders as they seek to be faithful disciplemakers for our Lord and Savior Jesus Christ.

Introduction Notes

[1]Donald A. McGavran to Mary McGavran, September 8, 1961, from Costa Rica. Collection 178: 81-1, Billy Graham Center Archives, Wheaton College, Wheaton, IL.

[2]Robertson McQuilkin, *How Biblical Is the Church Growth Movement?* (Chicago: Moody Bible Institute, 1973), 61.

[3]Wilbert R. Shenk, ed., *The Challenge of Church Growth* (Scottdale, PA: Herald, 1973), 103.

[4]Orlando E. Costas, *The Church and Its Mission* (Wheaton: Tyndale House, 1974), 124.

[5]Wilbert R. Shenk, ed., *Exploring Church Growth* (Grand Rapids: Eerdmans, 1983), 89.

[6]Walter Russell III, "Forty Years of Church Growth: A View from the Theological Tower," *Journal of the American Society for Church Growth* 6 (1995): 18.

[7]George G. Hunter III, "The Theological Roots, Vision, and Contribution of the Church Growth Movement" (paper presented at the annual meeting of the American Society for Church Growth, Indianapolis, IN, November 11–13, 1999), 1.

[8]Ibid., 2.

[9]Os Guinness, *Dining with the Devil: The Megachurch Movement Flirts with Modernity* (Grand Rapids: Baker, 1993), 24.

[10]Johannes Verkuyl, *Contemporary Missiology* (Grand Rapids: Eerdmans, 1978), 21.

[11]Donald McGavran's maternal grandparents, Mr. and Mrs. James H. Anderson, sailed from London for India in July 1854, a journey that took them around the Cape of Good Hope and lasted about six months. Baptist missionaries, they were destined for Bengal. In 1891, McGavran's father, John Grafton McGavran, twenty-four and single, sailed from the United States for India, where he would serve for the next twenty years as an evangelistic missionary and, on a personal note, marry Helen Anderson in 1892, the daughter of Mr. and Mrs. James H. Anderson. Donald McGavran credited his early missionary training and experience to the friendship and guidance of his father. For further information on McGavran's missionary heritage, see "John Grafton McGavran—Scholar, Crusader and Saint," *World Call* 13, no. 3 (March 1931): 13–14. See also "India through a Century," *World Call* 36, no. 7 (July–August 1954), 16–17.

[12]For further study regarding McGavran's career, see Donald A. McGavran, "My Pilgrimage in Mission," *International Bulletin of Missionary Research* 10, no. 2 (April 1986): 53–58. See also George G. Hunter III, "The Legacy of Donald A. McGavran," *International Bulletin of Missionary Research* 16, no. 4 (October 1992): 158–62.

[13]Hunter, "The Legacy of Donald A. McGavran," 159.

[14]McGavran, "My Pilgrimage in Mission," 53.

[15]J. Waskom Pickett, "Donald McGavran: Missionary, Scholar, Ecumenist, Evangelist," in *God, Man and Church Growth*, ed. A. R. Tippett (Grand Rapids: Eerdmans, 1973), 6.

[16]J. Waskom Pickett, *Christian Mass Movements in India* (Lucknow, India: Lucknow Publishing House, 1933).

[17]Donald A. McGavran, ed., *Church Growth and Group Conversion*, 3d ed. (Lucknow: Lucknow Publishing House, 1962). Originally published as *Christian Missions in Mid-India* (1936).

[18]Hunter, "The Legacy of Donald A. McGavran," 158.

[19]McGavran, "My Pilgrimage in Mission," 54.

[20]Ibid.

[21]Ibid., 56.

[22]Donald A. McGavran, *The Bridges of God* (New York: Friendship, 1955).

[23]Donald A. McGavran, *How Churches Grow* (London: World Dominion, 1959).

[24]Donald A. McGavran, *Understanding Church Growth* (Grand Rapids: Eerdmans, 1970).

[25]"Interview with Dr. Donald McGavran," *OMS Outreach*, no. 3 (1982): 7.

[26]Church Growth thought can be summarized in seven foundational principles: people movements, pragmatic research, scientific research, social networks, receptivity, priority of evangelism, and the central purpose of disciple-making. See Gary L. McIntosh, "The Church Growth Movement," in *Leadership Handbook of Outreach and Care*, ed. James D. Berkley (Grand Rapids: Baker, 1994), 31–41.

[27]Donald A. McGavran and Win Arn, *How to Grow a Church* (Glendale, CA: Gospel Light, 1973).

[28]C. Peter Wagner, *Your Church Can Grow: Seven Vital Signs of a Healthy Church* (Ventura: Regal, 1976, revised 1984).

[29]By 1985, the Fuller School of World Mission had over 2,700 alumni serving in almost every corner of the globe.

[30]For information on the American Society for Church Growth or the *Journal of the American Society for Church Growth*, contact the American Society for Church Growth, Center for Lifelong Learning, c/o Fuller Theological Seminary, 135 North Oakland Avenue, Pasadena, CA 91182. Phone: 1-800-999-9578. E-mail: ascg@fuller.edu. Website: www.ascg.org.

[31]George Barna, *Marketing the Church* (Colorado Springs: NavPress, 1988).

[32]Gary L. McIntosh, "Thoughts on a Movement," *Journal of the American Society for Church Growth* 8 (Winter 1997): 46–47.

[33]Os Guinness and John Seel, eds., *No God but God* (Chicago: Moody Press, 1992), 152.

[34]"We've Only Just Begun: An Interview with C. Peter Wagner," *Global Church Growth* 22, no. 1 (January–March 1985): 9.

[35]Jim Cymbala, *Fresh Wind, Fresh Fire* (Grand Rapids: Zondervan, 1997).

[36]Christian A. Schwartz, *Natural Church Development: A Guide to Eight Essential Qualities of Healthy Churches*, trans. Lynn McAdam, Lois Wollin, and Martin Wollin (Carol Stream, IL: ChurchSmart Resources, 1996).

[37]Dan Simpson, ed., "Natural Church Development," *Ministry Advantage* 7, no. 4 (Fall 1997): 12.

[38]A study I conducted of nineteen accredited seminaries in 1999 found an average of 3.6 Church Growth courses offered at the master's level and 2.4 courses at the doctoral level per school. A review of book sales on Amazon.com in 1999 revealed that Church Growth books continue to be of great interest in three major categories: pastoral ministry, evangelism, and clergy/ministry. Twenty-six percent of the top fifty books in these three categories were Church Growth books or were written by Church Growth authors. Additionally, the Billy Graham School of Missions, Evangelism, and Church Growth was established at the Southern Baptist Theological Seminary in Louisville, Kentucky, during the 1990s, with Dr. Thom Rainer, noted Church Growth author, as dean.

[39]Elmer L. Towns, *The Ten Largest Sunday Schools and What Makes Them Grow* (Grand Rapids: Baker, 1969); Towns, *America's Fastest Growing Churches* (Nashville: Impact, 1973).

[40]Craig Van Gelder, ed., *Confident Witness—Changing World: Rediscovering the Gospel in North America* (Grand Rapids: Eerdmans, 1999).

[41]Craig Van Gelder, *The Essence of the Church: A Community Created by the Spirit* (Grand Rapids: Baker, 2000).

[42]Charles Van Engen, *God's Missionary People: Rethinking the Purpose of the Local Church* (Grand Rapids: Baker, 1991); Van Engen, *Mission on the Way: Issues in Mission Theology* (Grand Rapids: Baker, 1996).

[43]Gailyn Van Rheenen, *Biblically Anchored Missions* (Austin: Firm Foundation, 1983); Van Rheenen, *Missions: Biblical Foundations and Contemporary Strategies* (Grand Rapids: Zondervan, 1996).

[44]Howard A. Snyder, *The Problem of Wineskins: Church Structure in a Technological Age* (Downers Grove: InterVarsity Press, 1975); Howard A. Snyder with Daniel V. Runyon, *Decoding the Church: Mapping the DNA of Christ's Body* (Grand Rapids: Baker, 2002).

Chapter One

EFFECTIVE EVANGELISM VIEW

EFFECTIVE EVANGELISM VIEW

Church Growth effectively confronts and penetrates the culture

Elmer Towns

Church Growth is not a title that has been used throughout church history. The Church Growth movement burst on the religious scene in the United States during the 1960s and has gone through the inevitable cycle that faces any new movement. American Christianity has gone through a cycle consisting of seven basic questions in response to the Church Growth movement:

1. a question of curiosity leading to creative insight, What's Church Growth?
2. a question of focus, What will Church Growth accomplish?
3. a question to improve an innovative idea, What's the latest Church Growth idea?
4. a question of application, Everyone is using Church Growth, why aren't you?
5. a question of unappreciative benefactors, Have you heard what's wrong with Church Growth?
6. a question of repudiation, Why do you still need Church Growth? and
7. a question of ignorance, What's Church Growth?

Today we seem to be in the seventh phase of this cycle, asking again, What is Church Growth? Looking back, however, the Church Growth movement has given so much to contemporary American Christianity that it is hard to imagine how we did ministry before the movement was introduced.

Before the Church Growth movement introduced its workable principles of outreach and evangelism, young pastors did not have adequate resources of articles, books, and published research to give them accurate direction in reaching their "Jerusalem" with the gospel. Little authoritative direction existed to give starting pastors practical help and direction for their ministry. Much of ministry was trial and error, and often those pastors that had found a successful way of doing things took their insights to the grave with them.

Before Church Growth, young pastors did not have many different models of church ministry to motivate and guide them and to hold them responsible for effective ministry. A century ago, many may have looked up to pastors such as Charles Spurgeon of the Metropolitan Baptist Church of London, D. L. Moody of the Moody Church in Chicago, and perhaps a few other pastors. But these models did not provide insight on how a smaller church could apply the same principles of growth. There were few examples of churches that attempted to "capture their town" for Christ. Whether or not you agree with Bill Hybels, or Rick Warren, or Jerry Falwell, or John McArthur, or Robert Schuller, you will have to admit that these pastors have been able to "package" their ministry and help other churches do ministry in the same way. Many churches have grown the way these models have grown. (Note: all of these men represent a Church Growth type, each representing a different dynamic and different growth methods. The science of Church Growth has helped them develop and understand their uniqueness and communicate it to others.)

With the introduction of Church Growth thought came an explosion of megachurches. These larger churches were not necessarily better churches, but they were certainly bigger, and they had a greater influence on their neighborhoods and drew national and international attention. The megachurches inspired many church leaders to believe it was possible to carry out the

Great Commission in a greater way and reach more lost people for Christ. These larger churches demonstrated to many that the power of God was still available to influence multitudes, to attract financial resources, and to do more than ever before to transform lives.

Before the influences of Church Growth, young pastors often focused primarily on programs, committees, office duties, marriages, hospitals, burials, counseling, and a thousand other perceived duties that kept them from the priorities of evangelism, leadership strategy, and establishing vision. The research that has come from the Church Growth movement has given pastors great vision and confidence because it has provided tools, priorities, and the motivation to give aggressive spiritual direction to their churches.

WHY TAKE CHURCH GROWTH SERIOUSLY?

Young ministers entering ministry should eagerly take Church Growth seriously and keep up on the latest in Church Growth for several reasons:

1. to give them focus to carry out the Great Commission—effective evangelism—through their church and ministry;
2. to ground them in the biblical and spiritual principles of building a New Testament church in a modern technological world;
3. to give them a big view of ministry so they will know how and when to use their talents and to lead in the employment of the spiritual gifts of their members in the face of varied and ever-increasing challenges in ministry;
4. to help determine the best ministry strategy for a particular geographical and cultural setting;
5. to help them avoid making mistakes based on wrong preconceptions or ignorance;
6. to help them identify and deal with all the reasons churches do not grow, stagnate, and die; and
7. to help them build a Bible-based and data-driven ministry, a ministry that is based on the eternal truth of the Word of God yet is relevant to the modern challenges of the world in which we live.

THE FOUNDATION

The modern Church Growth movement was not born in an academic environment where scholars devised principles in an attempt to be more effective in evangelism. Rather, Church Growth was born and grew out of the experiences of those doing evangelism in the field, who wanted to do it better and to do it more effectively.

While there have always been spurts in the growth of churches throughout history (for instance, in the times of the early apostles, St. Patrick [385–461], John Wesley [1703–91], and the Southern Baptists in the twentieth century), the unique movement given the technical name Church Growth[1] was brought to life more by Donald McGavran (1897–1990) than by any other modern individual.

George Hunter III, professor of Asbury Theological Seminary, says of Donald McGavran, "History will probably see him as the most influential missionary statesman of the twentieth century."[2] Hunter's statement might be correct, in view of McGavran's influence and what has happened in the past century. Before the twentieth century, much of foreign missions work was done by Western missionaries, and the success of foreign missions was judged by what those missionaries did.[3] Several changes have been observed since the introduction of Church Growth thought:

- A shift of authority and leadership in local and mission churches to indigenous leadership and ministry by Christian nationals.
- A distinct surge in church planting as a missionary strategy.
- The worldwide emergence of the megachurch movement as a source for church planting, ministry communication by media, development of innovative strategies that influence smaller churches, educational and training development, vision stimulation, and the like.
- An evangelistic focus on receptivity among ethnic and cultural groups.
- A recognition of barriers that prohibit evangelism and the application of principles to overcome barriers and make evangelism more effective, including contextualization in missionary strategy.

While McGavran and the Church Growth movement did not accomplish all the above developments directly, a cause-and-effect relationship is perceptible. The ideas, principles, and strategies that grew out of McGavran's thinking and the Church Growth movement have made a distinct positive contribution to the continual growth and effectiveness of the international ministry of missions and evangelism.

HISTORY OF THE CHURCH GROWTH MOVEMENT

Donald McGavran and his wife, Mary, went to India in 1923 as missionaries with the Disciples of Christ. At that time, the Disciples of Christ had only twenty to thirty small churches, which were experiencing little or no growth. It seemed to McGavran that his denomination focused on all types of ministry except evangelism. When McGavran saw other denominations converting people to Jesus Christ—primarily the "untouchables," the lowest caste in India—he wanted to examine their methods carefully.

J. Waskom Pickett, a Methodist missionary, was sent by the National Christian Council of India to investigate the mass movements of people to Christ. Pickett publicized the Christian mass movements in India and indelibly influenced McGavran's view of evangelism.[4] "As I [McGavran] saw a thousand people being baptized at one time, I said, 'This could happen to us, too.'"[5] Donald H. Gill gives this commentary in an article titled "Apostle of Church Growth": "This led McGavran to further research which indicated many of the reasons why the church in 136 districts had grown by 11 percent in 10 years while in 11 other districts it had grown by some 200 percent in the same period."[6]

Prior to his experience with Pickett, McGavran had considered the individualistic, "one-by-one" approach to evangelism as the most biblically based and pragmatically fruitful approach. He had heard of large groups of people claiming to have undergone Christian conversion and baptism but was skeptical about whether these claims were biblical. In fact, his term for these mass conversions was "half-baked mission work." In an interview with John K. Branner for *Evangelical Missions Quarterly*, McGavran confided: "In 1934–35 I began to see that what we had heard was quite wrong. What we had deemed 'unsound, half-baked work' was really one great way in which the church was growing quite effectively. God was blessing that way of growth. They were becoming better churches than ours. It was heresy to say that in 1935."[7]

Earlier, in 1930, McGavran had written *How to Teach Religion in Mission Schools,* and in 1936, he collaborated with Pickett and G. H. Singh in writing the early classic on people movements, *The Mass Movement Survey of Mid-India.* This title was revised in 1956 to *Church Growth and Group Conversion.*[8]

Because McGavran had been elected field secretary for the Disciples of Christ but kept emphasizing evangelism, he was not reelected as field secretary. Instead he was appointed as an evangelist in a remote central India region. Some saw that as a demotion, but in God's sight, it laid a further foundation for the Church Growth movement. McGavran was able to put into practice some of the ideas he was developing about evangelism.

In 1953, Donald McGavran spent a missionary furlough writing *The Bridges of God,* considered by many as the first book on Church Growth because it contained several embryonic elements of the future Church Growth movement.[9] Rather than being an evangelistic thunderclap, it was largely ignored by the evangelical world.

After thirty years in India and while on a furlough, McGavran received a research fellowship from Yale University. Through the United Christian Missionary Society, he traveled to fields such as Puerto Rico, the Philippines, Thailand, Formosa, Japan, and Jamaica, studying the evangelistic endeavors of Baptists, Episcopalians, Methodists, Presbyterians, Pentecostals, and others. Out of this came his second major book on church growth, *How Churches Grow,* in 1959.[10]

In an address to the North American Society for Church Growth,[11] McGavran said he was searching for a new term to replace the word *evangelism,* because it was often confused with catechism classes, baptism, and/or church membership. McGavran chose to use the new term *church growth,* because it described what should happen when evangelism and the Great Commission were carried out: people were won to Christ, baptized, and taught the Word of God, and as a result, churches grew. He said that evangelism is an *input term,* gospelizing the lost, but church growth is an *output term*, meaning that when the lost are properly evangelized, churches grow.[12]

AMERICAN CHURCH GROWTH

In 1969, I wrote *The Ten Largest Sunday Schools and What Makes Them Grow*,[13] a volume that C. Peter Wagner has called the first American Church Growth volume because I applied the scientific principle of social research to determine the principles that made these churches grow. He also said it was the first book to identify and examine the emerging megachurch phenomenon.[14] I was doing graduate work at Garrett Theological Seminary (Evanston, Illinois) and was examining the influence of sociology on the church. Ernst Troeltsch's work *The Social Teaching of the Church* motivated me to develop the "sociological cycles of church growth and death," examining the church as a social institution, not just as a theological body.[15] To carry out my research, I examined the ten largest churches, drawing from them a data pool that could be examined for workable principles that, if applied to other churches, could lead them to grow. Therefore, I visited these ten churches, interviewed the pastor and staff, and tried to determine the dynamics that made them grow. I was thrilled with the evangelistic results I saw at their altars, the large auditoriums built to reach the masses, the influence these churches had on their cities, and the faith they stimulated in others. Using a lengthy questionnaire, I questioned the church leaders and compared the findings from the ten churches, trying to find causes for growth.

Even though *The Ten Largest Sunday Schools and What Makes Them Grow* was viewed as a popular book, I felt chapter 13, "Methods of Research," was the most important because it explained how the case-study research method was used on these churches and how I arrived at the conclusions and principles of Church Growth.[16]

I followed this book with other similar research projects: *America's Fastest Growing Churches; Church Aflame; Capturing a Town for Christ; Getting a Church Started in the Face of Insurmountable Odds, with Limited Resources, in Unlikely Circumstances; The World's Largest Sunday School;* and *Ten of Today's Most Innovative Churches*.[17]

In 1968, I was scheduled to address a pastors' seminar for the Evangelical Free Church Conference in Austin, Texas. I decided to give a sermon based on my research. The impact was immediate and opened the door for preaching that sermon at other denominational conferences, at pastoral fellowships in cities, and at local churches. In the next seven years, I preached that one sermon 617 times. To me, this indicated that the Church Growth movement had a message the American church was ready to hear.

In 1969–70, Donald McGavran spent a sabbatical teaching for one quarter at Trinity Evangelical Divinity School, where he was an associate professor of Christian Education. We had many conversations about Church Growth: he from the foreign missions perspective, and I from the American perspective.

In 1971, I became cofounder of Liberty University in Lynchburg, Virginia, with Jerry Falwell. Our primary vision was to train in Church Growth principles pastors who would endeavor to build superaggressive churches that would saturate their area with the gospel and capture their towns for Christ.

DEFINITION OF CHURCH GROWTH

From the early days, the definition of the title Church Growth had three separate aspects. First, the title was associated with numerical growth: the growth of the church by attendance, offerings, baptisms, membership, and so on. These areas of growth were observable, measurable, and repeatable. (Most who have criticized Church Growth have focused on this measuring aspect and have missed the major contribution of Church Growth: scientific research. Counting numbers is only the output of following correct principles.)

The second aspect was planting churches both within and across cultural and class barriers. McGavran often repeated the phrase "Matheteusate panta ta ethne," "make disciples of all the nations" (Matt. 28:19 NKJV).[18] When the Great Commission was properly implemented, people were won to Christ, baptized, and taught to obey Christ. This action of ministry was done in a local church and was best carried out by planting new churches. Therefore, the heart of Church Growth is to plant churches that will carry out both evangelism and edification.

Since the Great Commission targets "all people groups," *panta ta ethne*, then it includes cross-cultural ministry that recognizes the barriers of culture, race, and language—cross-cultural church planting.[19]

The third aspect of the Church Growth definition is seen in its scientific research base; that is, Church Growth is a discipline or science.[20] But Church Growth research does not take place exclusively in the realm of the sciences that are tied to the physical world, such as psychology, anthropology, and sociology. Rather, Church Growth begins with doctrine or systematic theology. Based on the truth it finds in the Bible, Church Growth then applies research to culture. As such, it uses the research methods of both science and theology. Thus, Church Growth is a "Bible-based ministry that is data-driven in strategy."[21]

While not generally recognized, the greatest influence of Church Growth is not in numerical growth or the phenomenon of the megachurch but in the discovery and dissemination of workable biblical principles that have led to the growth and increase of Christianity in North America and around the world. The greatest contribution of the Church Growth movement has been its awakening of church leaders to ask why and what, in search of workable biblical principles for ministry.

The scientific research method has helped Church Growth researchers determine the principles and methods of evangelism. In the course of their research, they go through the following stages:

1. Researchers begin with a problem that focuses their inquiry, such as, Why have our evangelistic methods not worked? or, Why are some churches growing faster than others?
2. They gather all possible data on the problem, beginning with the Word of God, but also examine the data of society, culture, and ethnicity.
3. They establish a hypothesis from the data (suggest a solution or solutions to the problem), an unproven principle that is suggested as a solution or solutions to the problem.
4. Researchers then test the proposed solution (hypothesis) to see if it is biblical, valid, and effective (a solution is tested by Scripture, consistency, correspondence, etc.).

5. When a hypothesis is confirmed, new laws or principles of evangelism and Church Growth are thereby established.

(The Church Growth movement has distinguished itself by giving titles to the principles it has established. In a magazine article in *Christianity Today*, the founders of the Church Growth movement were chided for their desire to always name their principles, with titles such as People Movement, or the Law of Three Hearings, or the Law of Receptivity, or the Engle Scale.[22])

Robertson McQuilkin, former president of Columbia Bible College, reduced the multitude of Church Growth principles into five areas. In his book *Measuring the Church Growth Movement*, McQuilkin presents these five areas as:

1. the importance of numerical growth
2. the necessity of focusing evangelism on receptive groups
3. people movements, or the homogeneous principle
4. use of science as a valid tool to determine strategy and principles
5. right method guarantees large response[23]

In the mid-1970s, C. Peter Wagner listed what he believed were six irreducible presuppositions on which Church Growth was founded.[24] He noted that those who disagreed with the Church Growth movement invariably disagreed with one of these six suppositions:

1. Nongrowth displeases God.
2. Numerical growth of a church is a priority with God and focuses on new disciples rather than decisions.
3. Disciples are tangible, identifiable, countable people who increase the church numerically.
4. Limited time, money, and resources demand that the church develop a strategy based on results.
5. Social and behavioral sciences are valuable tools in measuring and encouraging church growth.
6. Research is essential for maximum growth.[25]

After looking at the three definitions of Church Growth, which are more similar to descriptions, the following definition is used by the American Society for Church Growth: "A discipline which investigates the nature, expansion, planting, multiplication, function and health of Christian churches as they relate to the effective implementation of Christ's commission to 'make disciples of all peoples.' Church Growth advocates strive to integrate the eternal theological principles of God's Word concerning the expansion of the church with the best insights of contemporary social and behavioral sciences, employing as the initial frame of reference, the foundational work done by Donald McGavran."[26]

Wagner notes the following aspects of this definition of Church Growth:

1. It is scientific in nature.
2. Its scope is Christian churches.
3. It is related to the implementation of the Great Commission.
4. It combines eternal theological principles with insights from contemporary social and behavioral sciences.
5. Its initial frame of reference is Donald McGavran.[27]

TYPES OF CHURCH GROWTH RESEARCH

Various types of research in Church Growth have characterised the movement. Originally, McGavran began to analyze growing churches through observation and investigation. He traveled to observe growing churches around the world and examined local church records. He compared the things he saw in growing churches with other churches that seemed to be nongrowing.

Flavil Yeakley conducted one of the earliest in-depth statistical research projects to impact Church Growth. In his 1976 Ph.D. dissertation in Speech Communication, he compared churches that had high, medium, and low growth rates and the differences in their rates of converts, dropouts, and nonconverts.[28]

The information gathered in Yeakley's study was used in the broader study of persuasion in religious conversion, but several major parts of this research focused directly on the relation of the theory, practice, perception, and results of church growth.

George Hunter has done valuable historical research into the establishment and growth of the Irish church, again determining principles for growing churches. His paper presented to the American Society for Church Growth, "The Ancient Celtic

Way of Being and Doing Church for the Post-Modern West," reflected his research.[29]

Charles Van Engen, professor at Fuller Theological Seminary, has done valuable research into historical creeds. He has reminded us of the purpose of the church from the perspective of the early church fathers.[30]

Contemporary research has been done in the area of sociology regarding the methods of evangelizing different generations. Just as Church Growth teaches us to recognize barriers to evangelism and how to reach out cross-culturally, two contemporary leaders have suggested that generations are unique people groups and that unique methods will therefore be needed to reach each generation with the gospel. Thom Rainer, dean of the Billy Graham School of Missions, Evangelism and Church Growth at Southern Baptist Theological Seminary in Louisville, Kentucky, has written *The Bridger Generation,* and Gary McIntosh of Talbot Theological Seminary, Biola University, has written *One Church, Four Generations* and *Make Room for the Boom ... or Bust.*[31]

The list in the sidebar "Types of Church Growth Research" is just a sample of the types of research done by Church Growth leaders. The names of many leaders have been left out and many research projects are not mentioned.

Types of Church Growth Research	
Observation	Donald McGavran
Case Study	Elmer Towns
Statistical	Flavil Yeakley
Historical	George Hunter
Dogmatic	Charles Van Engen
Sociological	Gary McIntosh and Thom Rainer

THE MOVEMENT CALLED CHURCH GROWTH

Dr. McGavran isolated five key historical events that have contributed immeasurably to the expansion of the Church Growth movement.

1. The establishment of the Institute of Church Growth (1961) on the campus of Northwest Christian College (Eugene, Oregon) to develop students knowledgeable in growth concepts.

2. The publication of the *Church Growth Bulletin* (1964).
3. The relocation of the Institute of Church Growth from the campus in Eugene (1961) to Fuller Seminary at Pasadena (1965).
4. The establishment of the William Carey Library (1969) for the mass publication and circulation of Church Growth books.
5. The creation of the Institute for American Church Growth (1973) by Dr. McGavran and Dr. Win Arn.[32]

Another key historical event was when McGavran conducted a gathering of Church Growth leadership in the first annual Church Growth Colloquium at the Emmanuel School of Religion, Milligan College, Tennessee, June 16–20, 1969. This four-day conference included such topics as "The Scientifically Measurable Factors of Church Growth," "Why Churches Stop Growing," and "How to Activate Churches."[33]

In the early 1970s, Fuller Theological Seminary became the geographical focus for the movement. During these days, Donald McGavran and C. Peter Wagner instituted the Fuller Evangelistic Association Department of Church Growth at Fuller to apply Church Growth methodology to American churches.

In 1972, the Institute for American Church Growth was founded by Win Arn and McGavran to provide information and research on North American Church Growth. Win Arn had produced twenty-seven films and had served as director of religious education for the Evangelical Covenant Church. He used films, books, seminars, workshops, audiotapes, and curriculum to spread the good news of Church Growth. The Institute for American Church Growth, according to James H. Montgomery, reached nearly 30,000 key lay leaders and pastors representing 4,000 local congregations, giving momentum to the movement.[34]

The almost immediate acceptance of Church Growth by a majority of American churches came through the ministry and writings of C. Peter Wagner, from his influential platform as professor at Fuller Theological Seminary. He communicated his findings to the students at Fuller, and many became leaders of denominations or mission boards. Other students were nationals who returned to their homes around the world to influence their churches with Church Growth principles. For almost a decade, from approximately the mid-1970s to the mid-1980s, Wagner spearheaded a yearly seminar in church planting (emphasizing both American and foreign strategies), which attracted leaders from almost every major denomination and mission board executives. They came to learn how to plant and grow churches. Fuller Theological Seminary thus became the dominant influence of the Church Growth movement. John Vaughan coined the phrase "the Fuller Factor," referring to Fuller Theological Seminary, the Institute for American Church Growth, and the Charles E. Fuller Evangelistic Association as the center of Church Growth influence in America.[35]

In the early 1980s, Larry Gilbert and I established the Church Growth Institute in Lynchburg, Virginia, to publish Church Growth resources, conduct Church Growth seminars, and conduct research into church growth. This organization became the largest Church Growth organization (apart from denominational departments of Church Growth) in terms of products sold, budget, and number of seminars conducted. The intent of the Church Growth Institute was to make the principles of Church Growth practical to the pastor and laypeople of local churches and to spell out the principles in methods and programs. The institute produced and sold over 250 resource packets, including over 40,000 *Friend Day* resource packets, and 10,000 programs to help churches add a second worship service. The institute also sold over four million spiritual-gifts inventories.

KINDS OF GROWTH

When the concept of *growth* is added to the word *church*, the question is naturally asked, What kind of growth? A church can experience several kinds of growth, and most growing churches may experience some growth in each category.

The first kind of growth is *internal growth*, which is qualitative growth in the Word of God, the Lord, grace, and/or spiritual maturity. This is also called the "spiritual factors of church growth."

The second kind of growth is *external growth*, or *numerical growth*. Numerical growth deals with growth in those qualities that can be objectively measured: attendance, membership, offerings, baptisms, enrollment, and so on. This growth relates to data that are observable, measurable, and countable. Those who strive for numerical growth without seeking spiritual growth are limiting the effectiveness of their ministry.

A third type of growth is *biological growth*. As church members have babies, the attendance figures of the church swell.

A fourth kind of church growth is *conversion growth*. This is sometimes called "making sheep." Evangelism is winning people to Christ and his church. If a church is effectively reaching its community with the gospel, this will also result in a numerical increase in the church.

Transfer growth is the fifth kind of church growth experienced by many churches. Some object to this kind of growth, calling it "sheep stealing," but others realize that mobility is increasingly a part of Western society and prefer to call this kind of growth "finding lost sheep." Approximately 22 percent of Americans move every year. The adjustments involved in a major move make a person more receptive to changes, including a change in attitude toward a church or denomination. If a church is serious about reaching people, it should have a strategy for reaching Christians moving into its community.

Expansion growth is yet another kind of growth experienced by many churches. This sixth type of growth results in a church beginning another church like themselves. Rather than build new facilities, many churches have opted to begin a mission Sunday school or a new church plant in another part of town or in a nearby community. They expand their ministry into the same type of community.

The seventh type of growth is *extension growth*. This means a church begins a new ministry geared at reaching another culture or ethnic group moving into the community. In communities experiencing changes in ethnic character, churches are developing strategies that produce expansion and extension of growth. This type of church growth also applies to a church that plants a church different from itself in a community that is different from the community in which the planting church is located. This is truly cross-cultural church planting or cross-cultural evangelism.[36]

SOCIAL SCIENCE OR THEOLOGY?

Although Church Growth uses social science research, it is based on theological research. Church Growth must also be considered under the area of theology called ecclesiology, which relates to the doctrine of the church. Just as the term *church* must be defined in ecclesiology, so the term *Church*

Growth must also be defined following the same guidelines. Previously, I suggested that science or research contributed to defining Church Growth. Does science or research have a role in defining terms in systematic theology? To answer that question, look at the nature of systematic theology both in its definition and in its method of theologizing. Systematic theology is defined as "the collecting, scientifically arranging, comparing, exhibiting and defending of all facts from any and every source concerning God and His works."[37] In this definition, the term "scientifically arranging" suggests the role of research in arriving at theological definitions. Therefore, when Church Growth is seen through the eyes of theology, many of the criticisms against it can be answered, because true church growth will always be grounded in both natural and supernatural revelation. Understanding church growth theologically will keep many from pushing Church Growth into fringe ministries that embarrass the movement or try to make it something it is not.

The Church Growth movement must recognize the following principles to remain on track:

1. The Word of God is the ultimate standard of faith and practice, and no principle of Church Growth that contradicts Scripture, even if it produces numerical growth, is a biblical Church Growth principle.
2. The Scriptures have not given a systematic presentation of church growth principles, but rather have given the Great Commission, describing how the principles and circumstances influence churches to grow. In addition, the Scriptures have offered solutions to church problems and other aspects of ministry that come with growth.
3. Where the Scriptures are silent, it is possible to gather insight from natural revelation to determine or verify Church Growth principles. These principles, however, must be consistent with models, commands, and principles that are explicitly found in Scripture.
4. There is a difference in basing one's Church Growth principles on those that are explicit in Scripture and basing them on those that are implied in Scripture. Church Growth researchers should recognize the absolute nature of explicit principles, but when principles are only implied, they should seek more data, test them to see if they correspond to other Scripture, test them through

internal consistency, and then wait for confirmation through scientific research.

5. Where Scripture is silent, scientific research can determine Church Growth principles. These, however, must be in harmony with those explicit principles previously established.

6. Theological and Church Growth research are not two mutually distinct methods of research that lead to separate sets of principles. Rather, both theology and Church Growth thought grow out of the same orientation to research, and harmonizing should be integrated in the total process.

7. Church Growth research and principles are not addenda to theological methods and principles but are at the heart of theology and its methods.[38]

Once Church Growth researchers have identified principles, they must be careful to distinguish between principles and methods.[39] The focus of the research is to establish principles, not just programs or methods.[40] In the first twenty years of the movement, research focused on principles; lately the focus has been on discovering new techniques, programs, or methods.

When viewing Church Growth, we must remember the following:

1. Methods and programs are not the same as biblical principles. While a technique or program may accomplish a biblical result because it contains some biblical principles, techniques and programs are not the same as absolute truth.

2. Methods and programs may be used effectively by certain people at certain times in certain circumstances but will not be equally effective overall.

3. Principles alone are biblical; they transcend programs and methods.

4. Methods and programs tend to change with time and culture.

5. Methods and programs may be effective in one contemporary setting but not in the next.

6. Some programs may be effective when used in a specific time frame but become ineffective with changing circumstances.

The method or program, although effective because it applies some biblical principles, becomes less effective when changing circumstances make the method ineffective. Principles do not change, but the way principles are applied changes. Therefore, the church worker must be grounded in biblical principles and yet be flexible to determine what program and technique will best help a specific church to grow.[41] McGavran suggests, "Analytical tools are available for pastors and concerned laypeople to determine whether their own churches have desirable growth patterns."[42] In an attempt to explain the tension between methods and principles, Church Growth authorities and others have quoted the following motto:

> Methods are many,
> Principles are few;
> Methods may change,
> But principles never do.

Biblical principles will lead to Church Growth strategy, which can become a practical approach or tool for carrying out the Great Commission. Church Growth strategy is to be based on the biblical objective of the church—the Great Commission—applying the biblical principles of Church Growth, and identifying a biblical paradigm to evaluate the effectiveness of Church Growth.[43]

THREE HISTORICAL STAGES

The Church Growth movement seems to have gone through three stages in its growth. The first stage involved the original pioneers, who were motivated by the discovery of new principles and the perceived potential growth or revival in the Christian church. These pioneers were mostly located in the academic community: McGavran, Wagner, and Gibbs at Fuller Theological Seminary, Towns at Liberty University, Vaughan at Southwest Baptist University, Yeakley at Harding University, George Hunter at Asbury Theological Seminary; add to that list Kent Hunter of the Church Growth Center and Win Arn of the American Church Growth Institute. It seems that for the first twenty years of the movement, every new book introduced new ideas or principles to the corpus of Church Growth understanding. (Note: the books that followed this period did not add new material to the original findings but were applications and methods of using the original corpus.)

The second generation of Church Growth influencers were primarily leaders who were practitioners, those who understood and put the principles into practice. For the most part, these influencers were pastors of growing churches who conducted seminars and wrote books to perpetuate Church Growth principles.[44] These were leaders such as Bill Hybels of Willow Creek Community Church, South Barrington, Illinois; John Maxwell of Skyline Wesleyan Church, Lemon Grove, California; and Rick Warren of Saddleback Community Church, Orange County, California. A number of influencers wrote and published material, including Bill Sullivan of the Church Growth Department of the Nazarene Church, Kansas City, Missouri, and Larry Gilbert of Church Growth Institute, Lynchburg, Virginia. Beside the practical books that appeared during this stage, there was an emergence of supplementary material in the form of resource packets and seminars that communicated the principles of Church Growth.

The third and present stage of Church Growth could be called the "Babel stage."[45] Today many individuals and centers are the influencers of Church Growth. The influencers are made up of pastors (large and small, growing and nongrowing churches), denominational publishers and book publishing companies, academic leaders, interdenominational church leaders, and others. This stage takes its name from the story of the Tower of Babel (Gen. 11:1–9), when each spoke a different language. Today each Church Growth authority seems to have a different niche, and each one seems to emphasize different principles or follow different methods in suggesting how to grow churches and make them effective. Some of these authorities turn on the movement and criticize its principles, usually claiming they have found a new or better way of growing the church. Most of the influencers in this Babel stage seem to care little about defending the movement against its critics; if anything, some in this third stage are critical of others in the movement. (Sometimes I wonder if they are critical so they can hold up their "product" or if they are critical because they are attempting to find the truth.)[46]

This third stage, while seen by some as diluting the movement, was the logical and mature next step for Church Growth.

Each local church must take the eternal principles of Church Growth and work them out in application to its context and within its resources. Hence, the term *niche* for Church Growth applies to each different local church, both in North America and in Third World cultures. Also, each local church represents a different theological system, from the various views of Calvinism to the various views of Arminianism, plus those churches that represent Wesleyanism, Lutheranism, Pentecostalism, charismatics, and so on. Each shade of doctrine will have some influence on the way Church Growth is expressed and applied. Thus, it was only natural that Church Growth be applied in many ways in this Babel stage.

With the death of McGavran and the move of C. Peter Wagner into the "apostolic and charismatic" movement, away from being a defender of the Church Growth movement, the stabilizing influence of the "Fuller Factor" was no longer the dominating influence of the Church Growth movement. The annual meeting of the American Society for Church Growth did not apply the direction needed to keep all factors focused on the original tenets of Church Growth. Therefore, "Babel" means each authority and/or group now looks to itself and its interpretation of data to certify the true meaning of Church Growth.

CRITICISM OF THE MOVEMENT

When the Church Growth movement was growing in influence during the 1970s, it was not without its critics. Most of the original criticism pointed out the stress on numerical growth, proselytism, priority of the church over interdenominational agencies, priority of evangelism over ministry, undue emphasis on removing barriers that prohibit evangelism, pragmatism versus scriptural authority, and manipulation and/or unbiblical motivation. Some also criticized the homogeneous unit principle as cultural exclusivism in the church, viewing it as a racial membership policy rather than understanding it as an evangelistic outreach strategy when applied to cross-cultural evangelism.[47] With a proper understanding of the true nature of Church Growth, most of the criticisms were answered.

Every new movement has its blind spots, however, and Church Growth was originally a growing movement that had some immature characteristics. These involved:

1. Some enthusiastic promoters who claimed Church Growth could do much more in producing growth than was humanly and divinely possible or intended.
2. Some writing in the name of Church Growth who did not know or understand its principles.
3. Some who pushed growth in churches for the wrong purposes (money, ego, non-Christian doctrine, etc.).
4. Some critics who were against any change in Christianity.
5. Some who were ignorant of basic New Testament essentials.

The contemporary criticism of the Church Growth movement (twenty years later) seems to be much more explicit and exact in nature. John Vaughan, in his presidential address to the American Society for Church Growth, best summarized the current accusations. He attempted to identify the criticism against the movement with the following list:[48]

1. the movement has abandoned the foundational principles of Donald McGavran;[49]
2. excessive application of pragmatism to the exclusion of Scripture results in a ministry that says any means of growing a church is justified by its ends;[50]
3. the argument against contextualization of the gospel into contemporary terms, such as "user friendly" churches;[51]
4. attempting to determine ministry from the "felt needs" of people, then formulating the gospel to meet those needs;[52]
5. the Church Growth movement has neglected to examine its law or principles through modern objective research techniques (validate by statistical research);[53]
6. the systematic replacement of biblical preaching and teaching with such things as audience ratings, preoccupation with corporate image, statistical growth, financial profits, opinion surveys, celebrity status, and Top 10 lists of churches;[54]
7. focusing on "churching" the already converted of Christianity rather than reaching the unconverted;[55]
8. failure to distinguish between the numerical growth of the orthodox churches and those teaching false doctrine;[56] and
9. making the size of a church the measure of success.[57]

The Church Growth movement cannot ignore these criticisms. While they come from well-meaning, yet at times self-serving, sources, these criticisms should only sharpen the focus of those in the movement to do a better job of carrying out the Great Commission. The problem is that the leaders of the Church Growth movement have not done an adequate job in answering the critics: Why have the leaders not addressed these issues?

Perhaps the original leaders of the first stage of the Church Growth movement were so focused on discovering new principles and writing their findings that they did not give attention to their detractors, especially when their detractors were influencing public opinion against their movement. In the second stage of Church Growth, perhaps leaders were so busy building churches that they cared little about pure theoretical principles or any attacks against the movement. They just kept doing what worked for them. It seems that many of the current Church Growth leaders may not really care about answering the criticisms against the movement or keeping the movement going.

SUMMARY AND FUTURE

When the explosion of growing churches occurred, many people took note, including J. Waskom Pickett and Donald McGavran. Everyone seemed to rejoice when churches evangelized the masses, baptized new converts, and grew numerically. While most were excited about effective evangelism, not many took note when McGavran first began writing about the principles that caused church growth. Perhaps they were turned off by the addition of scientific research to evangelism. They should not have been. After World War II, the use of science and research was giving insight into improving most every area of life. Why not church ministry?

With time, however, church leaders began to see a link between growing a church and the employment of correct principles. The Church Growth movement gained some acceptance, but not without its critics and detractors who opposed some of its principles. Also, Church Growth has always had some who identify themselves with the movement but advocate growth for the wrong reasons and with questionable methods. These people presented a negative model for Church Growth that was rightfully rejected.

As the church of Jesus Christ has moved into the twenty-first century, she has more enlightenment than in past ages. The church has a better understanding of what causes growth—biblical evangelism—and how to go about growing churches. The church has a better understanding of barriers, receptivity, and how to present the gospel of Jesus Christ. But correct knowledge has not always led to correct practice. Is correct practice not connected to the will? We have to want to do right before we can minister better. This means the church will not always do right because it knows what to do. We must recognize that the church's outward obedience to principles and methods will not always work. Biblical Church Growth will always include spiritual factors that lead to spiritual life and growth, such as prayer, fasting, revival, and the power of God.

The discipline of Church Growth faces some major questions in the future. As the United States faces postmodernism, what principles will the church follow in evangelism? As the world faces new threats of terrorism, secularism, and internationalism, what will be the workable principles of evangelism that will effectively reach twenty-first–century citizens and build churches in this new century? If this age is coming to an end, and if Christ is coming soon, what will be the role of Church Growth in the age of growing apostasy (1 Tim. 4:1–3; 2 Tim. 3:1–7)?

These and other questions face Church Growth leaders. While some feel the major corpus of Church Growth principles has been discovered and established, others do not agree. Since truth is as deep as the knowledge of God, leaders should expect to continually discover new principles that will help them grow and mature churches. On the other hand, since we know all we need to know about God for salvation and following him, we should expect that God has told us all we need to know about evangelism. Therefore, there is much work to be done; the church has not completed the command "Matheteusate panta ta ethne" (Matt. 28:19). Until a church has been established among every people group, we have not fulfilled the Great Commission. May all of us recommit ourselves to Church Growth—effective evangelism.

A CENTRIST RESPONSE

Charles Van Engen

Elmer has provided us a very helpful historical overview of the American Church Growth movement. I especially appreciate the emphases that Elmer has chosen to highlight. He is right that Donald McGavran's fundamental motivation had to do with a search for effective evangelism. In fact, it may be said that what McGavran articulated in the 1960s and 1970s was essentially a restatement of classic mission theology: God desires that men and women of all cultures be reconciled to God through Jesus Christ and become responsible members of Christ's church through the work of the Holy Spirit (2 Corinthians 5). This classical understanding of mission has prevailed in the church throughout the twenty centuries of its history.

Towns also accurately states that McGavran was the one to coin the term *Church Growth*. McGavran was intentional in emphasizing the role of the congregation and of the church; he was, after all, a committed churchman in conversion and mission. And he rightly considered the local congregation of believers to be the most fundamental building block of the church of Jesus Christ. On the one hand, he emphasized the importance of the universal church and of the local congregation over against the heavily individualist emphasis of evangelism movements (especially campaign evangelism) worldwide and especially in North America. These movements stressed individual conversion and were significantly weak with regard to the person's incorporation into and involvement in the church. On the other hand, McGavran stressed Church Growth over against the dominant ecumenical view of the 1950s and 1960s, spearheaded by J. C. Hoekendijk, which downplayed, and nearly negated, the importance of the church in favor of a strong sociopolitical and economic agenda of social transformation.[58] McGavran's denomination was a charter member of the World Council of Churches, and McGavran feared that the social concerns of the ecumenical movement would eclipse a committed emphasis on the conversion to Jesus Christ of the (then) two billion people who were not yet Christians. As I read McGavran's writings, I believe he coined the term *Church Growth* as a way to speak to both ends of the spectrum: to those who emphasized individual conversion with little concern for social change and to those who emphasized social change with little concern for the spiritual conversion and faith development of individuals.

Over the years of our friendship and collaboration, I have deeply appreciated Elmer's emphasis on principles as being more significant than methodologies. Elmer describes clearly and forcefully the way certain missiological principles flow from specific assumptions in the Church Growth movement.

However, Elmer's chapter left me with a number of unanswered questions. In drawing the principles of Church Growth from the assumptions in this chapter, Towns does not pursue an in-depth examination of the assumptions from which the principles are derived. The North American context is radically different from India or the various global contexts where much global Church Growth theory was born. Yet when McGavran teamed up with Win Arn to promote, popularize, and develop Church Growth theory in the North American context, the differences in the contexts were left relatively unexamined. I believe these differences had significant impact on the assumptions, the missiological theory, and the evangelistic practice of Church Growth in North America. Some of the more pertinent differences are:

- North American society is heavily individualistically oriented; much global Church Growth research was carried out (and the theory elaborated) in the midst of relatively self-contained people groups in relation to group conversion.
- Until recently, evangelism in North America has been predominantly monocultural, people sharing their faith with others who were like them; global Church Growth

was developed in the context of cross-cultural mission endeavors.

- North American church-based evangelism has been heavily impacted by its ties to the work of denominations and might be seen to some extent as denominational expansion through the ministry of pastors; global Church Growth involved predominantly the work of mission agencies through the ministry of cross-cultural missionaries.
- Church Growth in North America drew heavily from sociology and the sociology of religion for the creation of much of its theory; global Church Growth drew most heavily from anthropological worldview studies.
- The growth of the church in North America occurs in the midst of a rich and confusing smorgasbord of church forms; global Church Growth theory (especially considering the place of its birth—India) was developed in a context in which Christians are a small minority of the population in the midst of a majority of people who are adherents of many other faiths.

In addition to noting these differences, I have seven questions that I want to ask by way of self-examination, for I consider myself an integral part of the American Society of Church Growth, having served as one of its officers during the past six years and having presented numerous papers to the society prior to that.

First, I wonder what the theoretical relationship is between the Church Growth movement as such and concern for the growth of the church? Not all who study and foster the church's growth (however we might define that) are part of the Church Growth movement. The Church Growth movement does not have a corner on, and is not the only network of persons committed to, the growth of churches.

Second, why did North American Church Growth end up emphasizing white, Anglo-Saxon, suburban churches? In 1973, McGavran and Arn published *How to Grow a Church*. The next year, Arn produced a 16-millimeter film of the same title. The faces of the church members and others in the film are almost exclusively white. Over the past thirty years, the membership of the American Society for Church Growth has come almost entirely from this ethnic group (with notable exceptions), and thus the society has ghettoized itself within this shrinking ethnic group in North America.

Third, what assumptions prompted North American Church Growth to become enamored with very large churches in suburbia, raising them up as examples and giving the most emphasis to the publications written by the pastors of those types of churches?

Fourth, what theological, missiological, and ecclesiological assumptions were behind North American Church Growth's rather strong emphasis on a certain type of entrepreneurial pastoral leadership, downplaying other types and models of pastoral leadership?

Fifth, what assumptions led the North American Church Growth movement to essentially ignore small, rural congregations, storefront city congregations, and older churches in transitional neighborhoods? Why has the American Society for Church Growth seemed to ignore the growth of, for example, African American, Filipino, South Indian, Korean, Chinese, Spanish-speaking, Taiwanese, Eastern European, Carribean, South Pacific, multicultural, and so many other non-Anglo congregations in North America?

Sixth, what assumptions have kept North American Church Growth from researching and emphasizing the place, role, and pastoral leadership of women in the life and growth of congregations?

Finally, what assumptions may have prompted the silence of North American Church Growth with regard to a call for Christians to share their faith with persons who are adherents of other faiths? Given the plural religious contexts in which global Church Growth theory was born and developed, it strikes me as strange that this has not been a primary arena of research, teaching, and publication on the part of North American Church Growth.

Once again, let me express my deep admiration and respect for Elmer Towns and my appreciation for his chapter. The North American Church Growth movement has had significant influence in the life, development, growth, strategic planning, and administrative decisions of churches and denominations in North America. This significance should not be underestimated. Because of this, the movement also deserves thoughtful examination and critique. Where to from here?

A REFORMIST RESPONSE
Gailyn Van Rheenen

I will describe in chapter 4 of this book the missional helix, illustrating the intertwining, inseparable nature of theological reflection, cultural analysis, historical perspective, and strategy formation in preparation for the practice of ministry. Christian leaders develop their practices of ministry by first reflecting on the will of God as revealed in Scripture. For example, in preparation for church planting, the practitioners will not only study a theology of mission to discern God's mission in the world but will study texts, like 1 Peter and Ephesians, that describe what God desires the church to be. They will concurrently reflect on how the Good News of God, revealed in Scripture, will be incarnated in the new cultural context. They will also study the historical narratives, which describe how things got to be as they are, based on the interrelated stories of the particular nation, lineage, church, and God's mission. Using this process, strategies that reflect the will of God are appropriately developed for the missional context.

From this perspective, Elmer Towns's chapter focuses primarily on strategy without adequately reflecting on the other three items. Theological formation is assumed rather than accepted as the first step toward strategy formation. Strategic principles are evaluated based on efficacy (Do our principles make the church grow?) rather than on theology (Do our principles reflect the nature and will of God?"). He believes that empirical reasoning, rooted in Enlightenment thinking, enables church leaders to devise previously unknown strategies to make churches grow.

Of all the chapters in the book, this chapter has been the hardest to evaluate, because I disagree with many of its basic premises. I believe that the guidelines presented in this chapter are a recipe for church demise. Towns recounts that the end result of the Church Growth movement has become "Babel." The reason for this, I believe, is that differing humanistic approaches have sought to grasp a corner of the Church Growth market to help churches become large, healthy, and successful. The emphasis is on growth rather than on becoming people of God's kingdom.

APPLICATION OF THE SCIENTIFIC METHOD TO MINISTRY

Towns believes that applying the scientific research method to missions provides Church Growth practitioners with principles that enable the church to grow. As he says, "The use of science and research was giving insight into improving most every area of life. Why not church ministry?" There are at least two basic problems with this approach.

First, the research has to do with methods and growth rather than the intrinsic nature of the gospel as it intersects with culture. Towns asserts that the Church Growth practitioner must begin with the Word of God. However, theology is not the first step of his scientific process. The beginning questions are concerned with methodology and growth. These questions then lead the researcher to look to Scripture to evaluate methods and reasons for growth and nongrowth. Biblical theology, therefore, does not form the basic questions of Church Growth research.

Second, there is an immense pride, rooted in the optimism of modernity, that humans need only to determine the right methodology to access the answers to their problems. Thus, the beginning point of Church Growth ministry is social research and strategy planning rather than theological reflection.

SYSTEMATIC THEOLOGY AND NATURAL REVELATION

Towns affirms the need for both theological and social research. He acknowledges "the Word of God is the ultimate standard of faith and practice." He believes that Church Growth research and principles are "not addenda to theological methods and principles but are at the heart of theology." His theological methods, however, indicate otherwise. He seeks to reconcile social and theological research in two ways. First, he builds scientific inquiry into his definition of systematic theology, and secondly, he differentiates natural and special (or "supernatural") revelation.

In regard to the first, Towns defines systematic theology as "'the collecting [and] *scientifically arranging* . . . of all facts from any and every source concerning God and His works.'. . . The term 'scientifically arranging' suggests the role of research in arriving at theological definitions." Rather than seeking to prove Church Growth assumptions by superimposing a scientific grid on Scripture, missiologists must exegete texts within their own historical and cultural setting. They must allow the story line and messages of the Bible to speak for themselves rather than using scientific grids as interpretive models.

Towns's attempt to reconcile social and theological research by differentiating natural and supernatural revelation necessitates an understanding of natural revelation. Passages such as "The heavens declare the glory of God" (Ps. 19:1) and "God's invisible qualities—his eternal power and divine nature—have been clearly seen, being understood from what has been made" (Rom. 1:20) illustrate that natural revelation serves as a general testimony of God and his nature. The purpose of natural revelation is to testify of God. Social research, although valid in its proper place, should not be thought of as an analysis of natural revelation by human reason.

OPTIMISM

Towns has supreme confidence that a knowledge of Church Growth principles provides Christian leaders with models of church planting and tools for ministry "to motivate and guide them and to hold them responsible for effective ministry."

I agree that the Church Growth paradigm has helped by emphasizing incarnational identification, stressing pioneer evangelism, and accentuating the missionary nature of the church. Towns, however, overstates the case by truncating effective perspectives of ministry to Church Growth. One also wonders how the New Testament church grew without special knowledge of missions derived through social research.

Towns believes that the megachurch movement was birthed by the Church Growth movement and should be studied to provide models for other churches to follow. While I am neither for nor against big churches as such and study their theologies, strategies, and structures, I question whether the megachurch is really the wave of the future. Great growth gained using the seeker model will dwindle unless these churches become distinctive, countercultural communities of faith. Large numbers alone do not equate success. Churches who plant new churches every two or three years will likely have more cohesion than megachurches, unless these churches are extremely intentional about discipling and community development.

A RENEWAL RESPONSE
Howard Snyder

Elmer Towns's historical overview is a valuable contribution to our understanding of Church Growth theory and approaches. It is helpful to have this history documented and put into perspective and the varied contributions of a number of leaders and writers duly noted.

While I generally affirm Towns's perspective, I will highlight three areas where I either have reservations or feel that some clarification is needed.

MEGACHURCHES?

Towns, who has helpfully studied the growth of very large congregations, accents the "explosion of megachurches" as a key development in the evolution of Church Growth theory and practice.

While I am thankful for the redemptive ministry that many megachurches have, I believe these superchurches are less significant than many in the Church Growth movement seem to think. Any evaluation of the megachurch phenomenon, it seems to me, must keep several things in mind. First, megachurches have existed throughout church history, but they have been the exception rather than the rule. We can of course learn from these churches, but it is a mistake to take megachurches, or any particular megachurch, as the preferred model for churches today.[59]

The main cautions I would raise about megachurches are two: First, a focus on megachurches reinforces the tendency to be awed by the spectacular and to think that when it comes to churches, bigger is better. This tendency is not cured simply by entering a disclaimer (as Towns does) that "these larger churches [are] not necessarily better churches."

Second, the megachurch focus obscures the fact that most church growth historically does not come from huge churches but from small to medium-sized congregations. That is, overall, the church grows more from dynamic smaller churches that multiply themselves than from the numerical growth of megachurches. Thus, the focus on megachurches tends to put the emphasis in the wrong place.

THE GREAT COMMISSION?

Secondly, I have reservations about defining the mission of the church exclusively in terms of the Great Commission of Matthew 28:19–20. Historically, there has been a tendency in Church Growth thinking to define the church's mission (and therefore growth and success) too much in terms of the church and not enough in terms of the kingdom of God. This leads to churches that celebrate their own growth but often have little vision for the justice, socioeconomic, and ecological dimensions of God's reign in the present order.

This does not *need* to be the case, because Jesus defined making disciples as "teaching them to obey everything I have commanded you" (Matt. 28:20). What Jesus taught, above all, was the kingdom of God. Jesus' disciples were to "seek first" the righteousness and justice of God's reign and to keep right on praying that God's will would be "done on earth as it is in heaven" until their prayer was answered. There would be nothing wrong with defining the church's mission (and therefore growth) in terms of the Great Commission if the Great Commission were understood biblically—that is, in terms of the kingdom of God.

BIBLICAL PRINCIPLES?

Finally, I have some uneasiness with Towns's level of assurance that more or less objective biblical principles of Church Growth can be identified in Scripture and applied in various cultural contexts. Clearly the Bible reveals fundamental truths about the church and the gospel that are normative for all times and cultures. Whether these yield "Church Growth principles," however, is less clear.

My concern here is that we not lose the dynamic nature of Scripture and of the Spirit's application of the Word in diverse contexts. The way we define a particular Church Growth principle reflects not only the Bible but also our own cultural context and worldview assumptions. If we are not aware of this, we may end up with principles, and hence strategies and methodologies, that we are sure are biblical but in fact are largely shaped by our own cultural presuppositions and perceptions.

Towns says, "Principles do not change, but the way principles are applied changes" according to the context. But can we really discern or know biblical Church Growth principles with that degree of certainty and objectivity? If in some sense "principles do not change," certainly our understanding or apprehension of such principles will be shaped by our cultural context.

Key hermeneutical issues here are often ignored or overlooked. Sound interpretation of Scripture may be, in fact, the biggest ongoing challenge to healthy Church Growth thinking. New Testament professor William Webb distinguishes between *redemptive spirit* and *underlying principles* when working with biblical texts. "The principle underlying a text relates to the degree of abstraction needed to cross between two worlds in the application process."[60] In other words, discerning principles already involves us in some degree of interaction with our own cultural understandings or biases, consciously or unconsciously.

In sum, my response to this fine chapter by Elmer Towns is, "Yes, but . . . !" The three areas highlighted above are the places where, in my view, some qualification or reservation is needed.

A GOSPEL AND OUR CULTURE RESPONSE
Craig Van Gelder

The presentation by Elmer Towns is extensive in covering a wide range of themes associated with church growth and the Church Growth movement. As such, this chapter represents somewhat of a challenge in terms of knowing how best to respond briefly. I have chosen two items to address that represent, I believe, several of the more important issues where the author's presentation might be further refined or reframed.

First, I would like to address the author's view and use of Scripture in relationship to his approach to the development and understanding of Church Growth. The author asserts, "Based on the truth it finds in the Bible, Church Growth then applies research to culture. As such, it uses the research methods of both science and theology. Thus, Church Growth is a 'Bible-based ministry that is data-driven in strategy.'" There are several issues within this assertion that raise concerns for me. One issue has to do with equating the discovery of Bible truths with the doing of theology. In the Church Growth literature, the former is usually done by listing certain verses or texts and then formulating a principle. But once this has been done, one has not necessarily done theology sufficiently. Doing theology requires the testing of one's biblical insights or assertions against the whole of scriptural teaching, as well as against the historical theological perspectives that have developed over the centuries.

Another issue that needs to be considered is the methodology of correlating the discovery of Bible truths and/or principles with the data-driven discoveries of scientific research. Embedded in this practice is the claim that the research in which these folks engage is in fact based on solid social science principles. The author lists a variety of types of Church Growth research. My experience has been that much of the content that becomes known as the principles or laws of Church Growth are largely based on personal observation and case study. I have read few Church Growth studies that have used careful sampling procedures and sound controls to test hypotheses, although these methods are readily available from the social sciences.

The discussion of research methodology leads to a second item I would like to address: the extent to which Church Growth seems to reflect the ethos of modernity. Towns builds a case that Church Growth has helped many pastors by providing them with tools and strategies to improve the effectiveness of their ministry efforts (what I would label as human agency). This combination of tools, strategies, and human agency is at the heart of Church Growth, at least as presented by the author, but it is also at the heart of the ethos of modernity. The world of modernity views life primarily in functional and instrumental terms. Reality is defined by discovering cause-and-effect relationships, usually through social scientific research that generates objective facts that can be conceptualized as hypotheses, principles, and eventually laws. Human agency becomes the intervening variable to utilize this information to effect change among people and within organizations. The key to ministry becomes, then, the discovery of helpful tools and strategies that improve ministry effectiveness. One can see this ethos woven into Church Growth with what many of its critiques have named a "fierce pragmatism."

It is important to raise the question of whether the church and its ministry can be conceived primarily in functional and instrumental terms. Or does doing so diminish or marginalize something about the very nature of the church? This is at the heart of much of the critique that has been brought against the Church Growth movement. What has been named as a fundamental issue of a difference in ecclesiology is in reality rooted in the fundamentally different epistemological approach. While the church needs to always take seriously the worldview and context within which it lives, it does not necessarily need to adopt such a worldview as its own. It would seem, according to the author's presentation, that the epistemology of modernity has become the methodology of Church Growth for both its biblical studies and its social research on the church.

One final note that I would offer regarding the author's presentation concerns his summary of the phases of Church Growth. He suggests that we have been through two phases in the development of Church Growth—original pioneers and leader-practitioners—and are now in a third phase, the Babel stage. This choice of metaphor probably conveys more than the author intended. He uses the image to note that many persons today who come under the Church Growth umbrella tend to speak different languages and that they do not understand one another. He goes on to state his conviction that this probably represents a maturing of the movement. Without necessarily dismissing the point he is trying to make, I would suggest that if this metaphor is descriptive of the present phase of Church Growth, perhaps on a deeper level, it illustrates a lack of integration and coherence within the core theology and theory that is at the heart of the movement. This fragmentation appears to be more the result of diverse methods and strategies than one that is giving birth to diverse perspectives of what constitutes among these persons an understanding of church growth in particular and ecclesiology in general. It would be interesting to test among these diverse languages of Church Growth today whether chapter 3 in this book, in which Charles Van Engen proposes a comprehensive Church Growth theology, in fact, might effect a new Pentecost that enables each to hear the same gospel in their own tongue. But I confess up front that I have my doubts. I am not convinced that you can get to where you want to go from there.

Chapter 1 Notes: Effective Evangelism View

[1]The term *Church Growth* was capitalized by early Church Growth leaders, and the practice has continued. They maintained that the term should be capitalized because it represents a social science or a discipline, an entity. They have said it is a movement because it has (1) a founder, Donald McGavran; (2) a seminal book, *Understanding Church Growth;* (3) a research journal, *Church Growth Bulletin;* (4) a research institute, the original Institute of Church Growth in Eugene, Oregon, which moved to Fuller Theological Seminary in 1965; and (5) a publishing company, the William Carey Library (1969), for the mass publication and circulation of Church Growth books. See C. Peter Wagner, "American Church Growth Update," *United Evangelical Action* 33, no. 1 (Spring 1974): 15–16, 34. Early Church Growth leaders said the term was accepted and capitalized in the dictionary; however, in 2002, an examination of the six leading dictionaries did not reveal the term or definition.

[2]George Hunter III, quoted in Dan Simpson, ed., "Celebrating Donald McGavran and Church Growth," *Ministry Advantage* (Fall 1997): 1. This article is based on the works of Tim Stafford, "The Father of Church Growth" *Christianity Today* (21 February 1986); Herbert M. Works Jr., Kent R. Hunter, Neal Browning, and Peter Wagner, *Global Church Growth* 27, no. 3 (July–September 1990); Thom S. Rainer, *The Book of Church Growth: History, Theology, and Principles* (Nashville: Broadman and Holman, 1993), 33–49; Gary L. McIntosh, "The Church Growth Movement," in *Leadership Handbook of Outreach and Care,* ed. James D. Berkley (Grand Rapids: Baker, 1994), 31–37.

[3]The term *foreign missions* was once the dominant term used to describe ministry done in other nations; that term is seldom used today, except by those who hang on to past strategy.

[4]Elmer L. Towns, John N. Vaughan, and David J. Seifert, *The Complete Book of Church Growth* (Wheaton, IL: Tyndale House, 1981), 106. Pickett's findings were published in J. Waskom Pickett, *Christian Mass Movements in India* (Lucknow, India: Lucknow Publishing, 1933).

[5]Simpson, "Celebrating Donald McGavran and Church Growth," 2.

[6]Donald H. Gill, "Apostle of Church Growth," *World Vision* 12, no. 7 (September 1968): 11.

[7]John K. Branner, "McGavran Speaks on Roland Allen," *Evangelical Missions Quarterly* 8, no. 3 (Spring 1972): 173.

[8]Donald A. McGavran, *How to Teach Religion in Mission Schools* (Jubbulpore, India: Mission Press, 1934); J. W. Pickett, Donald Anderson McGavran, G. H. Singh, *The Mass Movement Survey of India* (Jubbulpore, India: Mission Press, 1937); J. Waskom Pickett, *Church Growth and Group Conversion* (Lucknow, India: Lucknow Publishing House, 1956).

[9]Donald A. McGavran, *The Bridges of God* (New York: Friendship, 1955).

[10]Donald A. McGavran, *How Churches Grow* (London, England: World Dominion, 1959).

[11]This is the original name of the American Society for Church Growth. The name was changed at the request of persons forming a Canadian Church Growth society to reflect a distinction from the Canadian society.

[12]Elmer L. Towns, *A Practical Encyclopedia of Evangelism and Church Growth* (Ventura, CA: Regal, 1995), 76.

[13]Elmer L. Towns, *The Ten Largest Sunday Schools and What Makes Them Grow* (Grand Rapids: Baker, 1969).

[14]Elmer L. Towns, *America's Fastest Growing Churches* (Nashville: Impact, 1972), 77.

[15]Ibid., 154.

[16]Towns, *The Ten Largest Sunday Schools*, 147–51.

[17]Elmer L. Towns, *Church Aflame* (Nashville: Impact, 1971); Jerry Falwell and Elmer L. Towns, *Capturing a Town for Christ* (Old Tappan, NJ: Revell, 1973); Elmer L. Towns, *Getting a Church Started in the Face of Insurmountable Odds, with Limited Resources, in Unlikely Circumstances* (Nashville: Impact, 1975); Towns, *The World's Largest Sunday School* (Nashville: Thomas Nelson, 1974); Towns, *Ten of Today's Most Innovative Churches* (Ventura, CA: Regal, 1990).

[18]Towns, *A Practical Encyclopedia*, 76.

[19]As never before, the present focus of worldwide evangelism is on planting new churches to evangelize unreached people groups. While other types of evangelism have their place (radio, TV, internet, tracts, colportage, street preaching, public education, etc.), the most effective type of evangelism has been church planting.

[20]McGavran originally used the phrases *scientific research* and *science*. At meetings of the American Society for Church Growth, however, members have tended to use the term *discipline* to identify it with theological disciplines.

[21]Towns, *A Practical Encyclopedia*, 79.

[22]Ibid., 76. To see an illustration of these laws or principles, there are forty-nine Church Growth principles by titles and definitions in John Vaughan, "The Fuller Factor," in Towns, Vaughan, and Seifert, *The Complete Book of Church Growth*, 100–33. Vaughan studied the principles of early Church Growth pioneers and concluded McGavran had found sixty-seven principles; C. Peter Wagner, fifty-one principles; and Win Arn, twenty-eight principles (p. 109).

[23]J. Robertson McQuilkin, *Measuring the Church Growth Movement* (Chicago: Moody Press, 1973), 110.

[24]C. Peter Wagner, "Church Growth: More Than a Man, a Magazine, a School, a Book," *Christianity Today* (December 7, 1973): 11–14.

[25]Towns, *A Practical Encyclopedia*, 78.

[26]This definition is taken from *New Wineskins for Effective Ministry in the Twenty-first Century*, a brochure advertising the American Society for Church Growth annual gathering held November 9–11, 2000 (Pasadena, CA: American Society for Church Growth, Fuller Theological Seminary, 2000).

[27]Towns, *A Practical Encyclopedia*, 79.

[28]Flavil Yeakley, "Persuasion in Religious Conversion" (Ph.D. diss., University of Illinois, 1976).

[29]George G. Hunter III, "The Ancient Celtic Way of Being and Doing Church for the Post-Modern West," *Journal of the American Society for Church Growth* 10 (1999): 3–28.

[30]Charles Van Engen, *God's Missionary People: Rethinking the Purpose of the Local Church* (Grand Rapids: Baker, 1991), 59–71.

31. Thom S. Rainer, *The Bridger Generation* (Nashville: Broadman and Holman, 1997); Gary L. McIntosh, *One Church, Four Generations* (Grand Rapids: Baker, 2002); McIntosh, *Make Room for the Boom . . . or Bust* (Grand Rapids: Revell, 1997).

32. Towns, *A Practical Encyclopedia*, 76.

33. Ibid., 76–77.

34. Ibid., 78.

35. Ibid. The phrase "the Fuller Factor" first appeared as a chapter title in Towns, Vaughan, and Seifert, *The Complete Book of Church Growth.*

36. Ibid., 81.

37. Lewis S. Chafer, *Systematic Theology*, vol. 1 (Dallas: Dallas Theological Seminary, 1947), 4. This definition for systematic theology is used because of the strong element of methodology that is included—*theologizing*.

38. Towns, *A Practical Encyclopedia*, 81.

39. Principles are the laws of evangelism that are transcultural and transtemporal. "Evangelism is communicating the Gospel in an understandable manner and motivating a person to respond positively to Christ and become a responsible member of His church." This definition of evangelism is used by the editors of *A Practical Encyclopedia of Evangelism and Church Growth*, 407. A method is an approach or technique used within culture to present the gospel with a view to getting people saved.

40. Why the recent focus on techniques, programs, and methods? Because the primary influencers are no longer academic personnel, who tend to be more concerned with abstract truth or principles. Rather, the primary influencers are now local church pastors, who tend to be more pragmatic, asking questions like, What will help my church become effective? The business community has also become a primary influencer, asking What can sell? Pastors and Christian businesses tend not to be as interested in abstract truth when applied to principles and methods.

41. Towns, *A Practical Encyclopedia*, 82.

42. Donald A. McGavran, *Understanding Church Growth* (Grand Rapids: Eerdmans, 1970), 162.

43. Towns, *A Practical Encyclopedia*, 82.

44. For the most part, the books written by second-generation Church Growth influencers did not contain the discovery of new principles of Church Growth, nor did they expand the boundaries of Church Growth truth. Rather, they were applying the principles that had already been established.

45. I use the word *Babel* in the sense that many languages were spoken, rather than in the negative sense of disobedience to God's directions.

46. Christian A. Schwarz, *The ABC's of Natural Church Development* (Carol Stream, IL: ChurchSmart Resources, 1998). Christian Schwartz is one who is critical of the Church Growth movement, yet he is a part of the movement. He claims that his "Natural Church Growth" has discovered new principles, but the principles seem to be only new terminology for existing principles.

47. Towns, *A Practical Encyclopedia*, 77.

48. John Vaughan, "The Church Growth Movement: Offense to the Cross," *Church Growth Today* 10, no. 2 (1995): 2.

[49]Os Guinness, *Dining with the Devil: The Megachurch Movement Flirts with Modernity* (Grand Rapids: Baker, 1993), 20–21. With this criticism, Guinness points out excesses by some who advocate the growth of churches. Guinness is probably correct; not everyone who advocates that churches should grow properly understands or applies the principles originally suggested by McGavran.

[50]Ibid., 51–52. Again, Guinness is describing growth methods that are contrary to Church Growth principles. He should have pointed his attack at the guilty individual and not at the movement.

[51]Charles Colson et al., *Power Religion: The Selling Out of the Evangelical Church?* (Chicago: Moody Press, 1992), 145. I doubt if Colson fully understands the biblical ramifications of contextualization, perhaps because of his legal training and lack of theological training.

[52]Ibid., 144. See also John F. MacArthur Jr., *Ashamed of the Gospel: When the Church Becomes Like the World* (Wheaton, IL: Crossway, 1993), 65. In this book, MacArthur argues that only principles identified in the Scriptures should be followed. He focuses most of his discussion on 1 or 2 Timothy. MacArthur does not understand the role of natural revelation (truth found outside of biblical revelation) in determining truth and principles of evangelism.

[53]C. Kirk Hadaway, *Church Growth Principles: Separating Fact from Fiction* (Nashville: Baptist Sunday School Board, 1991), 13.

[54]MacArthur, *Ashamed of the Gospel*, 80. Guinness, *Dining with the Devil*, 81. This argument against Church Growth does not deal with principles or applied methods, but rather deals with personalities and contemporary expressions of Christianity. These are not the essence of Christianity, and critics are not fair in attributing these contemporary expressions to Church Growth.

[55]MacArthur, *Ashamed of the Gospel*, 81. MacArthur does not recognize the valid role of transfer growth as only one element of the Church Growth movement.

[56]Ibid., 78. This is a valid criticism and must be honestly addressed by the movement.

[57]Charles Colson et al., *Power Religion*, 145. Why is it that critics seem to reject numerical growth, no matter what kind? The movement accepts the criticism that some church growth is not biblical. Yes, the movement has its fanatics, and there are non-Christian churches that are growing. But God loves growing things. From the beginning, God decreed all living things shall reproduce, "according to its kind" (Gen. 1:11–12, 21, 24–25). Perhaps the critics are convicted for their nonevangelism and are justifying their disobedience.

[58]See J. C. Hoekendijk, *The Church Inside Out* (Philadelphia: Westminster, 1966). Hoekendijk's missiology was strongly influenced by his pessimism over the church, which stemmed from difficult personal experiences he had while growing up in a very conservative church in the Netherlands. His post–World War II desire for the church to be a relevant instrument for social change (contra the events in Germany during that time) moved him further in a negative assessment of the importance of the church. As the secretary for the World Council of Churches' Commission on World Mission and Evangelism, and later as a professor in the United States, Hoekendijk made a strong case in *The Church*

Inside Out and in other articles that the best thing the church in its present form could do would be to die and be reborn through the presence of believers acting out the gospel in the world in which they lived. At most, the church's existence could only be justified as being a possible instrument for social change on the way to the establishment of shalom on earth. Hoekendijk's perspective was very influential in the ecumenical project *The Church for Others and the Church for the World* (Geneva: World Council of Churches, 1968). See also Thomas Wieser, ed., *Planning for Mission: Working Papers on the New Quest for Missionary Communities* (New York: U.S. Conference for the World Council of Churches, 1966).

[59]I elaborate on this in *Decoding the Church*, especially pp. 62–67 (Howard A. Snyder with Daniel V. Runyon, *Decoding the Church: Mapping the DNA of Christ's Body* [Grand Rapids: Baker, 2002]). It is instructive to remember that throughout history, megachurches have often grown rapidly precisely because they were doing something novel or innovative for their times.

[60]William J. Webb, *Slaves, Women and Homosexuals: Exploring the Hermeneutics of Cultural Analysis* (Downers Grove, IL: InterVarsity, 2001), 53.

Chapter Two

GOSPEL AND OUR CULTURE VIEW

GOSPEL AND OUR CULTURE VIEW

*Church Growth lacks a sufficient view
of the church, which hinders it
from effectively engaging the culture*

Craig Van Gelder

"And Jesus answered him, 'Blessed are you, Simon son of Jonah! For flesh and blood has not revealed this to you, but my Father in heaven. And I tell you, you are Peter, and on this rock I will build my church, and the gates of Hades will not prevail against it'" (Matt. 16:17–18 NRSV).

"Day by day, as they spent much time together in the temple, they broke bread at home and ate their food with glad and generous hearts, praising God and having the goodwill of all the people. And day by day the Lord added to their number those who were being saved" (Acts 2:46–47 NRSV).

"But speaking the truth in love, we must grow up in every way into him who is the head, into Christ, from whom the whole body, joined and knit together by every ligament with which it is equipped, as each part is working properly, promotes the body's growth in building itself up in love" (Eph. 4:15–16 NRSV).

"They sing a new song: 'You are worthy to take the scroll and to open its seals, for you were slaughtered and by your blood you ransomed for God saints from every tribe and language and people and nation; you have made them to be a kingdom and priests serving our God, and they will reign on earth'" (Rev. 5:9–10 NRSV).

These Scripture passages indicate there is a clear expectation in the New Testament that the church will grow. The basic premise is it is part of the very nature of the church, as the body of Christ on earth, to grow both spiritually and numerically. However, I do not believe this premise necessarily translates into what has come to be known as "church growth" as introduced by the Church Growth movement within the discipline of missiology over the past fifty years. How, then, are we to understand church growth?

This chapter will engage in a discussion of church growth and the Church Growth movement from the perspective of another recent movement within the discipline of missiology, the Gospel and Our Culture (GOC) conversation. My method will be to first clarify how church growth and the Church Growth movement are being understood within this chapter. Second, I will outline some of the basic tenants associated with the GOC conversation. This will be followed by some biblical perspective on the issues associated with the growth of the church. Finally, I will engage in a summary critique of church growth and the Church Growth movement from the viewpoint of the GOC conversation.

UNDERSTANDING CHURCH GROWTH AND THE CHURCH GROWTH MOVEMENT

It is necessary for me to acknowledge a bit of a surprise in relation to the focus of this book. Since the early 1990s, I have viewed church growth and the Church Growth movement as somewhat passé. Robert E. Logan's 1989 book, *Beyond Church Growth*, signaled some of the shifts taking place among the movement's advocates, toward a more holistic understanding of discipleship and church health.[1] Changes also took place in the leadership of the movement in the 1990s, as a new generation of leaders emerged to redefine what had been the North American Society for Church Growth into the American Society for Church Growth.[2] In addition, during the late 1980s, the best-known spokesperson for the movement in the United States, C. Peter Wagner, surprised many as he made a move toward power encounters and spiritual warfare as his new interest.[3] And finally, proposed as a textbook for Church Growth, *The Book of Church Growth: History, Theology, and Principles* was published in 1993 by Southern Baptist Thom Rainer, who had, as Wagner pointed out, never been part of the "Fuller connection."[4] The book reads largely like a summary of a movement that had already peaked. My perception was that the Church Growth movement was receding into the backwaters of missiological importance.

On one level, this perception was correct, especially in relation to the discussion about church growth by persons working in the discipline of missiology. Critique of the Church Growth movement began to surface in the early 1970s, especially after the publication in 1970 of Donald McGavran's foundational work, *Understanding Church Growth.*[5] A more public conversation about the movement took place in 1974 at the International Congress on World Evangelization, held in Lausanne, Switzerland. Some of the presenters were professors at the Fuller School of World Mission whom McGavran had recruited.[6] Accompanying this more public conversation was the beginning of a more focused criticism of Church Growth from among Third World evangelicals.[7] Substantial published critiques of the Church Growth movement began to surface in missiological circles by the mid-1970s.[8] Of theological significance during this period was Charles Van Engen's doctoral thesis at the Free University in Amsterdam, which was published in 1981 as *The Growth of the True Church.*[9] This work attempted to reconcile Church Growth thinking with Reformation ecclesiology.

It was *Exploring Church Growth*, however, a 1983 volume of essays edited by Wilbert R. Shenk, that best summarized a decade of missiological critique of the theology, theory, and methodology embedded in the Church Growth movement.[10] By the early 1990s, Shenk's efforts to update and reprint this volume fell on deaf ears at the publishing house. The basic question was, "What is new?"[11] While various evangelical mission organizations continued to focus their mission work around a church growth approach, the Church Growth movement was increasingly marginalized within the discipline of missiology and the wider missiological community. In addition, within the United States, most of the popular literature that might be associated with Church Growth was no longer being published directly under that title. The earlier literature that had stressed "how to grow a church" was now shifting to more nuanced themes, such as "church effectiveness," "church health," and "transformational leadership."[12]

On another level, however, my perception about Church Growth having become passé is not accurate. A quick web search using the Google search engine illustrates the continued popularity of the terms *church growth* and *Church Growth movement*.[13] I was surprised to find the following results:

Church Growth: 1,140,000 hits
Church Growth movement: 356,000 hits

In addition, a continuous stream of literature has been published that is at least associated with the words *church* and *growth*, even if the phrase *church growth* does not always appear in the title. When one enters "church growth" as the search category on amazon.com, one finds that over 800 books have been published on this topic since 1985.[14] One also finds that there are 46 different publishers involved in the printing of the last 100 of these books, published during 2001–02. The majority of these companies published only one such book each, while the two largest publishers of the last 100 were Zondervan (14 volumes) and Baker Book House (13 volumes).

Clearly the terms *church growth* and *Church Growth movement* have become deeply embedded within North American church culture. But the meanings associated with these terms have become broader and more diffuse than their original meanings within the specific Church Growth movement founded by the late Donald McGavran. It is evident, however, that much of the impulse embedded in the earlier movement is still shaping a larger conversation about how congregations function in the North American context.

NEW MOVEMENTS THAT ARE SHIFTING THE FOCUS

A number of movements have sprung up that have at least some of their roots in the earlier Church Growth movement. But these recent movements, which arose in the 1980s and 1990s, have broadened the understanding of what is meant by Church Growth. First, a new style of church has emerged, along with a new literature about these congregations, that moves beyond the earlier emphasis on numerical growth. This style of church might best be described as "market-driven." These market-driven congregations take more seriously the specific context of the United States and focus not just on growth but on growth in a particular way, or of a particular kind. These congregations include, for example:[15]

> *The Seven-Day-a-Week Church,* Lyle Schaller
> *The MetaChurch,* Carl George
> *The User-Friendly Church,* George Barna
> *A Church for the Twenty-first Century,* Leith Anderson
> *The Seeker Sensitive Church,* Bill Hybels
> *The Church for the Unchurched,* George Hunter
> *The Purpose-Driven Church,* Rick Warren
> *Natural Church Development,* Christian Schwarz
> *The AquaChurch,* Len Sweet

A second recent movement, which interrelates with these market-driven congregations, is the rise of what have come to be known as "teaching churches." These are usually large congregations, many of which are independent or loosely affiliated with their denomination. They offer numerous seminars and training processes for other congregations and are increasingly serving as centers for educating a new generation of pastors to engage in congregational vitalization and new church development. While there are scores of such teaching churches today, perhaps the most well-known examples are Willow Creek Community Church in South Barrington, Illinois, led by Bill Hybels, and Saddleback Church in Lake Forest, California, led by Rick Warren. Thousands of pastors and church leaders attend their annual seminars.[16]

A third recent movement that has broadened our understanding of what is meant by Church Growth is the expanding number of organizational networks and consultants that are seeking to foster the health and growth of congregations through seminars, publications, and on-site consulting. Some of the more influential organizations of this type are Leadership Network, operating out of Dallas, Texas; Easum, Bandy and Associates, operating out of Port Aransas, Texas; and Barna Research Group, located in Ventura, California.[17] Thousands participate in the numerous seminars offered each year by these organizations. Also of note as consultants and consulting organizations are

Charles Arn, with Church Growth, Inc.; Carl George, with the MetaChurch Project; George Hunter III; Kent Hunter, with the Church Doctor; Gary McIntosh, with the McIntosh Church Growth Network; and Elmer Towns. All of these consultants continue to be active members of the American Society for Church Growth.

A fourth movement having roots in Church Growth that has helped reshape the church landscape in the United States is the increasing number of congregations focusing on new church development. New church development collapsed within most denominations by the early 1970s after the growth caused by the baby boomer generation began to wane. By the 1980s, however, strategies for starting new, mission-driven congregations began to take hold. This movement does not have a clearly identifiable center, although a key influence is Robert E. Logan, formerly with Church Resource Ministries and now with ChurchSmart Resources, who along with his colleague Steven L. Ogne developed the *Church Planter's Toolkit*.[18]

THE CONGREGATIONALIZATION OF THE CHURCH GROWTH MOVEMENT—1985 TO THE PRESENT

Clearly an activism seeking to influence the growth of the church is at work today within U.S. denominations and congregations. The several movements outlined above illustrate this activism. In some ways, these movements can be viewed as the successors of the Church Growth movement and serve as representatives, at least to some extent, of the practice of Church Growth today. My perception is that the four movements outlined above have moved Church Growth into its current phase, which is lodged primarily with congregations, what I refer to as the congregationalization of the movement.

As discussed earlier, Church Growth as a movement in the United States went through a period of transition, beginning in the mid-1980s and continuing into the 1990s. In the field of missiology, apart from various evangelical scholars, Church Growth became somewhat marginalized. But as noted above, at least four different movements in the United States, all of which focus on congregations, continued to stress many of the basic premises of Church Growth. What appears to have happened is that Church Growth as a discipline has moved out of the academy and into the life of the church. In doing so, it diversified into a wide range of movements, many of which no longer used the terms *church growth* and *Church Growth movement*.

Given this diffusion of movements, in what sense does the phrase *church growth* function as an identifiable concept today, either through a published literature or among identifiable spokespersons? I do not believe that either exists today in the sense of there being a clearly defined movement, as was once true of Church Growth. But it is evident that the ethos of the present activism shares important connections with the impulses embedded in the earlier Church Growth movement and its understanding of church growth.

THEMES ASSOCIATED WITH CHURCH GROWTH

The current phase of the Church Growth movement, the congregationalization of Church Growth, is the primary focus of this chapter. While the lines of demarcation that define Church Growth in this phase are less clear than in earlier phases, some of the basic premises that have historically been associated with church growth and the Church Growth movement still seem to be at work.

Great Commission Theology and the Priority of Evangelism

The primary missiology that appears to undergird both the Church Growth movement and the recent derivative movements is the classic mission theology of evangelicalism stemming from the nineteenth century. This theology is founded on the Great Commission and is usually expressed as the obligation of the church to evangelize the world.[19] This understanding was embedded in the emergence of the Church Growth movement as "harvest theology."[20]

Understanding the Church Primarily in Functional Terms

The primary ecclesiology that appears to undergird both the Church Growth movement and its recent derivative movements is one that conceives of the church in functional terms— what the church does. This ecclesiology, with its emphasis on the functioning of the church, is related to the missiology of

Great Commission theology, with its emphasis on obedience. The church is defined by what it is supposed to do. Historically, ecclesiology has first focused on the nature of the church and its attributes (what God has done) and then discussed the functionality of the church in relation to its attributes (what we do in light of what the church is).[21] One of the implications of taking a primarily functional approach to ecclesiology is the tendency to conceive of the church in malleable terms as an instrument that we are responsible to build.

Learning from Experience and Focusing on What Works

The primary epistemology that appears to undergird both the Church Growth movement and its recent derivative movements is one that draws deeply on experience in relation to biblical practices. A clear pragmatism pervades Church Growth thinking and practice.[22] This stems from exercising a hermeneutical approach to Scripture that looks for biblical principles and identifies biblical practices as the basis for shaping Church Growth principles.

Mature Believers and Church Health

The primary focus of Church Growth appears to have shifted in recent years. One of the distinctions McGavran initially made was between the practices of "discipling" and "perfecting."[23] Discipling dealt mainly with conversion and was viewed as the primary responsibility of the church, while perfecting, or the maturing of believers, was relegated to secondary status. This distinction, though difficult to establish on a careful reading of Matthew 28,[24] is perhaps understandable for one who is working in a mission context in which millions of persons have never heard of Christ. But the distinction between discipling and perfecting appears to have collapsed in recent decades, at least within the recent movements in the United States that are derived from Church Growth. Holistic discipleship and healthy systems, what McGavran would have thought of as "perfecting" emphases, are increasingly becoming the expectation for every congregation. They are also the primary focus of the recent movements discussed earlier.

UNDERSTANDING THE GOSPEL AND
OUR CULTURE MOVEMENT

The decline of mainline U.S. denominations in the midst of resurgence in the evangelical sector of the church has been documented by numerous authors.[25] These shifts have been paralleled by an increased awareness of the emergence of the postmodern condition in the broader culture.[26] Accompanying these changes has been an increased turbulence within society as the result of globalization, the new immigration, and the emergence of the information age.[27] By the end of the century, it was becoming commonplace for the United States to be defined as a mission field in much the same way that the West had previously viewed other locations in the two-thirds world.[28]

The Influence of Lesslie Newbigin

In response to these changes, a movement emerged in the 1980s that came to be known as the Gospel and Our Culture (GOC) conversation. It surfaced first in England and then in the United States among missiologists and church leaders who were seeking to address the West as its own unique mission location. The person who most influenced the formation of this conversation was the late Lesslie Newbigin, whose career in mission within India paralleled that of Donald McGavran. But Newbigin's focus took a different direction than that of Church Growth. Newbigin was sobered by the secularity of Western society when he retired and moved back to England in the 1970s after years of service with the former International Missionary Council (IMC) and later with the Commission on World Mission and Evangelism (CWME) of the World Council of Churches. The question that began to intrigue him was, "What would be involved in a missionary encounter between the gospel and this whole way of perceiving, thinking, and living that we call 'modern Western culture?'"[29]

Newbigin's missiology was shaped by the mission theology given birth within the IMC conferences during the 1950s. This was a Trinitarian understanding of mission, what is commonly referred to as the *missio Dei* (the mission of God). Growing out of the emphasis on biblical theology, this mission theology was first articulated by Wilhelm Anderson at the

Wellingen Conference of the IMC in 1952 and was later given fuller expression by Johannes Blauw in his 1962 publication *The Missionary Nature of the Church*.[30] Newbigin articulated his own expression of this mission theology in his 1978 publication *The Open Secret*.[31] Central to Newbigin's understanding of mission is the work of the triune God in calling and sending the church, through the Spirit, into the world to participate fully in God's mission within all of creation. In this theological understanding, the church is the creation of the Spirit. It exists in the world as a sign that the redemptive reign of God's kingdom is present. It serves as a foretaste of the eschatological future of the redemptive reign that has already begun. It also serves as an instrument under the leadership of the Spirit to bring that redemptive reign to bear on every dimension of life.[32]

While stressing many helpful contributions that McGavran offered to the growing discipline of missiology, Newbigin expressed three points of concern. The second point has been largely addressed within the later developments of Church Growth, but the substance of the first and third points still holds merit today within contemporary congregational expressions of Church Growth in the United States. Newbigin's three points were:

1. Numbers in the New Testament are not so much a goal driven by a strategy for measuring the effectiveness of a church as they are the result of the faithful witness of Christian communities to the good news of the resurrected Lord.

2. Conversion in the New Testament is about more than just coming to faith in Christ, what McGavran refers to as "discipling." It also involves ethical dimensions that are intrinsic to the gospel, what McGavran refers to as "perfecting," which he wants to separate from discipling as a separate and later activity.

3. In the relationship of gospel and culture, culture as the sum total of ways of living involves negative as well as positive dimensions. A biblical understanding of culture needs to include a discussion of the powers—created, fallen, and redeemed. Fitting the gospel to the existing mosaic of a culture can, in reality, be a capitulation of the gospel to the more conservative, and often unethical, dimensions of that culture.[33]

The British GOC Programme

The British version of the GOC conversation was a movement that developed during the 1980s and was referred to as a "programme." It was shaped largely by the writings of Newbigin during this period, which included *The Other Side of 1984* (1983), *Foolishness to the Greeks* (1986), and *The Gospel in a Pluralist Society* (1989).[34] Newbigin's intellectual leadership of the programme was joined by the administrative and organizational contributions of Dr. Dan Beeby and Bishop Hugh Montefiore. An occasional newsletter began publication in 1989, but in many ways, the programme culminated in 1992 with the National Consultation at Swanwick. A volume of essays edited by Montefiore, titled *The Gospel and Contemporary Culture*, served as the agenda for discussion at that consultation.[35] During the early 1990s, the British GOC programme floundered somewhat, due primarily to its failure to secure sufficient funding and to find an institutional home within the church. In 1994, a move was made to merge the GOC programme with the C. S. Lewis center, but this merger proved short-lived and was disbanded in 1996.[36] The death of Lesslie Newbigin in 1998 brought an additional sense of closure to the symbolic leadership of the GOC movement in England.

The Gospel and Our Culture Network in the United States

As the British programme began to gain public recognition, a version of the Gospel and Our Culture conversation began to emerge in the United States. Several consultations sponsored in the mid-1980s by the Overseas Study Mission Center stimulated interest in the question Newbigin had posed in the Warfield Lectures at Princeton in 1984 (later published as *Foolishness to the Greeks*): "Can the West Be Converted?" Growing out of these early events, a network began to take shape by the late 1980s under the leadership of Dr. George Hunsberger, who in 1990 accepted a position as professor of mission at Western Theological Seminary in Holland, Michigan.

By the early 1990s, the Gospel and Our Culture Network (GOCN) was publishing a quarterly newsletter and convening a yearly consultation. During the 1990s, grants from the Pew Charitable Trusts and the Lilly Endowment provided helpful funding for study and writing projects. In addition, Western Theological Seminary provided an institutional home. By the mid-1990s, the U.S. movement began to find its own voice beyond the influence of Newbigin as Eerdmans began publishing a series of books under the moniker of the Gospel and Our Culture series. Included in this series are the following volumes:

> George Hunsberger and Craig Van Gelder, eds., *The Church Between Gospel and Culture: The Emerging Mission in North America*, 1996.
> Darrel L. Guder, ed., *Missional Church: A Vision for the Sending of the Church in North America*, 1998.
> George R. Hunsberger, *Bearing the Witness of the Spirit: Lesslie Newbigin's Theology of Cultural Plurality*, 1998.
> Craig Van Gelder, ed., *Confident Witness—Changing World: Rediscovering the Gospel in North America*, 1999.
> Darrel L. Guder, *The Continuing Conversion of the Church*, 2000.

Related to this series, but published by Baker Book House, is my own volume *The Essence of the Church: A Community Created by the Spirit*.[37] This growing body of literature represents the current perspective of the U.S. version of the GOC conversation. Central to this perspective is an understanding of the missional nature of the church within a missional ecclesiology.

THEMES ASSOCIATED WITH THE GOC CONVERSATION

There are a number of key premises that stand out in the literature that has been produced by the GOC conversation.

Missio Dei

The primary missiology that undergirds the GOC conversation is the *missio Dei,* which is understood as the triune God being in mission within all the world. This GOC understanding of mission theology is about the church as a called community of the triune God being sent into the world to participate fully in God's mission. The social reality of the Godhead in three persons is understood as the foundation of the church's being missionary by nature as the creation of God. Just as the Father sent the Son to accomplish salvation, so also the Father and the Son continue to send the Spirit into the world to guide and teach the church to participate fully in God's redemptive reign in Christ.

Kingdom of God

The primary identity of the church that undergirds the GOC conversation is founded on God's kingdom. The church's identity is formed out of God's work in the world in terms of the kingdom of God that Jesus announced and inaugurated in his person and work. This kingdom, what might be referred to as "the redemptive reign of God in Christ," is what the church lives within and now bears witness to in the world. The mission of the church must be understood in light of the mission of God that is present in the world as God's kingdom. This kingdom belongs to God. The church is to receive, enter, and seek the kingdom that it will one day inherit, but the church is never instructed to build, promote, or extend it. The work is of God's design, not that of humans, although humans fully participate in God's work.

Church

The primary ecclesiology that undergirds the GOC conversation is rooted in an understanding of the nature of the church as being the creation of the Spirit. It is a missiological ecclesiology, usually referred to as the "missional church." The church is understood to be a unique community in the world that is missionary by nature, created by God through the Spirit as both holy and human. Mission is not primarily something the church does, but rather defines what the church is, which means that everything the church does has a missional dimension to it. The church is created as a called and sent community, responsible for participating fully in the redemptive reign of God in Christ. What the church does is understood to stem from what the church is. The functionality of the church grows out of its essence, or nature.

Culture

The primary hermeneutic for understanding the church that undergirds the GOC conversation relates to how we understand culture. Culture is what comprises the whole of our existence and provides meaning for how we understand life. How we understand God, read the Bible, interpret the gospel, and live as a church is all embedded in a cultural perspective. This makes the meanings we construct perspectival in character. We are always in process of growing into a fuller and deeper understanding of God, of ourselves, and of the world around us. But our meanings can become captive to dimensions of the culture within which we live. This makes it imperative to understand one's particular cultural context. Different cultural contexts develop different behaviors and systems of meaning, and from the point of view of the gospel, every cultural context functions as a mission location. But culture is not neutral. Our behaviors and the systems of meaning we construct have ethical dimensions. This means that the gospel brings critique to a culture even as the gospel searches for bridges to build on. This dialectic introduces a constant tension into the life of the church as it seeks to bear witness to the redemptive reign of God in a particular context.

CHURCH GROWTH OR THE GROWTH OF THE CHURCH?

In many ways, the placement of the word *growth* makes all the difference in how one thinks about these matters. Whenever the word *church* is used as an adjective to describe something else, there is a tendency to turn the church into a functional entity that ends up serving primarily an instrumental purpose. While the church is an instrument of the Spirit intended to bear witness to the kingdom of God and to bring redemption to bear in every dimension of life, this is not the primary basis of the church's identity. The church is more than its functionality, a set of purposes to be performed. Its core identity is related to its nature, which is the creation of the Spirit. Thus, when phrases like *church renewal, church growth,* or *church effectiveness* are constructed, the tendency is to place the focus on the function that is being described by the noun—renewal, growth, or effectiveness. This can end up subverting the character of the church by turning it into a malleable tool that is intended primarily to accomplish a particular function. Instead of the church's character, through its nature, giving expression to what the church does, it is not uncommon for one dimension of what the church does to become the criterion for constructing an identity for the church. Thus, what becomes most important is the church's renewal, growth, or effectiveness. What is often lost in this approach is an understanding of the richness of what God has already created within the very nature of the church that exists in the world.

Taking a functional approach, with its instrumental view of the purpose of the church, is problematic when trying to come to an accurate understanding of the church. From a biblical perspective, the church, rather than themes such as renewal, growth, or effectiveness (or whatever), needs to function as the noun. Qualitative words that deal with functionality or instrumentality need to define the church. Thus, it is more biblical to speak of the "growth of the church" rather than "church growth," or the "effectiveness of the church" rather than "church effectiveness." This shift in emphasis is not just a matter of semantics; profoundly important ecclesiological issues are embedded in this distinction.

It is important to note that the Bible does, in fact, speak about the growth of the church. Gaining a biblical perspective on growth in relationship to the church is a matter of ecclesiology, how we view the church, and it is also a matter of pneumatology, how we view the person and work of the Spirit. Biblically, a case can be made for the growth of the church as the work of the Spirit. It is the Spirit who creates the church to bear witness to the redemptive reign of God in Christ, and it is the Spirit who leads the church into bringing redemption to bear on every dimension of life.

The Gospels

In the Gospels, one finds the expectation that a movement will be born as a result of the announced presence of the kingdom of God in the person and work of Jesus Christ. This kingdom is present in our midst: "The kingdom of God is among you" (Luke 17:21 NRSV). It is to be received (Mark 10:15), and persons are invited to seek it (Matt. 6:33) and enter into it (Matt. 23:13), while also looking toward that day when they will inherit it (Matt. 25:34). The coming of the kingdom is about God's power confronting and defeating the power of the enemy, the evil one (Matt. 4:1–11). Living in the presence of the kingdom, God's redemptive reign in Christ, means that illnesses may be healed (Matt. 11:2–5), evil spirits may be cast out (Mark 1:39), and natural circumstances may be changed (Mark 6:47–51), even as the poor hear the gospel of the kingdom as good news (Luke 4:18–19). Parables are used to explain the kingdom as a mystery that only some have ears to hear and eyes to see (Matt. 13:10–17). The Father gives the kingdom as a gift to the followers of Jesus. Accepting this gift radically changes the way one looks at material possessions (Luke 12:32–33). While the presence and influence of God's kingdom will grow dramatically in the world (Matt. 13:31–32), there are many who think they are part of God's kingdom that will miss it (Matt. 21:33–44).

As Jesus announced the presence of the kingdom, he gathered around himself followers who would learn to "fish for people" (Mark 1:17 NRSV). The expectation is that these followers will serve as the foundation of the church that Jesus himself would build (Matt. 16:18). Anticipating his death, Jesus prayed not only for his followers but also for all who would come to believe in him through their testimony (John 17:20). Following his death and resurrection, Jesus made it clear to his followers that they were to take the message of salvation, rooted in God's kingdom, to all people and to the ends of the earth (Matt. 28:19–20; Luke 24:47). Jesus also conveyed to these followers that they would be led in this work and empowered to carry it out through the presence of the Spirit among them (Luke 24:49; John 14:25–26; 20:22). Jesus clearly anticipated that a movement would grow out of the work of these followers as they were led and taught by the Spirit.

Acts

The Acts of the Apostles (probably better titled "the Acts of the Spirit") gives an account of what the followers of Jesus experienced after the Spirit came upon them. The author clearly lays out a growth hermeneutic for the church as one of the organizing themes of this book. There are regular references to growth taking place, both in terms of people and regarding the broader influence of the gospel. These references include the following (NRSV):

Acts 1:8	"... you will be my witnesses ..."
Acts 2:41	"... that day about three thousand persons were added."
Acts 2:47	"And day by day the Lord added to their number those who were being saved."
Acts 4:4	"But many of those who heard the word believed; and they numbered about five thousand."
Acts 5:14	"Yet more than ever believers were added to the Lord, great numbers of both men and women."
Acts 6:7	"The word of God continued to spread; the number of the disciples increased greatly in Jerusalem."
Acts 9:31	"Meanwhile the church throughout Judea, Galilee and Samaria ... was built up ... [and] it increased in numbers."
Acts 11:21	"The hand of the Lord was with them, and a great number became believers and turned to the Lord."
Acts 12:24	"But the word of God continued to advance and gain adherents."
Acts 13:48–49	"... as many as had been destined for eternal life became believers. Thus the word of the Lord spread throughout the region."
Acts 14:1	"... a great number of both Jews and Greeks became believers."
Acts 14:21	"After they had proclaimed the good news to the city and had made many disciples ..."
Acts 16:5	"So the churches were strengthened in the faith and increased in numbers daily."
Acts 17:12	"Many of them therefore believed, including not a few Greek women and men of high standing."
Acts 18:8	"... and many of the Corinthians who heard Paul became believers and were baptized."
Acts 19:10	"This continued for two years, so that all the residents of Asia ... heard the word of the Lord."
Acts 19:20	"So the word of the Lord grew mightily and prevailed."

This growth hermeneutic in the book of Acts anticipates the expansion of the church throughout the ages. In the midst of the reports of this growth are indications that some intentional strategies were used. Being sent necessitates making strategic choices. The growth of the church, however, under the leading of the Spirit, is characterized as much by conflict, disruption, and surprise as it is by any planned strategy. Examples of this stand out in the book of Acts.

Growth from Conflict in Acts 6

The complaint of the Hellenists that their widows were being neglected in the daily distribution of food led to a decision to add additional leadership to the church. This resulted in expanded ministry, which in turn facilitated even more growth, and even many in the priesthood became Christians.

Growth from Persecution in Acts 8

Jesus had made it clear that the apostles were to go from Jerusalem to the ends of the earth, but they remained in Jerusalem. Finally a persecution scattered the disciples throughout Judea and Samaria, although interestingly, the apostles still remained in Jerusalem. The disruption caused by this persecution led to substantial growth, bringing into the church many from among those whom Jewish Christians tended to look down on, the Samaritans.

Growth from Ministry on the Margins in Acts 11

Also as a result of this persecution, some of the Gentile converts to Judaism, who later became Christians, returned home to Antioch. They started sharing the faith directly with other Gentiles without requiring them to become Jews in order to become Christians. This ministry was a surprise to the church in Jerusalem and, following the Jerusalem council, eventually became the foundation for the mission to the Gentiles and redefined both the gospel and the church in the New Testament period. What began on the margins came to the center.

Growth from Divine Intervention in Acts 16

In working their strategy of taking the gospel to the next province to the West, Paul and the mission team were blocked by the Spirit from entering Asia and Bithynia. Through a vision to Paul, God redirected the team to go to Macedonia. This divine intervention shifted the location of the planting of churches from the East to the West when the Aegean Sea was crossed.

*Growth from New Insights into Gospel and
Culture in Acts 10 and 15*

Peter's understanding of the gospel was dramatically reframed by two encounters, first with God in a vision and then with Cornelius, a Roman centurion. While Peter wanted to claim that certain practices were theologically grounded, God made it clear that they were, in fact, culturally bound. What God called clean was to be understood as clean. Peter's strategy, in light of his understanding of the gospel as being shaped by the ceremonial practices of Judaism, would never have taken him to the Samaritans or to Cornelius. God intervened to disrupt and reframe Peter's understanding of gospel and culture, although for some time, Peter still continued to struggle with fully accepting Gentiles as fellow believers in Christ.

In all of the examples given above, the church encountered significant change that was neither planned nor anticipated. No strategy was in place that directly led to the growth of the church from these influences. The church was led by the Spirit to move in new directions, which resulted each time in growth taking place. Two patterns are evident. The first is planned activity—a strategy—that leads to growth, as illustrated in the work of Paul's mission team. A second pattern is the Spirit's leading the church through disruption into new and unanticipated directions that result in growth.

A FRAMEWORK FOR DISCUSSING THE ISSUES AND OFFERING A CRITIQUE

While points of convergence exist between Church Growth and the GOC conversation, it should be evident by now that there are also contrasting perspectives between these two movements. Suggestions regarding these contrasting perspectives have been made throughout this chapter, but it is now time to summarize and reflect more critically on the differences. My method will be to first contrast the two movements in terms of how they approach making strategic choices. This will be followed by a summary critique of how the two movements differ in their understanding of the interaction between the gospel, the church, and a cultural context.

CONTRASTING APPROACHES TO MAKING STRATEGIC CHOICES

There is a clear contrast, I believe, between how the two movements of Church Growth and the GOC conversation approach the matter of making strategic choices. As mentioned earlier, having to make strategic choices is part of the very character of what it means to be church. Every congregation has to make choices in implementing its ministry. But the key question is, How should a congregation approach this responsibility?

Strategic Choices from a Church Growth Perspective

It should be noted that the Church Growth movement has contributed numerous helpful insights regarding the various strategic choices that a congregation must make. I have regularly drawn on many of these insights in my own teaching and consulting work. It is important, however, to address not only the content related to such choices but also the method used to formulate such insights. The clearest statement I have been able to identify of an approach to strategic choices from a Church Growth perspective comes from C. Peter Wagner in his 1986 book, *Strategies for Church Growth*. In this work, Wagner addresses the criticism that Church Growth is overly pragmatic. He notes: "I believe that God is genuinely concerned with the practical implementation of His great commission. . . . He wants us to choose the means which will best accomplish these ends . . . , and this is another way of saying He wants us to be pragmatic. . . . I call this approach 'consecrated pragmatism.' While the Church Growth Movement has come in for its share of criticism for being pragmatic, I believe the critics are not understanding it properly as *consecrated* pragmatism . . . [in which] doctrinal and ethical principles revealed in the Word of God must never be compromised."[38]

This consecrated pragmatism clearly sets the agenda in motion toward strategic action. Something must be done to get at implementing God's plan. We must choose. We must act. We must select the best available strategy and use it. But how does one go about determining which strategy is the best available strategy? Wagner further comments: "The classical approach judges the validity of any experience on the basis of previously established principles. In contrast, church growth leans toward a phenomenological approach which holds theological conclusions somewhat more tentatively and is open to revise them when necessary in light of what is learned through experience. It is open to the possibility that theological expressions might vary from culture to culture and yet all be faithful to the Word of God."[39]

The basic approach of a congregation making strategic choices from a Church Growth perspective would appear to be the following:

- We must act in order to accomplish what God has called us to do.
- We commit ourselves and our work to God in prayer, believing that God's Spirit will actively guide our actions and inform our choices.
- Guided by biblical principles and informed by insights from the social sciences, we choose strategies that are available within our cultural context and that seem wise from the perspective of our experience.
- We adjust these strategies as needed, based on information learned from further experience, to become more effective in achieving our original goal of being obedient to God's command.
- We regularly check our choice of strategies against biblical teaching to ensure that we are not contradicting God's revealed intent.

In summary, congregational decision making from a Church Growth perspective is a prayerful reliance on the Spirit to help develop and implement a workable strategy for action that is informed by experience and that is supported by, or at least does not contradict, biblical principle.

Strategic Choices from a Gospel and Our Culture Perspective

In contrast to Church Growth, the Gospel and Our Culture conversation approaches strategic choices in a somewhat different way. One spokesperson for the GOC conversation who has given attention to these matters is George Hunsberger. He outlines the decision-making task in the following manner.

> If our practical missiology points us toward developing patterns of life, deed, and word, the wider missiological task includes the attention we give in three other directions.
>
> First, we must *pay attention to the culture*. For us to assume we know it has cost too much. It has led too easily to accommodation. Only an insightful analysis of the cultural and social systems shaping, and being shaped by, life in North America can enable us to keep our missiology contextual. . . .
>
> Second, we must *pay attention to the gospel*. A theological agenda here must correspond to the phenomenological one. The central question of theology—What is the gospel?—must be asked in more culturally particular ways. And the more particular the question, the more will be our sense that the answer will emerge in unexpected ways. . . .
>
> Third, we must *pay attention to each other*. It will require of us a new range of "ecumenical" partnerships if we are to hear the gospel as it takes form in the variety of cultures, subcultures, denominational cultures, and ethnic cultures of North America. There is no substitute for that breadth of listening if the forms of our common mission are to be seriously directed toward the dominant undercurrents of the culture as a whole.[40]

The basic approach of a congregation making strategic choices from a GOC conversation perspective would appear to be the following:

- As a called and sent community by the Spirit, we must act in order to live more fully into our participation in God's mission in the world.
- We recognize that there are always elements of our cultural context that can subvert the gospel in terms of God's intent.

- We pray and listen carefully to the gospel to allow the Spirit to bring God's truth into fresh perspective in our cultural context.
- We utilize social science insights to develop a better awareness of our culture but always keep these insights subject to the gospel.
- We communally discern how God's creation of the church as a community of the Spirit continually invites us into deeper faithfulness, even as we learn from diverse Christian communities around us how they are making strategic choices in light of the gospel.
- We make strategic choices in community regarding how best to structure our lives and participate in God's mission in the world.

In summary, congregational decision making from a GOC perspective is our prayerful listening to the gospel as a community, discerning together how God is leading us to act within our particular cultural context as we reflect on:

1. the gospel,
2. the nature of the church,
3. the perspective offered by our fellow Christians, and
4. insights from the social sciences.

CONTRASTING VIEWS REGARDING GOSPEL, CHURCH, AND CULTURAL CONTEXT

This part of the discussion draws on a framework in common use within the GOC conversation. It envisions the interrelationship of three dynamics: the gospel, the church, and a cultural context.[41]

The Gospel

It is clear that the two movements have different understandings of how the Bible functions in terms of both the method and content.

Regarding Method

Church Growth appears to view the Bible primarily as a set of revealed truths that can be codified into principles and used to make decisions in determinative ways within any cultural context. These biblical principles are usually documented by particular passages or texts that either reference the principle as a concept or illustrate it as a practice. In contrast, the GOC conversation views the Bible more as a dynamic story of God's purposes in relation to creation, redemption, and a final consummation. Learning to live into this story, so that God's story continues to shape our story, is seen as an ongoing journey in which new insights into the meaning of the gospel are regularly unfolding within the Christian community, especially in light of the changing character of cultural contexts.

Regarding Content

Two matters need to be addressed here. First, we need to address the mission of God in the world. As noted earlier, a Trinitarian understanding of mission was developed during the 1950s that reframed what was then the current mission theology. This theology focused on the fulfillment of the Great Commission as the primary mission of the church in the world, with a priority being placed on evangelism in order to accomplish this. A Trinitarian approach to mission, what is referred to as the *missio Dei*, effected two shifts in thinking. One was the shift from the church being at the center of the discussion to the world as a whole coming center stage. God's actions of creation and redemption were about all of life; therefore, the mission of God needs to be understood in terms of all of God's works in the world. The second was the shift from thinking primarily in terms of Christology and the offer of salvation to the lost through the crucified and risen Christ to thinking in terms of the sending work of the Spirit. As the Father and the Son sent the Spirit into the world to accomplish God's purposes, so also the Spirit is sending the church into the world to participate fully in the mission of the triune God. This mission includes, but is not limited to, the offer of salvation to all through the crucified and risen Christ.

The second matter we need to address is the issue of the kingdom of God. From the perspective of the GOC conversation, the Great Commission has to be understood in the context of the relationship between *church and kingdom*. This is in contrast to the Church Growth perspective, which conceives of the Great Commission as a relationship between *church and mission*. The

GOC conversation understands that God is at work in the world through the presence of the kingdom, the redemptive reign of God in Christ. This kingdom presents a gospel in holistic terms, as bearing on every dimension of life. In kingdom thinking, conversion and ethics can never be separated. The church is to participate in God's mission by bearing witness to the redemptive reign of God and openly inviting persons into the community of faith to experience the fullness of God's grace. In kingdom thinking, salvation and community can never be separated. Coming to know the living God through the crucified and risen Christ also means that a person is simultaneously being introduced to the body of Christ, the church.

The Church

Ecclesiology is increasingly being recognized as the critical issue of the day. Earlier in this chapter, the point was made that the Church Growth perspective tends to see the church in functional terms, which corresponds, I believe, to viewing the Great Commission as the primary starting point for defining the mission of the church. It is essential to come to clarity regarding what the church is to do. But foundational to understanding the functionality of the church is to also come to clarity on what the church is—the nature of the church.

God creates the church through the Spirit. The church as the creation of the Spirit has been given a new nature. There is a duality to the nature of the church; it is both holy and human. The good news is that through the Spirit, God's holiness indwells our humanness and provides the community of God's people with a new nature. There is no other organization like it in the world. Coming to understand the nature of the church is foundational to understanding the relationship of the church to God's mission in the world. The church is missionary in its very nature. Mission is not just something the church does; it is something the church is.

This has profound implications for how one understands mission in relation to the church. Engaging in mission is not so much a matter of trying to motivate Christians to be obedient to the biblical imperatives as it is helping them to understand what God has already made them to be—the biblical indicatives. The empowerment of the imperatives is embedded in the indicatives.

This is where the scores of images and metaphors used by the New Testament authors to describe the church come into play.[42] The ninety-six images and metaphors used in the New Testament to describe the church provide powerful insights into the nature of the church. As we come to understand what God has already made us to be, participating in God's mission becomes more a matter of living into and out of the new nature that God has already given us through the Spirit.

From a GOC perspective, the *horizon* of mission is defined by the *missio Dei*, the mission of the triune God in the entire world. The *motivation* for mission is coming to understand more fully the reality of what God has already made us to be as the creation of the Spirit. The *content* of mission is determined by bearing witness to the fullness of the kingdom of God, God's redemptive reign in Christ, within a particular context. The *strategy* for mission is our prayerful listening to the gospel as a community, discerning together how God is leading us to act within our particular cultural context in light of the gospel, the perspective offered by our fellow Christians, and insights from the sciences.

Cultural Context

The third dimension of this summary critique addresses the important issue of the cultural context within which the church is located. From a GOC perspective, we need to first ask two questions: (1) To what extent is our cultural context shaping our own understanding of the gospel? and (2) Are the strategic choices we make and the methods we use being subverted by our cultural context in a negative way? As Newbigin noted in *The Open Secret*, culture is not neutral. The fallen powers are at work within culture to challenge and subvert the work of redemption.[43] Every cultural context is filled with bridges to the gospel but is also laden with barriers to that same gospel.

The Cultural Context and the Gospel

In answering the question of the extent to which our cultural context is shaping our own understanding of the gospel, it is important to note the influence of culture in shaping our understanding of the gospel. An example of this can be found in the way many in the evangelical movement, which includes most in the Church Growth movement, conceive of the gospel as a defined message that invites a person to make an individual decision to receive Christ and that results in the primary benefit of receiving eternal life. This view of the gospel is deeply rooted in Western individualism, an Enlightenment understanding of the self, and the conservative reaction to the social gospel at the end of the nineteenth century. It is an understanding of the gospel that is significantly shaped by influences from the cultural context. A more biblical understanding of the gospel calls for understanding conversion to Christ as being communal in character, where a person enters not only into a relationship with the living God through Christ but also into a living relationship with Christ's body on earth, the church. A more biblical understanding also calls for understanding salvation as living life in all of its abundance within the present world, through the power and presence of the Spirit, while looking toward the final consummation.

The Cultural Context and Strategic Choices

In answering the question of whether the strategic choices we make and the methods we use are being subverted by our cultural context in a negative way, it is important to note that a cultural context can influence how we make our strategic choices and develop our methods. Our choices and methods can sometimes work to subvert the intent of the gospel. An example of this can be found in the popular methodological approach of targeting a particular generational age group with a cultural-sensitive worship service.[44] While the rationale of targeting has merit in trying to provide focus, the result is often the development of a congregation that is mainly composed of a particular age group. When the methodology is successful in reaching a particular group of persons, this success is then used to justify the validity of the method. But this begs some important biblical and theological issues regarding the nature of the church as a reconciled community of diversity that seeks to include the "other." It also begs an important critique of our cultural context, which endlessly promotes, and almost seems to require, the segmentation of society according to generations and lifestyle choices. While Church Growth has focused on being culturally relevant, the GOC conversation has sought to address the church's tendency to become captive to cultural patterns that subvert biblical intentions. I believe the views of these two movements need to inform one another. A larger issue is how to be culturally relevant while maintaining biblical integrity.

SUMMARY

This chapter has attempted to offer a critique of the Church Growth movement from the perspective of the Gospel and Our Culture conversation. I believe these two movements have much to offer each other, and it is my hope and prayer that constructive dialogue will take place. Perhaps this book will help to serve this purpose. The challenge of being the church in our current postmodern context is too great and too important not to pursue such a dialogue.

A CENTRIST RESPONSE

Charles Van Engen

Van Gelder is accurate in beginning his chapter with the observation that he thought Church Growth as a missiological movement to be passé. There is a sense in which interest in, and enthusiasm for, Church Growth theory might be thought to have peaked around the middle of the 1980s and to be passé today. It seems that the creation of the theoretical foundations and the elaboration of the major components of the theory had been accomplished by the mid-1980s.

Church Growth has given rise to a host of new approaches, initiatives, perspectives, movements, and programs. Craig is also accurate that Church Growth's influence in terms of mission in North America can hardly be underestimated. Thus, I find very helpful Craig's overview of all the new movements that have directly (and in a number of cases, quite indirectly) arisen from Church Growth theory.

Such a branching or twigging into a multitude of derivative initiatives is typical of activist sociological movements like Church Growth. On the positive side, this expands and deepens their influence and contributes to their impact in diffusing innovation. On the negative side, as Elmer Towns also notes, such branching can create significant confusion with regard to the core of the movement's theoretical framework. So we now have a situation where many folks in North American church culture assume that congregations are supposed to grow numerically and that folks ought to work toward that. Yet many of these same people do not seem to be familiar with the original theoretical framework of the Church Growth movement and may even want to distance themselves from it. Thus, many people who seem positive about the growth of churches might be negative about Church Growth.

These developments make it important not to create a false dichotomy between the "growth of the church" and "church growth." I would not distance these as far from each other as Van Gelder seems to do. McGavran was interested in the growth (and decline) of churches and the factors that contributed to that. Both McGavran and Peter Wagner would emphatically state their major commitment to be the growth of the church, with little interest on their part in the development of a movement called Church Growth. The primary architects of "church growth" would be found standing on the side of "the growth of the church." Thus, we need to avoid this kind of artificial dichotomy.

I find confusing Van Gelder's comment that Church Growth theory in the North American context has undergone what he calls "congregationalization." From its inception, with McGavran's publication of *Bridges of God*, throughout its entire development up to the present, the Church Growth movement has been strongly committed to, and heavily focused on, the local congregation. In fact, until recently, Church Growth was one of the major missiological initiatives in North America specifically focused on the health and growth of congregations.

I believe Craig's comment is on target, however, that there has been a perceptible shift from an emphasis on "discipling," in the McGavran sense of making disciples (that women and men be converted and become disciples of Jesus Christ by grace through faith), to "perfecting," in the McGavran sense of the spiritual development of those who are already believers. The increased emphasis today on a kind of spiritual self-help of those already Christian would be a source of major concern for Donald McGavran.

I appreciated very much reading Van Gelder's reference to Lesslie Newbigin's critique of Church Growth that he wrote in *The Open Secret*. I consider Newbigin's critique to be accurate and appropriate. I also share Craig's concern that much Church Growth theory has fueled a functional view of the church, to the extent that churches (and congregations) are only significant as they are useful tools to achieve some other goal. The Church Growth movement has not been immune to the temptation to look at the church primarily as a tool through which more churches could be planted and grown. Though I recognize this danger as being very real, Church Growth has also viewed the church as a *goal*, not merely as a useful means to an end.

I also share Van Gelder's sadness over the way the Church Growth movement has used the Bible. It is terribly unfortunate that the Church Growth movement, beginning with McGavran, had a nasty habit of using Bible texts to buttress a host of pre-conceived agendas, methods, and goals with little consideration given to the emphases of the texts themselves. One of the clearest examples of this abuse of Scripture can be found in the way that proponents of Church Growth used the parable of the sower (what McGavran, Ralph Winter, Peter Wagner, and others called the "parable of the soils") to provide what they supposed as a biblical justification for selective targeting.[45]

I was helped by Van Gelder's summary of the missiological emphases developed by the Gospel and Our Culture Network (GOCN). This network has also spawned a number of new initiatives that seek to develop a new understanding of the mission of the church in North America. I also found it encouraging to read Van Gelder's list of references in the book of Acts to the growth of the church and the "broader influence of the gospel" on the surrounding cultures of the day.

It is instructive to compare the emphases of the Church Growth movement with those of the Gospel and Our Culture Network. Van Gelder's writing stimulated me to do so, and I was surprised by the degree to which the two perspectives overlap—considering also important differences. As I see it, the two views would contrast as follows:

The GOC View	The Church Growth View
Listening to culture.	Examining the cultural mosaic.
Listening to the gospel.	Women and men should become disciples of Jesus Christ.
Use the social sciences for a better awareness of culture.	Social sciences should be used to understand the worldview of those who are not yet disciples of Jesus: contextualization, cross-cultural communication.
The church as a community of the Spirit.	Congregations as growing, organic, corporate groups of disciples of Jesus.

Christians should structure their lives in order to transform their culture.	Christians should intentionally cross barriers so people not yet Christian may come to know Jesus.
Ethical living by Christians is the goal.	Evangelization of the unreached is the goal.
Is this viewpoint too introverted?	Is this viewpoint too extroverted, producing a church that is a mile wide in extension and an inch deep in spirituality?

There are two areas where I am uncomfortable with the emphases of the GOCN. The first has to do with the language about culture. In Van Gelder's chapter, I see the same lack of precision I have noticed in most of the GOC publications. I am not clear as to what is meant by "culture" as it is used by folks in the network. In North America, we can no longer use the word in the singular. North America is a complex mosaic of many cultures that represent quite radically different worldviews. Thus, we need to consider how in North America the gospel will be preached to "cultures." The word *our* will therefore refer to persons who represent a host of different languages, perspectives, and worldviews. I do not see enough awareness of, or intentional response to, this cultural diversity of the multiple contexts of North America in the GOC publications. Here is an area where the GOCN would profit from the work of Church Growth missiologists.

Second, I wonder about the lack of an emphasis on conversion in the publications of the authors in the GOCN. Clearly, the GOC folks are concerned over the state of the church and of congregations, especially as that translates into the nearly nonexistent influence of the church on public life in North America. I share this concern. However, I do not believe ethical living and the social impact of the gospel on public life in North America is possible without the spiritual conversion of the members of the congregations. Philosophical analysis is important, but it does not translate into social change unless the Holy Spirit radically transforms the lives of church members.

I want to express my deepest respect and appreciation for Craig Van Gelder's informative and stimulating comparison of the GOC viewpoint with that of the Church Growth movement. He has pointed out a number of issues that call for the attention of all who are concerned about, and committed to, the reevangelization of North America.

A RENEWAL RESPONSE

Howard Snyder

Viewing Church Growth theory from the perspective of the Gospel and Our Culture conversation, as Van Gelder does, is very helpful. The critique of dominant North American Church Growth thinking is on target. I agree that niche-generational churches are an abomination whenever the market or numerical-success orientation overrides the church's calling to be a visible demonstration of the cross-generational, multiethnic nature of the true church of Jesus Christ.[46]

I will comment on three points: the use of "church growth" as a term, the question of the nature of the gospel, and the issue of strategy.

CHURCH GROWTH OR GROWTH OF THE CHURCH?

Van Gelder's point about the language we use to speak of the church and its growth is not a superficial one. Language is not neutral; it conveys biases and subtly reinforces unexamined presuppositions. To speak of "church growth" puts the accent on *growth,* not on the church. I have often said that we cannot speak intelligently about "church growth" until we define what *church* means, and this, I think, is the issue Van Gelder is getting at. (The same pertains to "church renewal" or "church vitality"; Van Gelder convinces me that these terms are problematic.)

WHAT IS THE GOSPEL?

Van Gelder believes that Church Growth theory and the GOC conversation are operating with "different understandings" of the gospel, or at least of "how the Bible functions" in revealing the gospel to us. Here he invokes *missio Dei* theology, noting two "shifts": from a church focus to a world focus discussion and from Christology to pneumatology—less emphasis on "the offer of salvation to the lost through the crucified and risen Christ" and more on "the sending work of the Spirit."

It is problematic to put the theological issue in these terms. A biblically faithful understanding of the gospel will not permit any wedge between Christology and pneumatology, nor between a proper focus on the church itself and on God's concern for all of creation. I assume that Van Gelder does in fact want to hold these together, but his language implies a certain one-sidedness. He is certainly correct, however, in suggesting that people's response to Church Growth thinking often reflects deeper theological issues.

Biblically, these different accents must be held together. Certainly salvation *does* concern and center in the redemptive, atoning work of Jesus Christ for our sins. But it *also* concerns God's redemptive plan for all of creation; the full range of what God reveals to us through Jesus Christ (embodied in his incarnation, life, and ongoing reign, as well as in his death and resurrection). It involves as well the continuing active work of the Holy Spirit animating the church, preceding the church in mission, and sending God's people in mission to all the world. Church Growth thinking would be enriched by a broader (more biblical) focus on God's plan through the church (for example, Eph. 1:10; 2:10; 3:10). Similarly, GOC discussions would be strengthened by more emphasis on the church's specific mission to go and make disciples. (In the salutary GOC focus on the North American mission field, is there at times a tendency to forget God's mission to all earth's peoples?)

I would make the same comment with regard to world focus versus church focus. Some *missio Dei* theology, especially in the 1960s and 1970s, did the very thing Van Gelder warns against: saw the church in a mere functionalist (even obstructionist) way. The focus, it was said, was to be the world, not the church; *that* is where God is at work; the world sets the agenda. Clearly this is wrong, or at least one-sided. "Christ loved the church and gave himself up for her" (Eph. 5:25). But it is precisely this well-beloved church to which Jesus says, "As the Father has sent me, I am sending you" (John 20:21). Perhaps we could say that God always loves the church, but *especially* when it really is the missional church, the church in mission!

Church Growth thinking is right to focus on the church, even on its growth. But the church with which God is especially pleased, it seems, is the church that gives itself for the world, not for itself—the church that ultimately is more concerned about the growth and manifestation of God's reign in the world than about its own expansion.

Because of these considerations, I think it is a mistake to say, as some have claimed, that Church Growth thinking is theologically neutral, that it can function equally well within any theological tradition. Van Gelder is right in identifying the set of missiological, soteriological, and ecclesiological assumptions that are generally presupposed in much Church Growth thinking and methodology.

THE QUESTION OF STRATEGY

Church Growth thinking is strong on pragmatic strategy (though how effective such strategy has really been, even on its own terms, is in many cases an open question). In general, I agree with Van Gelder's critique here and with his insistence that each church needs to "come to clarity on what the church is."

I would want to push the issue further, however. "Engaging in mission is not so much a matter of trying to motivate Christians to be obedient to the biblical imperatives," Van Gelder writes, "as it is helping them to understand what God has already made them to be—the biblical indicatives." Granted, but this can be understood much too cognitively and much too passively. Jesus' disciples need not only to *understand* but to *experience deeply* the reality of the church as the body of Christ and the *koinonia* of the Holy Spirit. It is true that "participating in God's mission [is] more a matter of living into and out of the new nature that God has already given us through the Spirit." But this does not happen automatically. It requires leadership, including sensitive strategy. It requires helping congregations grow in the gifts and graces of the Spirit, encouraging and channeling a wide range of spiritual gifts (for example, 1 Peter 4:10–11), and encouraging and strengthening a broad spectrum of ministry in the world.

AN EFFECTIVE EVANGELISM RESPONSE

Elmer Towns

In reading Craig Van Gelder's presentation, I found myself supporting some of his basic theses that address modern-day challenges and problems within the church from the perspective of a cultural and societal response. I agree that the very nature of the church is the body of Christ and that society reflects in the kingdom of God must be harmonized with the church to produce growth. However, I kept looking for basic terms of Scripture concerning evangelism, growth, and outreach but did not see them. I had the sense that I was not reading about Church Growth and evangelism from the basic observations I find in the Word of God.

Craig Van Gelder does an outstanding job of presenting the development of the Church Growth movement, beginning with McGavran, through the 1980s, and into the present expression. However, when he says the Church Growth movement was increasingly marginalized, this is his interpretation. He is speaking from his limited perspective, the missionary outreach of major denominations and the World Council of Churches. Remember, some of the largest forces of missions (as far as manpower is concerned) are the independent missions boards, evangelical denominational mission boards (including most of the Pentecostal denominations), and the Southern Baptists. These organizations would present a different perspective and strategy of missiology than that presented by Van Gelder.

Craig Van Gelder does understand the Church Growth movement, and when he summarizes the movement, he is mostly accurate. However, I do not agree with his assessment that the distinction between "discipling" and "perfecting" is disappearing. When McGavran made a distinction between discipling and perfecting, he was talking about the difference between accepting Christ to become a Christian and a second stage of growing in Christ, or becoming more like Christ. Perhaps Van Gelder is observing the obliteration of these two stages within his church perspective. The evangelical community, however, is characterized by those who emphasize evangelism and getting nonbelievers to become Christians. This emphasis is not found in Van Gelder's presentation, and I would like to see him develop answers to the questions, What is evangelism? and What is conversion, or regeneration?

It is important to understand why the church changes or reacts at certain times. Van Gelder correctly identifies many of the conditions that have changed in the culture of the United States and of the whole world: the emergence of postmodern conditions, increased turbulence within society, globalization, new immigration, the information age, and so on. However, the response of the church to these changes is the issue. The movement that became known as Gospel and Our Culture (GOC) involves itself in a missional encounter between the whole way that society thinks, perceives, lives, and encounters the gospel. The problem is that to understand Van Gelder, you must understand how he identifies the gospel, the church, and society. (I explain to my students that the foundation of understanding theology is to learn how each theologian defines his or her terms and then evaluate these definitions by the Word of God.)

When we use terms and define them according to traditional Church Growth movement definitions, there should be no difficulty. Van Gelder, however, has redefined these terms, hence giving us a different and new strategy for missions—a new paradigm of growing the church.

Central to Van Gelder's understanding of growing the church is his definition of the church. He says the church is made up of both the holy and of the people. It is not a commissioned body of believers, gifted and powered by the Holy Spirit. He does not see the church as having the task or the Great Commission of winning individuals to Jesus Christ and planting other churches. Rather, "the church ... participate[s] fully in God's mission within all of creation.... It exists as a sign that the redemptive reign of God's kingdom is present. It serves as a foretaste of the eschatological future of the redemptive reign that has already begun. It also serves as an instrument under the leadership of the Spirit to bring that redemptive reign to bear on every dimension of life." To Van Gelder, culture is not neutral, but rather subverts the work of redemption. Every culture has bridges to preach the gospel and barriers to block the gospel. This understanding of cultures shapes our understanding of the gospel. I ask, however, is not the Bible the source to understanding the gospel? Culture does not change the gospel, but culture does teach us how to communicate the gospel and how to implement the gospel. The acculturation of the gospel in lives and in culture is still an aim of evangelism, of Church Growth.

Van Gelder would have us believe that the culture is most important in formulating the gospel. He charges that the Church Growth approach is deeply rooted in "Western individualism, an Enlightenment understanding of the self, and the conservative reaction to the social gospel at the end of the nineteenth century." He reacts to the gospel being perceived as "a defined message that invites a person to make an individual decision to receive Christ and that results in the primary benefit of receiving eternal life." These statements best reflect his Church Growth orientation outside the traditional view and his theological orientation outside a biblical approach to evangelism. The Bible has reports of individual conversions as well as of a corporate growth of churches. The Bible has reports of community impact as well as of individual transformations.

Rather than beginning with a GOC orientation to influence my orientation to Church Growth, I would rather get my philosophy and principles of evangelism from the Word of God. The Bible does not take a scholarly orientation to evangelism, but rather average people have read its pages, applied its principles, and demonstrated how God can transform individuals and influence the culture where they live.

A REFORMIST RESPONSE

Gailyn Van Rheenen

Van Gelder's chapter is one of the most significant in this volume. He has enhanced our understanding of Church Growth by describing historical shifts in Church Growth thinking and has shown how these shifts have resulted in new movements and perceptions of ministry. One of the most interesting elements is Van Gelder's description of Church Growth's shift from the seminary to the local church, the "congregationalization of the movement." He has also noted the changing themes of Church Growth.

Above all, Van Gelder has greatly amplified the dialogue between the Gospel and Our Culture (GOC) movement and the Church Growth movement. He has done this by contrasting the beginning points of ministry, the use of Scripture, and approaches to making strategic decisions. For example, Van Gelder suggests that the word *church* should be used as a noun rather than as an adjective. When used as an adjective, the church becomes subservient to whatever it modifies, thus turning the church into a functional entity. Thus it is better to say "the growth of the church" rather than "church growth." When *church* is used as an adjective, "it is not uncommon for one dimension of what the church does to become the criterion for constructing an identity for the church."

It is this dialogue between movements that I will address in this response.

COMPARISON BETWEEN THE GOC AND CHURCH GROWTH MOVEMENTS

The table "Comparing the GOC and Church Growth Movements" seeks to contrast the two movements. The items listed are drawn largely from Van Gelder's article but also from other sources.

COMPARING THE GOC AND CHURCH GROWTH MOVEMENTS		
	Gospel and Our Culture	**Church Growth**
Orientation/ Perspective	Theocentric Theological	Anthropocentric Practical
	Postmodern	Modern
Theological Focus	*Missio Dei*	Great Commission
Beginning Point	Gospel	Growth
Perspective on Scripture	Narrative of God's purposes	Propositional truth
How does missions happen?	By the Spirit (God's "surprises")	By strategic planning
Nature of Community	Inclusiveness, unity of the body of Christ	People groups
Focus of Evangelism	Initiation of people into the kingdom of God; holistic understanding of "making disciples"	Differentiation between discipling and perfecting; individual salvation
Orientation toward Social Action	The gospel, evangelism, and social action cannot be separated	Priority of evangelism and church planting over social action; reactive to the social gospel
Advocating Forums	Academy, marginal influence in some churches	Field missionaries, then academy, now churches and parachurch agencies

The contrast between the two movements is stark. The beginning point for the Church Growth movement is anthropocentric. The focus is on strategy development and cultural analysis, with biblical passages appropriated to give validity to the perspectives. The GOC movement, on the other hand, begins theologically with the perspectives of the mission and kingdom of God. The concepts are ethereal, however, and are hard to apply to Christian ministry. Christian leaders read Church Growth books, like McGavran's *Understanding Church Growth* and Wagner's *Strategies for Church Growth*, or contemporary Church Growth literature, like Warren's *The Purpose-Driven*

Church and Schwarz's *Natural Church Development*, and make immediate application. The concepts of GOC, however, are too lofty, too difficult for local leaders to apply. For example, church leaders without a theological education will find *The Missional Church*, written by six GOC scholars and edited by Darrell Guder, hard to understand. The GOC desperately needs a popular guide to missional thinking.[47]

The central theological concern of GOC is "What is the gospel?" The gospel is thought to intersect with every theological and strategical question. Therefore, it cannot be relegated to the periphery, even when strategical decisions are being made. The beginning question of Church Growth is "Why do some churches grow in a particular context and others do not?" Deciding the primacy and order of questions will determine the missiological focus.

The Church Growth movement focuses on truth as proposition. On the other hand, in this chapter, Van Gelder maintains that the gospel cannot be contained in a set of propositions. The mission of God must be communicated as the dynamic story of God in relationship to his creation.

According to GOC, God's mission cannot be predicted by human planning. The book of Acts is full of God's surprises, which result when the Holy Spirit goes ahead of human messengers and directs them in God's mission. The GOC movement, however, appears to be passive, rarely entering into human contexts to actively minister. It appears that GOC scholars seek to actively interpret Scripture and do crisis management in existing churches but are passive in regard to strategy and evangelism. The Church Growth heritage has emphasized the mighty workings of God and the Holy Spirit. Its major focus, however, has been on human ingenuity in decision making, illustrated by the application of the scientific method to ministry.

The Church Growth movement has focused on the uniqueness and distinctiveness of people groups and the contextualization of the gospel among the *ethne* of the world. GOC, on the other hand, believes that the gospel breaks down socioeconomic and ethnic divisions between peoples so that all become one in Christ.

The GOC movement does not dichotomize evangelism and social action, discipling and perfecting, but views God's mission holistically. Church Growth adherents, reacting to the social gospel, argue that the primary task of missions is evangelism and incorporating new believers into the body of Christ. Evangelism and church planting, therefore, take priority over social action.

The Church Growth movement began in India with the reflections and research of Donald McGavran, then moved into the academy, with Fuller Theological Seminary's School of World Mission leading the way, and finally shifted into major evangelical congregations and agencies. At the present time, GOC is an academic movement seeking roots within congregational contexts.

Contrasting Emphases of the Gospel and Our Culture and Church Growth Movements

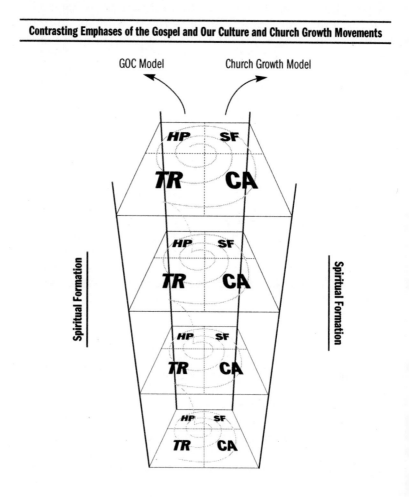

Gospel and Our Culture and Church Growth represent two very different emphases. As illustrated in the figure, GOC emphasizes theological reflection and historical perspective, and the Church Growth movement emphasizes cultural analysis and strategy formation.

These two movements have much to learn from each other. From the Church Growth movement, GOC must learn to study culture beyond the general impressionistic level and be more intentional in strategy formation. From the GOC movement, Church Growth must learn to rethink their discipline in integrative theological categories and to study culture, interpret history, and develop strategy through the lens of Christian theology.

Chapter 2 Notes: Gospel and Our Culture View

[1]Robert E. Logan, *Beyond Church Growth: Action Plans for Developing a Dynamic Church* (Old Tappan, NJ: Revell, 1989).

[2]Information about the American Society for Church Growth can be found at www.ascg.org.

[3]The book that most clearly signaled this shift was C. Peter Wagner, *How to Have a Healing Ministry without Making Your Church Sick* (Ventura, CA: Gospel Light, 1988).

[4]See C. Peter Wagner, preface to *The Book of Church Growth: History, Theology, and Principles,* by Thom S. Rainer (Nashville: Broadman and Holman, 1993).

[5]It is important to note that this foundational work is still being used as a standard textbook for an introduction to Church Growth. Donald A. McGavran, *Understanding Church Growth* (Grand Rapids: Eerdmans, 1970).

[6]Probably the most influential presentation was made by Ralph Winter, who spoke on "The Highest Priority: Cross-Cultural Evangelism," which can be found in *Let the Earth Hear His Voice: International Congress on World Evangelization, Lausanne, Switzerland,* ed. J. D. Douglas (Minneapolis: World Wide Publications, 1975), 213–45.

[7]An ad hoc group was formed during the conference by a number of these persons who wrote a short piece on "Theological Implications of Radical Discipleship," in Douglas, *Let the Earth Hear His Voice,* 1294–96.

[8]See, for example, Orlando E. Costas, *The Church and Its Mission: A Shattering Critique from the Third World* (Wheaton, IL: Tyndale House, 1974); and Harvie M. Conn, ed., *Theological Perspectives on Church Growth* (Nutley, NJ: Presbyterian and Reformed Publishing, 1976).

[9]Charles Van Engen, *The Growth of the True Church* (Amsterdam: Rodopi, 1981).

[10]Wilbert R. Shenk, ed., *Exploring Church Growth* (Grand Rapids: Eerdmans, 1983).

[11]Observation made to this author by Wilbert Shenk in 1989.

[12]Contrast, for example, the work of Donald A. McGavran and Win C. Arn, *How to Grow a Church* (Glendale, CA: Regal, 1973) with Kennon L. Callahan, *Effective Church Leadership: Building on the Twelve Keys* (New York: Harper and Row, 1990); Christian A. Schwarz, *Natural Church Development: A Guide to Eight Essential Qualities of Healthy Churches,* trans. Lynn McAdam, Lois Wollin, and Martin Wollin (Carol Stream, IL: ChurchSmart Resources, 1996); and Phillip V. Lewis, *Transformational Leadership: A New Model for Total Church Involvement* (Nashville: Broadman and Holman, 1996).

[13]This search engine can be found at www.google.com and presently searches almost 2.5 billion web pages.

[14]This search engine can be found at www.amazon.com.

[15]Books that are associated with these descriptions include: Lyle E. Schaller, *The Seven-Day-a-Week Church* (Nashville: Abingdon, 1992); Carl F. George, *Prepare Your Church for the Future* (Tarrytown, NY: Revell, 1991); George Barna, *User Friendly Churches* (Ventura, CA: Regal, 1991); Leith Anderson, *A Church for the Twenty-first Century,* (Minneapolis: Bethany, 1992); Mark

Mittelberg and Bill Hybels, *Building a Contagious Church* (Grand Rapids: Zondervan, 2000); George G. Hunter III, *Church for the Unchurched* (Nashville: Abingdon, 1996); Rick Warren, *The Purpose Driven Church* (Grand Rapids: Zondervan, 1996); Christian A. Schwarz, *Natural Church Development: A Guide to Eight Essential Qualities of Healthy Churches* (Carol Stream, IL: ChurchSmart Resources, 1996); and Leonard I. Sweet, *AquaChurch* (Loveland, CO: Group Publishing, 1999).

[16]Information on these two churches and their networks can be found at the following web sites: Willow Creek Church, www.willowcreek.com; Willow Creek Association, www.willowcharts.com. In 2001, there were 7,200 congregations in Willow Creek's network, with over 65,000 leaders attending the various seminars. Saddleback Church, www.saddleback.com; the Purpose Driven Seminar, www.purposedriven.com. Over 200,000 church leaders have attended the Purpose Driven seminar during the past fifteen years.

[17]For information on these organizations, see: Leadership Network, www.leadnet.org; Easum, Bandy and Associates, www.easumbandy.com; Barna Research Group, www.barna.org.

[18]The *Church Planter's Toolkit* is available online at www.church smart.com.

[19]The watchword of the student volunteer movement in the late 1800s was "the evangelization of the world in our generation." This theme set the stage for the Edinburgh missionary conference in 1910, and in many ways, the Church Growth movement seems to have viewed itself as the keeper of that vision.

[20]McGavran, *Understanding Church Growth*, 26–40.

[21]This was the case in what has come to be known as the Nicene Creed of 381, which lifts up the attributes of the church being one, holy, catholic, and apostolic.

[22]One should note here the position of C. Peter Wagner, who calls for us to utilize a "consecrated pragmatism" in our methodological approach. See C. Peter Wagner, *Strategies for Church Growth* (Ventura, CA: Regal, 1987), 29–32.

[23]Donald A. McGavran, *The Bridges of God* (New York: Friendship, 1955).

[24]See David J. Bosch, "The Structure of Mission: An Exposition of Matthew 28:16–20," in Shenk, *Exploring Church Growth*, 218–48.

[25]See Wade Clark Roof and William McKinney, *American Mainline Religion: Its Changing Shape and Future* (New Brunswick, NJ: Rutgers, 1987); and Robert Wuthnow, *The Restructuring of American Religion* (Princeton, NJ: Princeton University Press, 1988).

[26]See Stanley J. Grenz, *A Primer on Postmodernism* (Grand Rapids: Eerdmans, 1996); and J. Richard Middleton and Brian J. Walsh, *Truth Is Stranger Than It Used to Be: Biblical Faith in a Postmodern Age* (Downers Grove, IL: InterVarsity Press, 1995).

[27]See Leonard I. Sweet, *SoulTsunami* (Grand Rapids: Zondervan, 2001); and George Barna and Mark Hatch, *Boiling Point: It Only Takes One Degree* (Ventura, CA: Regal, 2001).

[28]See Craig Van Gelder, "A Great New Fact of Our Day: North America as Mission Field," in *The Church Between Gospel and Culture: The Emerging Mission*

in North America, eds. George H. Hunsberger and Craig Van Gelder (Grand Rapids: Eerdmans, 1996).

[29]Lesslie Newbigin, *Foolishness to the Greeks* (Grand Rapids: Eerdmans, 1986), 1.

[30]Johannes Blauw, *The Missionary Nature of the Church: A Survey of the Biblical Theology of Mission* (Grand Rapids: Eerdmans, 1962).

[31]Lesslie Newbigin, *The Open Secret: Sketches for a Missionary Theology* (Grand Rapids: Eerdmans, 1978).

[32]Ibid., 124.

[33]Ibid., 135–80.

[34]Lesslie Newbigin, *The Other Side of 1984: Questions for the Churches* (Geneva: World Council of Churches, 1983); Newbigin, *Foolishness to the Greeks* (Grand Rapids: Eerdmans, 1986); Newbigin, *The Gospel in a Pluralist Society* (Grand Rapids: Eerdmans, 1989).

[35]Hugh Montefiore, ed., *The Gospel and Contemporary Culture* (London: Cassell Academic, 1992).

[36]A brief history of the British GOC programme is available online at www.deepsight.org/articles/engchis.htm.

[37]Craig Van Gelder, *The Essence of the Church: A Community Created by the Spirit* (Grand Rapids: Baker, 2000).

[38]Wagner, *Strategies for Church Growth*, 29.

[39]Ibid., 38.

[40]George R. Hunsberger, "The Newbigin Gauntlet," in Hunsberger and Van Gelder, *The Church Between Gospel and Culture*, 24.

[41]Ibid., 3–25.

[42]See Paul S. Minear, *Images of the Church in the New Testament* (Philadelphia: Westminster, 1960).

[43]Newbigin, *The Open Secret*, 135–80.

[44]Warren, *The Purpose Driven Church*, 155–72, 251–78.

[45]See Van Engen, *The Growth of the True Church*, 354–57.

[46]As a minor point, I would take exception to classifying Christian Schwarz's *Natural Church Development* within the "market-driven" category.

[47]James V. Brownson, Inagrace T. Dietterich, Barry A. Harvey, and Charles C. West, *Storm Front: The Good News of God* (Grand Rapids: Eerdmans, 2003) partially fills this niche.

Chapter Three

CENTRIST VIEW

CENTRIST VIEW

Church Growth is based on an evangelistically focused and a missiologically applied theology

Charles Van Engen

As we think about Church Growth theory, we should remember that Donald McGavran began forming Church Growth theory as a way to respond to his fundamental research question: Why do some churches grow (he meant mostly numerical growth at that point) in a particular context and others do not? Some of the major aspects of Church Growth thought as developed from the 1960s to the 1990s by McGavran and those of us who consider ourselves his disciples is summarized in the table "Church Growth Theory as a Contextual Theology of Mission."

In this chapter, I would like to suggest an outline of a Church Growth theology that builds on and rearticulates the basic biblical and theological loci or concepts of theology from the point of view of a Church Growth paradigm. In other words, I wish to offer the reader vintage wine for new wineskins. Or we might say this chapter is "back to the future" in Church Growth theology.

We are presently at a stage in the development of the Church Growth movement in which many people use the term *church growth* with little or no relationship to the original theoretical foundation of the movement, and sometimes with seemingly little understanding of the theory itself. I am asked very often to explain to folks the foundational tenets of Church Growth theory. My answer is that Church Growth theory is founded on Donald McGavran's missiology as he articulated primarily in *The Bridges of God*[1] and in the first edition of his *Understanding Church Growth*.[2] This conceptual framework was popularized and applied specifically to the life of local congregations by Peter Wagner in a series of "seven vital signs," "four axioms," and "eight pathologies," as seen in the sidebar "Major Components of Church Growth Theory" (page 126).

CHURCH GROWTH THEORY AS A CONTEXTUAL THEOLOGY OF MISSION

Source	The loving heart of the God who seeks and finds the lost and who wills that the church grow
Context	The world of cultures and unreached peoples, receptive homogeneous units of cultural mosaics, contextual factors of growth and decline
Motivation	The Great Commission
Penultimate Goal	"Make disciples," to grow the church
Means	Crossing barriers, proclamation, persuasion, incorporation, many and varied strategies of church growth, both a sociological and spiritual mission process
Agents	The church—Jesus Christ, the Holy Spirit, the disciples, church growth experts, institutional factors of growth and decline
Mobilizer	The Holy Spirit, commitment, vision, and hard, bold plans for growth
Message	Proclamation of the gospel of the incarnation, life, death and resurrection of Jesus Christ; conversion, transformation, reconciliation, gathering into the church
Ultimate Goal	The kingdom of God (Arthur Glasser) The glory of God (J. H. Bavinck)

During the past thirty years, a number of folks in the Church Growth movement have contributed to an articulation of a theology of church growth. Among them (in order of their publication) would be the following:

Alan R. Tippett. *Church Growth and the Word of God* (1970).
Donald McGavran. *Understanding Church Growth* (1970).
Alan R. Tippett, ed. *God, Man and Church Growth* (1973).

Harvie M. Conn, ed. *Theological Perspectives on Church Growth* (1977).

C. Peter Wagner. *Church Growth and the Whole Gospel: A Biblical Mandate* (1981).

Elmer Towns, John Vaughan, and David Seifert. *The Complete Book of Church Growth* (1981).

Charles Van Engen. *The Growth of the True Church* (1981).

Donald McGavran and Win Arn. *Back to Basics in Church Growth* (1981).

Eddie Gibbs. *I Believe in Church Growth* (1985).

C. Peter Wagner, ed. with Win Arn and Elmer Towns. *Church Growth: State of the Art* (1986).

C. Peter Wagner. *Strategies for Church Growth* (1987).

Thom S. Rainer. *The Book of Church Growth: History, Theology, and Principles* (1993).

Christian A. Schwarz. *Paradigm Shift in the Church* (1999).

Unfortunately, these works tended to be fragmentary, dealing with only one or two loci of theology and predominantly giving a theological rationale for the particular Church Growth issues that the author or editor was concerned about in each book. This approach was a mostly apologetic and piecemeal attempt to offer a "theology of church growth" that usually presented a few admittedly important but selective biblical and theological foundations and rationale for particular aspects of Church Growth theory. This buttressing approach sought to give theological and biblical justification and underpinnings for particular emphases that the Church Growth movement had already adopted in its theory and action.

The apologetic approach is not enough. I believe we must construct the theological issues in Church Growth theory in a different way. We need to give careful thought to the loci or concepts of theology itself and ask how the theological assumptions they represent need to be rethought in the light of Church Growth theory. I would call this a "Church Growth theology." In what follows, I will suggest an outline of a Church Growth theology that redefines and rearticulates some of the basic biblical and theological loci and concepts of theology from the point of view of a Church Growth paradigm. That is, I am seeking to do theology "with Church Growth eyes."

Major Components of Church Growth Theory

Seven Vital Signs of a Growing Church

1. A pastor who is a possibility thinker and whose dynamic leadership has been used to catalyze the entire church into action for growth.
2. A well-mobilized laity which has discovered, developed, and is using all the spiritual gifts for growth.
3. A church large enough to provide the range of services that meet the needs and expectations of its members
4. The proper structural balance of the dynamic relationship between celebration, congregation, and cell.
5. A membership drawn basically from one homogeneous unit.
6. The use of evangelistic methods that have proven to work and focus on making disciples.
7. A philosophy of ministry which has its priorities arranged in biblical order.[a]

Four Axioms of Church Growth

1. The pastor must want the church to grow and be willing to pay the price.
2. The people must want the church to grow and be willing to pay the price.
3. The church must agree that the goal of evangelism is to make disciples.
4. The church must not [be suffering from] a terminal illness.[b]

Church Pathologies

1. Ethnikitis/Ghost-Town Disease
2. Old Age
3. People Blindness
4. Hyper-Cooperativism
5. Koinonitis
6. Sociological Strangulation
7. Arrested Spiritual Development
8. St. John's Syndrome[c]

---

[a] C. Peter Wagner, *Your Church Can Grow: Seven Vital Signs of a Healthy Church* (Ventura, CA: Regal, 1976).

[b] C. Peter Wagner, *Your Church Can Be Healthy* (Nashville: Abingdon, 1979), 24–28.

[c] Ibid., 29–121. Reprinted (with suggestions for how to heal these diseases) in Elmer Towns, C. Peter Wagner, and Thom S. Rainer, *The Everychurch Guide to Growth: How Any Plateaued Church Can Grow* (Nashville: Broadman and Holman, 1998), 10–17. In this latest form, a ninth pathology has been added, called "Hypopneumia."

I will offer five pillars of a Church Growth theology as I believe they can be found in McGavran's definition of mission, as follows: "Up to this point, mission has been widely defined as 'God's total program for [humanity],' and we have considered the alternatives arising from that definition. Mission may now be defined much more meaningfully. Since God as revealed in the Bible has assigned the highest priority to bringing men [and women] into living relationship to Jesus Christ, we may define mission narrowly as an enterprise devoted to proclaiming the Good News of Jesus Christ and to persuading men [and women] to become His disciples and dependable members of His Church."[3]

McGavran's definition of mission has been echoed by Peter Wagner in a number of places: "The central purpose of mission [in Donald McGavran's *The Bridges of God*] was to be seen as God's will that lost men and women be found, reconciled to himself, and brought into responsible membership in Christian churches."[4]

The best way I have found to understand the intricate complexity of Church Growth theory is by organizing the various factors of growth and decline in a grid, following the conceptual framework developed by Dean Hoge and David Roozen.[5] In the 1980s, Wagner used this same conceptual framework as the structure of a class he taught to hundreds of doctor of ministry students. This conceptual organization involves a grid of four quadrants that serves to interrelate four distinct types of growth and decline: national contextual factors, local contextual factors, national institutional factors, and local institutional factors. You can see this grid on page 129. Notice that I have given some examples of factors of growth and decline that are part of each quadrant in the grid, although it is beyond the scope of this chapter to give the entire theoretical foundation.

From his earliest research efforts in India, McGavran, in partnership with J. Waskom Pickett, was interested in how a group of Christians interfaced with the context (he called this being an "indigenous church") and what attitude those Christians exhibited toward each other and toward those in their context who were not yet Christians. As can be appreciated from a reading of *The Bridges of God,* McGavran was interested in numbers only as these represented the men and women who had come to faith in Jesus Christ.

McGavran was also very interested in the interrelation of the church with its surrounding environment, especially as that had come to his attention when he observed the withdrawn, fortress approach of many mission agencies who created mission stations and extracted their converts from the general population. Thus, the grid of four quadrants is, I believe, an accurate portrayal of the breadth of McGavran's missiological concerns regarding the growth and decline of churches (chart 1).

Thus, when McGavran founded the School of World Mission/Institute of Church Growth at Fuller Seminary in 1965, his aim was to gather a large group of researchers who would join him in seeking answers to his fundamental question: Why do some churches grow, some stay stagnant, and others decline in a particular context?

McGavran was interested in seeing the church of Jesus Christ grow at a more rapid pace than the general population did because he wanted to see more and more of the earth's inhabitants become disciples of Jesus Christ and responsible members of Christ's church. So in terms of numerical growth, McGavran was committed to conversion growth and not very interested in either biological or transfer growth.

Another way to present the same grid, using a Venn-diagram approach, might look like figure 1 (see page 130).

These factors individually and collectively become even more interesting—and more complex—when one takes into account the interaction between the four quadrants (figure 2, see page 131).

An additional complexity occurs when one takes into account the matter of spiritual issues in church growth. We could illustrate that by overlaying a grid with lines over the four quadrants (figure 3, see page 131).

Now in order to construct an outline of a Church Growth theology, I have taken the traditional theological loci as found in, for example, the Apostles' Creed and have arranged them to interface with the four quadrants of Church Growth theory (chart 2, see page 132).

FACTORS AFFECTING CHURCH GROWTH

National Contextual Factors	National Institutional Factors
· Crisis of change · Religious and social changes · Increase of religious interest · Lack of satisfaction with status quo · Loss of hope · Historical developments · Relation to other Christian nations · Hunger for an existential, experiential religion that is personal, practical, effective, transformational · Economic crises · Disasters · National revival/awakening	· Passive or active approach to church development and growth · Maintenance/preservation mentality versus evangelism and growth · A missional theology and view of evangelism · Extent of secularization and nominalism · Missionary vision locally and globally · Indigeneity of the church · Appropriateness of the denomination with reference to the groups being addressed · Self-determination and identity of church planters and pastors · Seminary education oriented toward evangelism and growth · Denominational publications, writings about church growth · Financial commitment for church planting and growth
Acts: Rome and "the nations"	Acts: Israel under Roman rule
Local Contextual Factors	**Local Institutional Factors**
· Contextually appropriate for local receptors · Local competition among churches · Natural bridges of human relationships · Are basic needs being addressed? · Planting new indigenous churches · Level of contextualization of the message · Human relationships with the receptors? · "Good testimony" of the local churches · Local revival/renewal movement · Local crisis · Local church cooperation/unity	· Vision and commitment of pastor and church members · Orientation toward the future, rather than the past or present · Missional approach to being church · Congregation is contextually appropriate to context and receptors—indigenous · Integral growth of the congregation · Stewardship of all the congregation's resources for evangelism and church growth
Acts: Jerusalem, the city	Acts: the disciples of Jesus

This concept is from Dean Hoge and David Roozen, eds., *Understanding Church Growth and Decline, 1950–1978* (New York: Pilgrim, 1979). I have drawn from several places in this groundbreaking work.

Chart 1

FACTORS AFFECTING CHURCH GROWTH

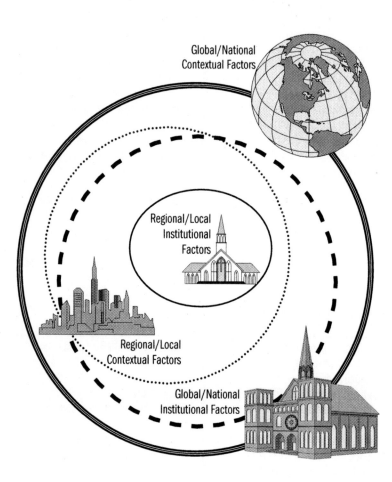

Global/National
Contextual Factors

Regional/Local
Institutional
Factors

Regional/Local
Contextual Factors

Global/National
Institutional Factors

Figure 1

This concept is from Dean Hoge and David Roozen, eds., *Understanding Church Growth and Decline, 1950–1978* (New York: Pilgrim, 1979). I have drawn from several places in this groundbreaking work.

FACTORS AFFECTING CHURCH GROWTH

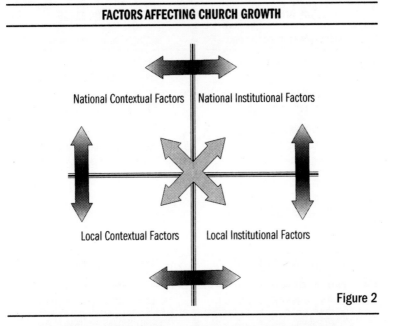

National Contextual Factors · National Institutional Factors

Local Contextual Factors · Local Institutional Factors

Figure 2

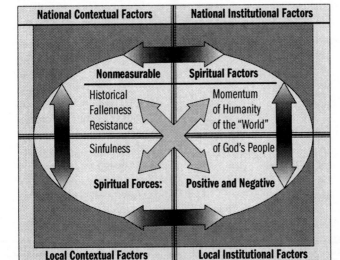

National Contextual Factors · **National Institutional Factors**

Nonmeasurable · **Spiritual Factors**

Historical
Fallenness
Resistance

Momentum
of Humanity
of the "World"

Sinfulness · of God's People

Spiritual Forces: · **Positive and Negative**

Local Contextual Factors · **Local Institutional Factors**

Figure 3

1. THE GOD WHO SEEKS IS THE MERCIFUL GOD WHO FINDS

National Contextual Factors	National Institutional Factors

2. Theology of the world
    Creation
    Providence
    Sin and Fall, resistance
 	
3. Theology of general revelation
    (Rom. 1:18–2:16)
    God's grace related to receptivity
 	
4. Theology of special revelation
    (Hebrews 1)
    Scripture and Church Growth
	7. The Holy Spirit and the church's witness
	    Pneumatological activity
	    Prayer for the nation
	    Spiritual influence of the
	    kingdom of light
	
	8. The church: the primary instrument
	    and penultimate goal of church growth

Acts: Rome and "the nations"	*Acts: Israel under Roman rule*
Local Contextual Factors	**Local Institutional Factors**

5. The Incarnation
    The Word made flesh: Jesus Christ
    (Ephesians 1, Colossians 1)
6. Pentecost: regeneration by the
    Holy Spirit
	9. The congregation: the locus of church
	    growth
	10. Congregational life, worship, holistic
	    growth (Orlando Costas)
	11. Mission: the church's:
	    Reason for being
	    Purpose of mission
	    Intention, priorities
	    Existence as a kingdom presence
	    Activities of
	        humanization/evangelization
	12. Eschatology
	    Hope in church growth
	    Vision, goal setting, mobilizing for
	    mission

Acts: Jerusalem, the city	*Acts: the disciples of Jesus*

Chart 2

In Luke's description of the growth of the church in Acts, all four quadrants are demonstrated.

- National contextual factors: Rome and "the nations"
- Local contextual factors: Jerusalem, the city
- National institutional factors: Israel under Roman rule
- Local institutional factors: the disciples of Jesus

In what follows, I will develop a brief outline of what I see as the "five pillars of a Church Growth theology." Each of the five propositions offered below involves a theological perspective that relates to a part of McGavran's definition of mission.

In Scripture, a pillar is used as a metaphor for the church, leaders in the church, and those who are faithful to the gospel. I believe it is also appropriate to use the metaphor to refer to foundational concepts of our understanding of the gospel. First Timothy 3:15 says, "If I am delayed, you will know how people ought to conduct themselves in God's household, which is the church of the living God, the pillar and foundation of the truth."

In Galatians 2:9, Paul writes, "James, Peter and John, those reputed to be pillars, gave me and Barnabas the right hand of fellowship when they recognized the grace given to me." And Revelation 3:12 states, "Him who overcomes I will make a pillar in the temple of my God."

Like a building constructed of five columns, Church Growth theory is grounded in a foundation of Scripture that draws from a classical reading of the Bible regarding God's mission *(missio Dei)*. The foundational value of McGavran and the Church Growth movement is that God does not want any to perish, but rather desires that all would come to repentance (2 Peter 3:9). Grounded in that biblical perspective, the five pillars we will review can be seen to hold up the roof of Church Growth theory and practice. This includes the use of all appropriate social sciences and many varied activities whose purpose is to see women and men become disciples of Jesus Christ and responsible members of Christ's church. When this occurs, the church grows. Thus, the five pillars we will survey contribute toward creating a Church Growth theology grounded in Scripture and contextually, culturally, and socially in touch with the people in each new context.

In figure 4, the five pillars we will survey in this chapter are related to the four-quadrant grid of Church Growth theory.

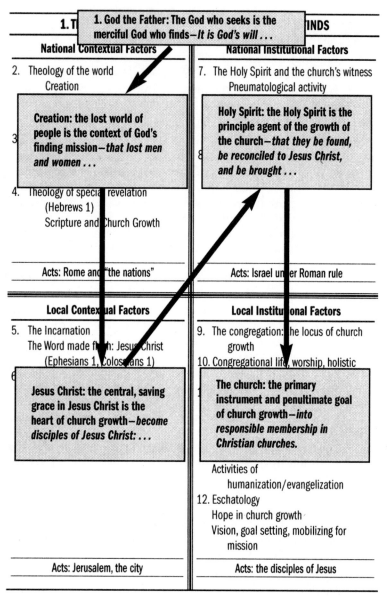

1. THE GOD WHO SEEKS AND FINDS

1. God the Father: The God who seeks is the merciful God who finds—*It is God's will . . .*

National Contextual Factors

2. Theology of the world
   Creation

Creation: the lost world of people is the context of God's finding mission—*that lost men and women . . .*

3.

4. Theology of special revelation
   (Hebrews 1)
   Scripture and Church Growth

Acts: Rome and "the nations"

National Institutional Factors

7. The Holy Spirit and the church's witness
   Pneumatological activity

Holy Spirit: the Holy Spirit is the principle agent of the growth of the church—*that they be found, be reconciled to Jesus Christ, and be brought . . .*

8.

Acts: Israel under Roman rule

Local Contextual Factors

5. The Incarnation
   The Word made flesh: Jesus Christ
   (Ephesians 1, Colossians 1)

6.

Jesus Christ: the central, saving grace in Jesus Christ is the heart of church growth—*become disciples of Jesus Christ: . . .*

Acts: Jerusalem, the city

Local Institutional Factors

9. The congregation: the locus of church growth
10. Congregational life, worship, holistic

The church: the primary instrument and penultimate goal of church growth—*into responsible membership in Christian churches.*

Activities of
   humanization/evangelization
12. Eschatology
   Hope in church growth
   Vision, goal setting, mobilizing for mission

Acts: the disciples of Jesus

Figure 4

A. THE GOD WHO SEEKS IS THE MERCIFUL GOD WHO FINDS.

It is God's will ...

As can be seen in this diagram, this first pillar of a Church Growth theology has to do with the nature of God. This affirmation overarches all four quadrants of Church Growth theory. All other mission endeavor derives and flows from the mission of God, who "so loved the world that he gave his one and only Son, that whosoever believes in him shall not perish but have everlasting life" (John 3:16).

Hendrikus Berkof speaks of the most fundamental attribute of God as being one of self-disclosure. "God is a self-disclosing God."[6] In 1 John 4:8, we are told that God is *agape* love. God always initiates his quest to reach humanity and embrace humans in a covenantal relationship. As I have mentioned in *Mission on the Way,* in my chapter on the covenant as a model of contextual theology, we could summarize the covenant formula that God establishes with God's people as follows: "I will be your God and you will be my People—and I will dwell among you."[7] This is the most foundational affirmation of the nature of God and God's relationship with God's people.[8]

This God is not the unmoved mover or the first cause of the Western Enlightenment. This is not the deist's God, who set in motion the so-called laws of nature. The God of the Bible is not only a God of the "omni's" (omnipresent, omniscient, omnipotent) of the Westminster Confession, though his nature includes those attributes. The God of the Bible is not the god of my subjective experience or of the numinous, à la Schleiermacher, nor the god of the categories of the mind as Emanuel Kant would have had us think. The God of the Bible is loving, compassionate, slow to anger, abounding in mercy, and always wanting to reach humans with his love and covenant with them.

I found it disconcerting to note that what Christian Schwarz calls the "biotic" approach is based on an Enlightenment paradigm that essentially assumes God created the world, placed in motion the so-called laws of nature, and then let those laws operate on their own. This assumption leads to a second: that once we can discover these "laws" in relation to the nature of the church and the local congregation, we can find a way to allow them to work "naturally" in bringing about the health and growth of the church. Christian Schwarz writes:

> Every student of God's creation—Christians and non-Christians alike—will eventually stumble upon something scientists call the "biotic potential." Ecologists define it as the "inherent capacity of an organism or species to reproduce and survive...." It was God's intent to build this perpetuity into His creation from the start. It is the secret of life, a divine principle of creation.... The same is true for church development. We should not attempt to "manufacture" church growth, but rather to release the biotic potential which God has put into every church.... Then church growth can happen "all by itself...." The principle of self-organization is found throughout creation.... What can be done to release the biotic potential...? The four building blocks of natural church development—quality characteristics, minimum strategy, biotic principles, new paradigm—try to supply an answer to this question.[9]

Scripture, on the other hand, portrays a God who is actively involved with his creation, revealing himself to humans, responding to human rejection of his love and grace, and in Jesus Christ, preserving all creation and holding all creation together, as Paul notes in the high Christology of Colossians 1.

The God of the Bible is a self-revealing, seeking, finding, and covenanting God—not a removed God, nor an imminent god who is the product of culture or of psychological hunger for meaning, nor the object of a religious search. He initiates the first move toward calling humans to reconciliation and calls humans to a relationship with himself. This Church Growth God is the God who creates humans to be in fellowship with God.

With his own hands, the God of Creation shaped humanity from the mud and then breathed his own breath into the lump of clay, carefully and lovingly sculpting humanity in the image of God. He cried with deep pathos "Adam, Adam, *where are you?*" This is the God who preserved Noah and promised never again to totally destroy humanity.

This is the God who called Abraham so that "all the families of the earth will be blessed through you" (Gen. 12:3). The God of Abraham, Isaac, and Jacob heard the cries of God's people in Egypt and worked through and around Moses to free the slaves so they might worship God at Sinai. This God is "The LORD, the LORD, the compassionate and gracious God, slow to anger, abounding in love and faithfulness, maintaining love to thousands, and forgiving wickedness, rebellion and sin" (Ex. 34:6–7).

This is the God of Psalm 23—"The LORD is my Shepherd"—and of Isaiah 6, the God who calls, "Who will go for us?" (v. 8). He is the seeking and finding God of the parables of Luke 15: the God who seeks and finds the lost sheep, who seeks and finds the coin, and who waits anxiously for the day when the lost son will return, and who celebrates with great joy when that which was lost is found.

About this God, the apostle Paul asked, "He who did not spare his own Son ... will he not also ... graciously give us all things?" (Rom. 8:32). This God "is patient ... , not wanting anyone to perish, but everyone to come to repentance" (2 Peter 3:9). This is the God who, we are told in Revelation, will gather people from every nation, tribe, people, and language into the New Jerusalem (Rev. 7:9).

We all know these truths in our heads. Too often we seem to forget their significance, as our actions testify. The bedrock foundation of Church Growth is God's seeking and finding activity in love.

Given the nature of this covenanting, loving, self-revealing God of the Bible, Church Growth is not optional; it is, rather, the most foundational aspect of the essence of our faith. If we are children of this God, we too will do all we possibly can to seek, find, and enfold persons, the *ethne*, calling them to "be reconciled to God" (2 Cor. 5:20).

Church Growth theory recognizes that we do not grow churches because it is the nature of the church; we grow churches because it is God's will. Christian Schwarz's relatively deistic approach may communicate well in the context of Western modernity, but it undervalues and misrepresents the Bible's foundational motivation for church growth: a loving God who seeks and finds. Church Growth is God's will.

B. THE LOST WORLD OF PEOPLE IS THE CONTEXT OF GOD'S FINDING MISSION.

That lost men and women ...

The second pillar involves the upper-left quadrant of our diagram, the one dealing with national contextual factors. McGavran's reference to lost men and women draws our attention outward to the world. Very early in the development of the Institute of Church Growth, McGavran invited Alan Tippett to join him. Already in 1965, in his book *Church Growth and Christian Mission*,[10] there is a profound awareness of the mosaic of cultures and of the need for the church to be indigenous to its context. Decades before that, McGavran had written about people groups and group conversion. An awareness of the world—and especially of the cultural characteristics of humans—is at the core of Church Growth theory.

Though I do not have space here to develop all the related theological issues, let me mention a few.

An awareness of creation and the world draws us to consider the matter of general revelation, of common grace, and in the words of the Wesleyan tradition, of prevenient grace. This also calls for awareness of sin and the fact that humans have a God-given option to say no to God.

McGavran talked about "lost" men and women. This in turn gives us a theological perspective on resistance and receptivity. In a presentation I made a few years ago to the Evangelical Missiological Society, my thesis was: "A missiological and theological understanding of 'resistance' or 'resistant people' must be grounded biblically in a recognition of human sinfulness that reflects the way humanity spiritually and relationally rejects God's loving self-disclosure to humankind. This would imply that a missiological discussion of 'resistance/receptivity' should deal primarily with issues of spirituality, theology, and reconciliation with God, self, others, and the world—and secondarily with matters of worldview, sociology, contextualization, and strategy."[11]

In that presentation, I made a case for the following points:

1. All humans are loved always by God.
2. All humans are receptive: they have a profound spiritual hunger to know God.

3. Because of Sin and the Fall, all humans are resistant to God all the time.
4. Some humans are resistant all the time, to all missional approaches.
5. Some humans are resistant some of the time to some things.[12]

I also offered the following comments: "Some groups are resistant because of contextual factors.... Some groups become resistant because of factors within the church.... [And] some groups become resistant because of the lack of cultural and spiritual interface between the church and the receptor group."[13]

A quick glance at the "eight essential qualities" that are the heart of Christian Schwarz's Natural Church Development (NCD) approach demonstrates that matters of culture and context are totally absent in this approach. These characteristics are:

1. Empowering leadership
2. Gift-oriented ministry
3. Passionate spirituality
4. Functional structures
5. Inspiring worship services
6. Holistic small groups
7. Need-oriented evangelism
8. Loving relationships[14]

With the possible exception of the seventh characteristic, these eight quality characteristics appear to be concerned almost exclusively with the internal life of a congregation. There is little or no awareness of the particularity of the contextual factors. Graphically, we could represent this by noticing that all NCD theory falls within the lower-right quadrant of our grid: the quadrant having to do with local institutional factors.

This disregard for contextual and cultural issues is a glaring weakness in the theoretical framework of *Natural Church Development*. You and I can rearrange the furniture within the church as much as we want, but if those changes are irrelevant to the congregation's interface with its context, they will make little or no difference. The lack of contextual awareness in NCD probably contributes to the erroneous assumption in NCD literature that the same principles can be applied in similar ways all over the world and in all cultures. This is simply not the case.

When we consider God's creation and humanity, we need to take sin seriously. We also need to take culture and contextualization seriously. We must realize that the world is not merely a deposit of souls from which we extract people to fill our churches. The world does not exist for the church. The church exists for the world. Jesus Christ sends us to the world.

On the other hand, McGavran was right when he stated that "men and women like to become Christians without crossing [unnecessary] linguistic, racial and class lines."[15] This affirmation is two-pronged. It recognizes the sinfulness of humans and their need for conversion (thus, there are necessary barriers) and yet people are to be free to become Christians within their own cultural modes (thus, there are unnecessary barriers).

The homogeneous unit principle arose from a recognition of the uniqueness of the cultural mosaics of the peoples of the earth and takes seriously the Tower of Babel. Most Western European theology has ignored the impact that cultural differences has on theology itself. The West has, until recently, assumed that theology is universally applicable to the whole world—a cultural superiority that must be dethroned. This lack of understanding of a plurality of cultures is evident in the Gospel and Our Culture Network in the United States, as well as in the Natural Church Development perspective, which seems to assume that what is good for Western Europe and North America is good for the church everywhere in the world.

Yet the quadrant dealing with national (and global) contextual factors also represents one of the glaring weaknesses of McGavran's missiology. He had a nasty habit of undervaluing social, economic, and political works of compassion in mission, relegating them to a category he called "other good things." Thus he steadfastly refused to support mission endeavors related to creation, development, health, agriculture, medicine, psychology, structural social and political change, and such. His missionary experience in India kept him from developing a holistic, kingdom-of-God understanding of mission. It tended to undermine McGavran's credibility in some missiological circles.

C. THE CENTRAL, SAVING GRACE IN JESUS CHRIST IS THE HEART OF CHURCH GROWTH

Become disciples of Jesus Christ: ...

The third pillar has to do with local contextual factors, the lower-left quadrant in our diagram. The gospel is always incarnated in a particular here and now, always in a unique time and place. God comes to the world through the incarnation of Jesus Christ (John 1). Church growth is always *local*. At its most foundational, Church Growth proclaims that "Jesus is Lord" and all else is negotiable. But this proclamation must be indigenous and local. The central issue is faith in Jesus Christ.

Church Growth Christology does not separate Christ's person (discussions regarding Christ's humanity and divinity) from Christ's work (theories of atonement, reflections concerning soteriology). Neither does Church Growth theory separate the Christ of faith from the Jesus of history. Rather, taking seriously Christ's threefold office, Church Growth missiology emphasizes the missional ministry of Jesus as sent by the Father for the salvation of the world. And that ministry and mission is transferred to Christ's disciples. "As the Father has sent me, I am sending you," Jesus said (John 20:21). We are to be prophets, priests, kings, liberators, healers, and sages who carry out the ministry of Jesus in the world as his body. And most important of all, we are to call people to become disciples of Jesus Christ, just as we see the disciples doing in all the sermons in Acts.[16]

Church Growth missiologists affirm that salvation is not to be found in church participation or in church membership. In that sense, fundamentally, our mission is not to plant churches; rather, we are called to "make disciples of Jesus Christ." Church planting too easily becomes church extension, an activity of opening new branch offices of the denomination, nationally and internationally. This was a problem with the understanding of *plantatio ecclesiae* of early Roman Catholic missionary orders.

Thus, Gisbertus Voetius and J. H. Bavinck affirmed that the goal of mission was first and foremost "the conversion of [people]" and ultimately the "gloria Dei." In between those two goals, and circumscribed, checked, and tested by them, we are involved in *plantatio ecclesiae*. The disciples we are called to make are not to be simply followers of our churches, nor of our pastors, but followers of Jesus Christ. We are to make disciples of Jesus Christ, not merely have people sign decision cards.

We need to draw from a full hermeneutic of Matthew 28, whereby the disciple-making is connected with our "going" and our "baptizing and teaching." All these activities are simultaneously included. This is where McGavran's distinction between what he called "discipling" and "perfecting" was very unfortunate. He used the term *discipling* in a way that no one else did at the time. Thus, he was mostly misunderstood. In addition, his use of these terms created an unnecessary and unbiblical split in the process of people growing in their discipleship in Jesus Christ. Where McGavran was right, however, is that what matters above all else is that women and men become disciples of Jesus Christ. Here is the Christological center of Church Growth theory.

This perspective helps us understand better what Church Growth is not. Though there is no space here to delve deeply into this matter, it is important to at least take note of what Church Growth is not. Church growth is not:

- individual conversion (nor only individualized campaign evangelism)
- private religion (Robert Bellah, et al., *Habits of the Heart*)
- acts of mercy with no incorporation
- mere sociopolitical pronouncements
- mere socioeconomic lift
- merely denominational programs
- exclusivism of any kind
- proclamation with no results
- nominal culture-Christianity

Notice the order in McGavran's definition of mission quoted at the beginning of this chapter. First the goal is that lost men and women become disciples of Jesus Christ. Only secondarily is it important that they become also "responsible members of Christ's Church." Thus, McGavran was in fact not ecclesiocentric, no matter how much J. C. Hoekendijk, Johannes Verkuyl, and Rene Padilla (among others) have said he was.

D. THE HOLY SPIRIT IS THE PRINCIPLE AGENT OF THE GROWTH OF THE CHURCH.

That they be found, be reconciled to Jesus Christ, and be brought . . .

Spiritual issues have dominated much of the thinking in some Church Growth circles during the past twenty years. And this concern for the spiritual factors that impact the growth and decline of the church attests to Church Growth's profound understanding that only the Holy Spirit can grow the church.

It may be good for us to remember what Acts affirms regarding the work of the Holy Spirit in the growth, health, and development of the church. A reading of Acts yields at least the following list. The Holy Spirit:

creates the church
reforms and transforms the church
empowers the church
unifies the church
gives new wisdom and illumination to the words of Jesus
sends the church
creates the deep desire to grow
accompanies the church
guides the church
prays for and through us and intercedes for us
gives us the words of witness
facilitates communication
develops receptivity
convinces of sin, righteousness, and judgment
converts persons to faith in Jesus Christ
gathers and unites Christians together in the church
builds up the faith community, edifies it, and helps it to grow
incorporates new arrivals
sends the church anew to the world so loved by God

One of the Holy Spirit's principle desires is to enable the church to grow. As I pointed out in my dissertation, "The Growth of the True Church," yearning to grow is a mark of the presence of the Holy Spirit and is part of the essence of the church's nature. This is more than an attitude. It is, rather, the bottom line, the bedrock commitment of the church's mission.

In developing his missiology, McGavran drew heavily from Roland Allen's concepts presented in the *Spontaneous Expansion of the Church*. The spiritual issues in Church Growth of the 1980s involved a pursuit of matters that had earlier been noted by McGavran and Tippett. Both emphasized that the growth of the church is a work of the Holy Spirit. For example, very early in the history of the Church Growth movement, Alan Tippett wrote about the concept of what he called "power encounter" in the Solomon Islands.[17]

No strategies can ultimately create the church. The church is the "mysterious creatio Dei" (Karl Barth) and is created by the work of the Holy Spirit. Remember that McGavran grew up in India, where everyone is deeply conscious of the unseen world. His early emphasis on pneumatology and spirituality was based on solidly biblical and evangelical theology. Wagner's *Look Out! The Pentecostals Are Coming* pointed to his early interest in these issues. Yet we also need to hear Samuel Escobar's concern that the Church Growth movement has too easily begun to attempt to engineer the Holy Spirit's work.

The recognition of the essential role of the Holy Spirit in the growth of the church seems to be a weak link in the theoretical framework of Schwarz's *Natural Church* Development. Although one can find some places where the Holy Spirit is mentioned (called "pneumatic functionality" by Schwarz,)[18] the "Ten Action Steps" have little space for the role of the Holy Spirit in the development of healthy churches.[19]

E. THE CHURCH IS THE PRIMARY INSTRUMENT AND PENULTIMATE GOAL OF CHURCH GROWTH.

Into responsible membership in Christian churches.

We come now to the fifth and last pillar, which is related to the lower-right quadrant of our diagram: local institutional factors. And this has to do with ecclesiology.

In the final analysis, the church is not an object, nor is it essentially an institution. The church is an event, as I noted in *God's Missionary People*. Christian Schwartz strongly critiqued the Church Growth movement, which formed and taught him, with regard to an overemphasis on numerical growth. He wrote, "In the last few years there have been a large number of publications on the theology behind church growth. However, most of these publications were surprisingly one-sided in their focus on the aspect of the 'numerical growth'—as if this were the theological key to understanding the essence of the subject. . . . Numerical growth seems to me to be just a side issue—albeit an important one—of church development. It is not the strategic goal, but one of many natural consequences of a church's health to experience growth."[20]

Schwarz adds a footnote here, saying, "The most thorough discussion of this subject I know of is still the dissertation by the Reformed theologian Charles Van Engen, 'The Growth of the True Church.'. . . Here, the concept of growth is related to the classical *notae* of the true church. This book, however, is a typical example of the way the numerical approach is seen as the essence of the church growth movement."[21]

Schwarz's comment shows an unfortunate misunderstanding of my writing. He apparently never read the last chapter in my rather long dissertation. In the last chapter, I critiqued McGavran's "harvest theology." In doing so, I was not ecclesiocentric, nor did I intend to measure the faithfulness or the essence of the church in relation to its numerical growth. On the contrary, the thesis of my dissertation was that it is a matter of the church's essence to yearn to grow (in oneness, catholicity, apostolicity, and holiness), and that any resulting numerical growth is a contextual matter that comes as a fruit of the interplay of many factors. While yearning to grow is an indispensible quality of the church's desire to reach out to those who do not yet know Jesus Christ, the resultant numerical growth depends on a host of contextual factors. The growth as such is not directly related to the church's desire to grow. It seems to me that this perspective is very close to what Schwarz himself advocates.

In terms of the larger Church Growth movement, one should also remember the contribution of Arthur Glasser to Church Growth theology, bringing forceful emphasis on the kingdom of God. McGavran's definition shows he never intended to be "ecclesiocentric," something that even Johannes Verkuyl missed.[22] On the contrary, notice the order of McGavran's definition. He placed the phrase "that men and women become disciples of Jesus Christ" in front of considering how they might "become responsible members of Christ's Church."

When McGavran talked about men and women becoming "responsible" members of the church, he meant it in two ways. First, for McGavran, "responsible" spoke of his hope that converted men and women would become a force for transforming the reality of their context, for social, economic, and political reconstruction. McGavran assumed that once there was a large number of Christians, they would change their social reality. He was probably idealistic and mistaken here. But if so, then he is in good company. Each in their own way, such an impact is assumed in the Gospel and Our Culture Network, in Neibuhr's emphasis, in John Calvin's work, and in the Christendom model of church in Western Europe. That the number of believers in Jesus does not have a direct bearing on the degree of sociopolitical and economic change in a context is acknowledged by most missiologists today. Yet "responsible" must in some way include Christians being a transforming presence in a lost and hurting world so loved by God.

Second, for McGavran, "responsible" spoke of the new converts becoming more like Jesus Christ (being baptized and taught). This was what, unfortunately, McGavran called "perfecting." The Church Growth movement has long emphasized its dream that new Christians would themselves become active in making disciples of Jesus Christ, in furthering world evangelization. This has been the heart of the DAWN movement that sprang out of the Church Growth movement.[23] Ultimately, the church exists for mission as fire exists for burning. And the church cannot grow except as it grows in its missional commitment and action to participate in God's mission in the world. Yet this dream has also been illusory.

CONCLUSION

In this chapter, I have sought to illustrate in a summary fashion that to construct a Church Growth theology, we do not need a host of biblical texts and theological affirmations to buttress the Church Growth movement. This apologetic approach is what people expected and what folks demanded of the Church Growth movement early on. That expectation was never fulfilled by the founders of the movement. This lack has often led to accusations that Church Growth is not theological or has no theology.

But maybe there was good reason for this lack. Maybe the real reason was that the heart of Church Growth theory is itself theological in its essence. Maybe the need has been something else: that we learn to articulate a Church Growth theology, rather than a theology of church growth. Clearly, we need to do much more work. We need to construct a paradigm of a biblical Church Growth theology whose heartthrob is the heart of God and whose deep desire it is that the church should grow.

Thus, a Church Growth theology may be constructed on at least these five pillars:

1. The God who seeks is the merciful God who finds.
2. The lost world of people is the context of God's finding mission.
3. The central, saving grace in Jesus Christ is the heart of church growth.
4. The Holy Spirit is the principle agent of the growth of the church.
5. The church is the primary instrument and penultimate goal of church growth.

The foundation of these pillars is God's mission as revealed in the Bible. The archway that holds the five pillars together is McGavran's definition of mission as I have paraphrased it in this chapter: it is God's will that men and women become disciples of Jesus Christ and responsible members of Christ's church. The roof of this building is the creative, entrepreneurial, freewheeling, open-ended, contextually appropriate, and biblically faithful proclamation that Jesus is Lord. Together, the five pillars begin to form a Church Growth theology. Here, then, is the superstructure of Church Growth, one of the most influential missiological movements of the past fifty years.

A RENEWAL RESPONSE
Howard Snyder

Donald McGavran's central thesis, as summarized by Van Engen, was: "It is God's will that men and women become disciples of Jesus Christ and responsible members of Christ's Church." In his chapter, Van Engen attempts to build a theological superstructure ("five pillars") on McGavran's "definition of mission" and thus to articulate "a Church Growth theology." Along the way, Van Engen makes a number of telling points, particularly in showing some of the limitations of McGavran's thinking and offering some correctives.[24]

Since the chapter is intended as an exercise in constructive theology, I focus my response primarily on issues of theological method.

I had to struggle first of all with a sense of artificiality in the structure of Van Engen's argument. The overlaying of the four quadrants, twelve theological points, and five pillars (depicted visually in the graphics) seemed to me unnatural and lacking in any clear logical coherence.

Van Engen rightly criticizes an "apologetic approach" to Church Growth theory. "We need to give careful thought to the loci or concepts of theology itself," he writes. This intent is laudable. Whether the chapter succeeds in doing this or not is another issue.

The key theological claim in the chapter, it seems to me, is the statement, "Like a building constructed of five columns, Church Growth theory is grounded in a foundation of Scripture that draws from a classical reading of the Bible regarding God's mission." This statement, however, raises several definitional and hermeneutical issues that are not spelled out: What is "a classical reading of the Bible" and how does one "draw from" such? In what way is Church Growth theory "grounded upon a foundation of Scripture"? And what exactly is being claimed here about the *missio Dei*? Apparently what the author means is that (1) Church Growth theory is soundly grounded in Scripture and that (2) the proper hermeneutic is "a classical reading of the Bible." Though such a reading of Scripture is not defined, Van Engen speaks of "traditional theological loci as found in, for example, the Apostles' Creed." Van Engen never defines what these "traditional theological loci," or "basic biblical and theological loci or concepts" (as he also calls them), consist of. In his graphics, however, he lists twelve doctrines, or doctrinal areas, beginning with a statement about "the God who seeks" and moving through such themes as general and special revelation, incarnation, Pentecost, the church, and finally, eschatology. Apparently the rationale for these twelve categories or topics is simply that they are in traditional Western theology. It is not clear that these doctrinal areas bear any inherent relationship to the four quadrants within which they are arranged.[25]

The approach here is essentially *deductive*—arranging theological points to support an *a priori* position. Thus, the approach is still essentially apologetic. This is clear when Van Engen says, "We need to give careful thought to the loci or concepts of theology itself and ask how the theological assumptions they represent need to be rethought in the light of Church Growth theory." Here Church Growth theory is the given; fundamental doctrines must be "rethought" so that they harmonize with it. One might have thought, rather, that the challenge would be just the opposite: to examine Church Growth theory in the light of classical doctrines—if that is the approach one is taking.

We can imagine a better approach, however—one that is inductive rather than deductive. We could start with Scripture itself, not with Church Growth theory or classical doctrines, and ask: What does the Bible teach or show us *theologically* as well as pragmatically about how churches grow?[26]

An inductive approach would not seek to support the thesis that "it is God's will that men and women become disciples of Jesus Christ and responsible members of Christ's Church." Rather it would ask, for example, What is the church and its mission, biblically understood? And it would ask this on the Bible's own terms, not by superimposing the grid of a "classical reading" or the four marks of the church or the formulations of later creeds. A key issue here is hermeneutics. Theologians and Church Growth advocates have from time to time done pieces of this task, but generally the results have been largely predetermined by grids brought to and laid over Scripture.

In this connection, Van Engen's criticism of Christian Schwarz's *Natural Church Development* misses the mark. Van Engen claims that Schwarz's "biotic" model "is based on an Enlightenment paradigm" and is "relatively deistic" because it assumes "laws of nature" that operate more or less autonomously and does not make sufficient room for the ongoing work of the Spirit.

This is a misreading of Schwarz and a misunderstanding of what Schwarz means by the "all by itself" principle. Though Schwarz does use (perhaps unfortunately) the term "laws of life," his focus is on the dynamic, organic nature of life, not on mechanistic laws. In this sense, *Natural Church Development* is actually a critique of Enlightenment thinking. "Learning from nature means learning from God's creation. And learning from God's creation means learning from God the Creator," says Schwarz. As he points out, this is analogous to what Jesus did in telling parables.[27] To use organic or "biotic" models may be premodern or postmodern, but it certainly is not modern in the Enlightenment sense.

Nor does Schwarz slight the work of the Holy Spirit. "The central concern of natural church development," he writes, "is to do as much as possible to enable God's Spirit to work unhindered in our churches, so that he can grow the church."[28] I see nothing unbiblical or "Enlightenment" or theologically suspect in recognizing that the Spirit works *through* dynamics built into the divinely created world and that we should cooperate with these dynamics. In fact, Church Growth theory has often acknowledged this.

I do have some problems with Schwarz's so-called "bipolar ecclesiology," but I do not see NCD as either mechanistic or deistic. In some ways, it is closer to emerging complexity theory than to the Enlightenment.[29] Schwarz's main point is a valid and biblical one: The church is a living organism that functions consistently with principles and dynamics God has built into it. We ignore these to our peril.

AN EFFECTIVE EVANGELISM RESPONSE

Elmer Towns

Years ago C. Peter Wagner and I had a conversation about the desperate need for a theology of Church Growth, or what Charles Van Engen has so aptly described as a Church Growth theology. Both Wagner and I decided that many had tried to do it, but no one had adequately approached the subject, and we thought no one had succeeded. Yet Van Engen has laid a foundation for a Church Growth theology in his chapter, and I trust he will one day put all of his thoughts into a complete systematic approach to all of Church Growth from a theological perspective. This chapter is a great beginning.

I assumed that Van Engen was approaching Church Growth from a different perspective from mine but found that we stand back-to-back in basic areas of our discipline. We are very close in most areas, although we may be looking in different directions. Most of our disagreement is peripheral or a matter of how we see and interpret the issues.

The premise of Van Engen's theology is that "it is God's will that lost men and women become disciples of Jesus Christ: that they be found, be reconciled to Jesus Christ, and be brought into responsible membership in Christian churches." This statement is faithful to the teachings of McGavran and becomes the foundation for Van Engen's Church Growth theology.

In Van Engen's discussion on "lost men and women" (section B), he dealt with resistance, what was called "barriers" by some Church Growth leaders. McGavran talked about cross-cultural evangelism, reaching from one culture "crossing barriers" to another culture. He dealt with resistance and difficulties in reaching people. Van Engen's focus in this chapter is more on the resistance of groups than on the resistance of individuals. Emphasis on both individuals and groups is needed to get a balanced approach to Church Growth; I am sure Van Engen will deal with individual barriers in other places in his theology.

I had difficulty understanding two concepts in Van Engen's chapter. First, he makes the statement, in section C, that "Church growth is always *local*," yet a few paragraphs later he says, "Our mission is not to plant churches." When he makes this statement, he is emphasizing bringing individuals to Jesus Christ, "making disciples of Jesus Christ," and that is necessary. However, Church Growth has always emphasized church planting as one of the most effective ways of evangelizing a city, state, or nation. As a matter of fact, church planting is indigenous and implied in the statement "Matheteusate panta ta ethne" (Matt. 28:19).

Beyond the five pillars of theology, I would encourage Van Engen to develop a strategy for Church Growth, which I know he has in his mind but which is not evident in this paper, explaining how these five pillars will be carried out. Part of that strategy is establishing those principles that carry out the Great Commission to reach all nations, since Church Growth must develop methods that evangelize each unique culture. After all, is not it the methods of Church Growth that many attack when disagreeing with Church Growth?

The strength in Van Engen's theology is his concern to incorporate "spiritual factors" into the heart of his theology. I like his statement, "Only the Holy Spirit can grow the church." Van Engen sees the evidence of "yearning to grow" as a mark of the presence of the Holy Spirit, and that is the bedrock commitment of the church's mission.

If I have any difficulty with Van Engen, it is his statement, "No strategies can ultimately create the church." Obviously, this is a focus on the body of Christ, the invisible church or the true church. This statement needs to be balanced within the context that the church is both universal and local, that is, the church is the spiritual body of Christ, and only the Holy Spirit can add to it. But at the same time, Church Growth deals with local churches attempting to carry out the Great Commission. So then strategies are necessary, as are principles and methods. Even though some, like Samuel Escobar, may criticize strategies as an "attempt to engineer the Holy Spirit's work," we must realize that we work in cooperation with the Holy Spirit.

Also, Van Engen needs to reconsider his definition of the church. He says, "The church is not an object, nor is it essentially an institution. The church is an event." Again, a balanced approach is necessary because the church is made up of both humans on this earth as well as the spiritual body of Christ. Therefore, the church is both a human institution and a spiritual entity. I define the Church as "an assembly of professing believers in whom Christ dwells, existing under the discipline of the Word of God, organized to carry out the Great Commission, administer ordinances and manifest spiritual gifts."[30]

Van Engen properly uses McGavran's term *harvest theology*, and in doing so, he focuses attention on evangelism and carrying out the Great Commission. In this matter, Van Engen supports the evangelistic implementation of the Great Commission. However, I always look for phrases related to local church outreach—such as *soul winning, evangelism, preaching*—which I did not find in his presentation.

Van Engen is correct that the ultimate mission in Church Growth is not the church but the expression of the kingdom of God as seen in the gathering of all believers in heaven, when every knee shall bow (some willingly and some unwillingly) before Jesus Christ.

A REFORMIST RESPONSE

Gailyn Van Rheenen

A PARADOX

I have great appreciation for the writings of Charles Van Engen because they have been formative to my missiological thinking, especially in the area of theology of missions. I respect him as a friend, mentor, and colleague.

I believe, however, that Chuck's defense of Church Growth presents an obvious paradox. He assumes two very different roles: Dr. Van Engen, the missiological theologian, and Dr. Van Engen, the theological advocate of Church Growth. As the missiological theologian, he insists that theology take precedence over pragmatism. As the theological advocate of Church Growth, he retrofits theology to undergird an existing anthropocentric model.

Chuck's writings on the theology of missions are astutely constructed based on biblical understandings and theological reflection. When writing about Church Growth, however, he has superimposed theology over an already existing set of cultural factors.

DOING THEOLOGY "WITH CHURCH GROWTH EYES"

Van Engen makes his methodological approach overt by saying that he seeks to "do theology *'with Church Growth eyes.'*"

I would say that biblical theology should form the lens through which we view culture, and culture provides the arena posing dilemmas and issues requiring further theological reflection. While praxis informs theology and surfaces cultural issues that must be theologically addressed, the beginning points of missiology must be developed biblically and theologically before the missionary moves on to consider contextual issues. Without this foundation, the discipline is easily swept back and forth by the ebbs and flows of cultural currents.

This book's major issue concerns the beginning point of missiology. In other words, does missiology begin with contextual factors and then reflect theologically, or does theology provide the foundational beginning points of the discipline? I believe that missiology must be formed by biblical theologies, such as the mission and kingdom of God and the incarnation and crucifixion, before moving to praxis, where new questions for theological reflection surface.

When people build a model with few theological underpinnings, it is easy for the agenda to be hijacked by practitioners who focus on strategy. These practitioners are guided by "What works?" rather than "What is of the will of God?" Van Engen (and before him McGavran) laments that "we are presently at a stage in the development of the Church Growth movement in which people use the term *church growth* with little or no relationship to the original theoretical foundations of the movement, and sometimes with seemingly little understanding of the theory itself." Should this not lead us to question the very foundations of a missiology in which cultural analysis and strategy formation precede biblical theology?

WHAT IS THE FUNDAMENTAL RESEARCH QUESTION?

Foundational to the Church Growth paradigm, according to Van Engen, is its fundamental research question: "Why do some churches grow ... in a particular context and others do not?"

Should *growth* be the foundational focus of the church? Does not this question naturally lead to pragmatics and an atheological approach to missions?

I suggest these alternative questions that prioritize theological formation: How does the church enter into the mission and kingdom of God? How does the church reflect the incarnation and crucifixion of Christ? Without negating growth, these questions more clearly prioritize the purposes of God.

THE PROCESS OF DEVELOPING A THEOLOGY OF CHURCH GROWTH

It is also important to note Van Engen's process for developing a theology of Church Growth. He first presents the classic Church Growth diagram describing factors affecting church growth, a model that is useful for cultural analysis. He then superimposes spiritual items over this analytical paradigm. Finally, he overlays classic doctrines of the Christian faith over the diagram, which by this time, appears highly confusing and cluttered.

His move from cultural factors to spiritual items to theologies does not demonstrate theological integration. It illustrates that spirituality and theology must be attached to an anthropological model of analysis.

In reality, however, Church Growth practitioners seldom follow Van Engen's entire process. Typically, they analyze culture without theological reflection and then make strategy plans. Afterward they add Scriptures that proof-text their plans.

I propose that the process be reversed. First, missionaries should be equipped to reflect theologically on the mission and kingdom of God in all of its spiritual dimensions. Their view of humanity and of Christian ministry, then, would be based on a theology of culture rather than on a static diagram of contextual factors.

APPRECIATION

The final pages of Van Engen's chapter are the most significant. Using McGavran's statement, "It is God's will that lost women and men become disciples of Jesus Christ: that they be found, be reconciled to Jesus Christ, and be brought into responsible membership in Christian churches," he develops five theological pillars of Church Growth. This attempt to theologize Church Growth is commendable.

The Church Growth movement would be stronger had these theological principles been foundational from the beginning. Moreover, while these pillars may be inferred from McGavran's statement, they are not frequently expressed by Church Growth adherents and seldom are they formative to developing strategy.

I would suggest that Van Engen, rather than trying to retrofit theology into Church Growth pragmatism, heed Valdir Steuernagel's advice: "As we move into a new century, I share the conviction that we need to reposition ourselves and to work once again on the agenda."[31] My own journey in missions has led me to believe that pragmatic ("What works?") and missional ("How do we enter God's mission?") approaches are different paradigms of mission and that the latter is preferable to the former. Let us "work once again on the agenda" with bibilical theology forming our initial agenda.

A GOSPEL AND OUR CULTURE RESPONSE
Craig Van Gelder

This chapter provides the reader with an opportunity to reflect on the theology of Church Growth after nearly fifty years as a missiological movement.

Perhaps the author does not include the development of the *missio Dei* missiology movement because he presumes the kingdom of God discussion to have been folded into Church Growth under the influence of his former Fuller School of World Mission colleague Arthur Glasser. Glasser's work is substantive in this regard, and Van Engen notes the relationship between the ultimate goal of the "the kingdom of God" and the "penultimate goal of church growth." While the relationship is stated in the right order at this point, it would be my assessment that Van Engen fails to frame his theology of Church Growth within the larger theology of the kingdom of God in relation to the *missio Dei*.

The core issue that the author seeks to address in his chapter is the development of a comprehensive missiological theology that can support the missiological theory of Church Growth. He notes the "fragmentary" character of much of the theology that has been presented to frame Church Growth. Nevertheless, he asserts that the core vision of Donald McGavran still stands as the central thesis for building a comprehensive theology for Church Growth. The author develops McGavran's vision, using five "pillars" in relation to the fourfold matrix of national-local and contextual-institutional factors.

Let me raise two concerns regarding the author's constructed proposal of "seeking to do theology 'with Church Growth eyes.'" First, I would raise a concern about the proposed framework: his matrix and the five pillars. While I have also found this matrix to be helpful in doing analysis of contexts and congregations, the author's efforts to frame mission theology within this matrix by folding the Apostles' Creed into its categories feels a bit arbitrary. For example, how does one determine if the incarnation and Pentecost are really local contextual factors, whereas the Holy Spirit is a national contextual factor? One could probably argue that the incarnation has both local and national (global) dimensions.

This approach is illustrative, it seems to me, of the dilemma that continues to plague many within the Church Growth movement. Rather than building a mission theology from a bibilical foundation that is tested with theological and historical perspectives, there is a tendency to use biblical, theological, and historical materials to support an assertion that is already assumed to be a representative summary of God's work in the world. This brings me to my second point of concern: the assertions embedded in the five pillars.

Van Engen uses McGavran's theological thesis as the foundation for framing the five pillars. While he takes note of some of the contextual realities that shaped McGavran's thinking, I am not sure that Van Engen has sufficiently unpacked the forces that gave birth to Church Growth as it was developed by McGavran. In this regard, Van Engen does not test the pillars against any biblical framework per se or against any other theologies regarding mission that have been developed in recent years.

In building on McGavran's work, the author asserts, for example, that the overriding theological premise that should be assumed about God is that "the God who seeks is the merciful God who finds, ... it is God's will ..." Is this the core theological assertion that one should start with in thinking about God? If one does start here, it is not difficult to see how one can move to the Great Commission as the core command of Scripture to be obeyed. What if one started from a slightly different angle, for example, along the lines of what Paul asserts in 2 Corinthians 5:16–21: that God as a creating God is also a reconciling God who seeks to reconcile all things in Christ? This would reframe the conversation about a seeking God to include God's mission to bring redemption to bear on every dimension of life within creation, in which the church is called, equipped, and sent to fully participate.

Such a move would relocate the primary activity regarding redemption to be the work of God in which the church participates. It would also reframe the understanding of the Great Commission from being seen primarily as an imperative to be obeyed through human agency to another perspective. The Great Commission would now become the natural response of a community of people whose identity has been framed by the earlier indicative in Matthew 5. Here God's people are informed that they are already the salt and light of the world because of what God has done and is doing through Jesus. From the perspective of grace and redemption, the indicatives of Scripture serve as the basis for understanding and responding to the imperatives. Such a shift has profound implications. Human agency is still deeply involved, but the activity now becomes the work of God through God's Spirit in leading and guiding the church to participate fully in God's mission in the world. This shift reframes the discussion from being about church growth to being about the growth of the church, a small shift of wording that has profound theological and missiological implications.

A similar critique could be offered of the other four pillars, but this short response does not allow for a fuller treatment. There are, however, two other matters I would like to touch on briefly. One has to do with the author's treatment of Schwarz's development of the church's "biotic potential." The author dismisses the concept of growth being part of "the nature of the church." I would note that Schwarz tends to be focusing more on the social organic nature of the church, which has its limits. But it is at this point that the author fails, I believe, to incorporate into his discussion a fuller understanding of the spiritual-social reality of the church as a community created by the Spirit. Such a community has within its very essence the reality of already being a seeking and growing community. The key is that this seeking and growing—what the author himself tried to establish in his doctoral thesis as being of the essence of the church, the yearning to grow—is not implemented out of some type of human obedience as the primary cause for action. Rather, it is implemented out of a human response to the divine realities that are already present within the very nature of the church as the living, dynamic community created by, and continuing to be led and taught by, the Spirit.

The other matter I would like to comment on is in reference to the author's critique and dismissal, on two occasions, of the movement that has come to be known as the Gospel and Our Culture Network (GOCN). The first occurs where the author suggests there is a "lack of understanding of a plurality of cultures" evident within this network, with the assertion being that the GOCN is still functioning with a Western universalizing theology. No examples are offered to support this critique, and as one who has participated in this movement for over a decade, I find just the opposite to be the case, although the "Our Culture" part of the GOCN does seek to address primarily North American Christianity. The second occurs where the author lists the GOCN, Neibuhr, John Calvin, and Christendom as holding on to the "idealistic and mistaken" assumption that converted persons might somehow influence and impact their social reality. Van Engen's assertion is that Christians can be a "transforming presence in a lost and hurting world" but that this is not to be correlated with the number of believers in Jesus. I know of no argument that has been published within the literature coming out of the GOCN that supports his critique of the network correlating social transformation with a certain number of Christians. The argument within the GOCN conversation is essentially the same as the author's, that Christians can be a "transforming presence."

Chapter 3 Notes: Centrist View

[1]Donald A. McGavran, *The Bridges of God* (New York: Friendship; London: World Dominion, 1955).

[2]Donald A. McGavran, *Understanding Church Growth* (Grand Rapids: Eerdmans, 1970).

[3]Ibid., 35.

[4]Donald A. McGavran, quoted in C. Peter Wagner, "Donald McGavran: A Tribute to the Founder," in *Church Growth: State of the Art*, ed. C. Peter Wagner (Wheaton, IL: Tyndale House, 1989), 16. Throughout the rest of this chapter, I will combine parts of both of these definitions as a shorthand way to refer to McGavran's conecpt of mission and the foundation perspective of Church Growth theology.

[5]Dean Hoge and David Roozen, eds., *Understanding Church Growth and Decline, 1950–1978* (New York: Pilgrim, 1979).

[6]Hendrikus Berkhof, *Christian Faith* (Grand Rapids: Eerdmans, 1979), 41–65.

[7]See, for example, Genesis 17:3–8; Exodus 4:32; 19:3–8; 24:1–11; 29:44–46; 34:2–28; Leviticus 26:1–45; Deuteronomy 26:16–19; Joshua 24:1–27; 1 Samuel 12:1–25; 2 Samuel 23:5; 7:14; 1 Chronicles 17:13; Psalm 2:7; 89:3, 26, 34, 39; Jeremiah 31:9–11; Romans 8:14; 2 Corinthians 6:16. See also Charles Van Engen, *Mission on the Way: Issues in Mission Theology* (Grand Rapids: Baker, 1996), 77.

[8]Charles Van Engen, *Mission on the Way: Issues in Mission Theology* (Grand Rapids: Baker, 1996), 71–89.

[9]Christian A. Schwarz, *Natural Church Development: A Guide to Eight Essential Qualities of Healthy Churches*, trans. Lynn McAdam, Lois Wollin, and Martin Wollin (Carol Stream, IL: ChurchSmart Resources, 1996), 11.

[10]Donald McGavran, *Church Growth and Christian Mission* (New York: Harper and Row, 1965).

[11]Charles Van Engen, "Reflecting Theologically about the Resistant," in *Reaching the Resistant: Barriers and Bridges for Mission*, ed. J. Dudley Woodberry (Pasadena, CA: William Carey Library, 1998), 23.

[12]Ibid., 37–59.

[13]Ibid., 59–68.

[14]Schwarz, *Natural Church Development*, 22–38.

[15]Donald A. McGavran, *Momentous Decisions in Missions Today* (Grand Rapids: Baker, 1984), 100. See also Donald McGavran, *Understanding Church Growth* (Grand Rapids: Eerdmans, 1970), 198.

[16]See Charles Van Engen, *God's Missionary People* (Grand Rapids: Baker, 1991), 119–30.

[17]See, for example, Alan R. Tippett, *Solomon Islands Christianity* (London: Lutterworth, 1967).

[18]Christian Schwartz, *Paradigm Shift in the Church* (Carol Stream, IL: ChurchSmart Resources, 1999), 70–72.

[19]See Schwartz, *Natural Church Development*, 24–41.

[20]Schwartz, *Paradigm Shift in the Church*, 8–9.

[21]Ibid., 9n. 2.

[22]See Johannes Verkuyl, *Contemporary Missiology* (Grand Rapids: Eerdmans, 1978), 188–92.

[23]DAWN is an acronym for Discipling a Whole Nation. For further information, write to DAWN, 5775 North Union Blvd., Colorado Springs, CO 80918. Phone (719) 548-7460. Website: www.dawnministries.org.

[24]Van Engen's pointed critique of the common Church Growth misappropriation of the parable of the soils (Matt. 13:1–13; Mark 4:1–20) is refreshing. This has long been of concern to me.

[25]In this connection, Van Engen seems to be making a theological point about the use of the term *pillar*. He cites three New Testament passages in which the term *pillar* occurs and suggests it is "appropriate to use the metaphor to refer to foundational concepts of our understanding of the gospel." No doubt it is appropriate to use the pillar metaphor in articulating "foundational concepts," but the mere fact that *pillar* occurs three times in the New Testament is not a theological argument and gives no additional biblical credibility to the concepts. Such use of Scripture makes one uneasy from the start about the theological depth and coherence of the position being advanced.

[26]This is, I think, essentially what McGavran attempted in his early classic *The Bridges of God*. Though he did not adequately achieve this (Van Engen notes the "discipling" / "perfecting" problem), the strength of the book is how McGavran brought Scripture to bear on current mission assumptions and practice.

[27]Schwarz, *Natural Church Development*, 7–8.

[28]Schwarz, *Paradigm Shift in the Church*, 260.

[29]See Howard A. Snyder with Daniel V. Runyon, "The Church: A Complex Organism," chap. 2 in *Decoding the Church: Mapping the DNA of Christ's Body* (Grand Rapids: Baker, 2002).

[30]Elmer L. Towns, *Theology for Today* (Fort Worth, TX: Harcourt College, 2001), 894.

[31]Valdir Steuernagel, "Learning from Escobar … and Beyond," in *Global Missiology from the Twenty-first Century—The Iguassu Dialogue*, ed. William D. Taylor (Grand Rapids: Baker, 2000), 127.

Chapter Four

REFORMIST VIEW

REFORMIST VIEW

Church Growth assumes theology but ineffectively employs it to analyze culture, determine strategy, and perceive history

Gailyn Van Rheenen

As we move into a new century, I share the conviction that we need to reposition ourselves and to work once again on the agenda.
—Valdir Steuernagel

PERSONAL CHURCH GROWTH INFLUENCES

I am deeply indebted to Donald McGavran and the Church Growth perspective. Donald McGavran was a personal, though distant, mentor. Throughout my years in Africa, he read our mission reports and occasionally sent personal replies and suggestions. I have always felt that our affinity stemmed from sharing a common heritage in the Restoration movement as well as his intense desire to see churches grow among all peoples of the earth.[1]

As our team saw local church leaders maturing and therefore contemplated phasing out our work, McGavran wrote, "Your ministry has demonstrated such receptivity that it is not time to retreat but to amplify forces. Instead of pulling missionaries out, you should amplify forces to win the winnable while they are winnable."[2] His message not only demonstrated his personal concern for us but also his urgency for growth as the major criterion for missions effectiveness.

As field missionaries, our mission team operated out of the Church Growth paradigm. We chose to minister to the Kipsigis because of their receptivity to the gospel at that particular time. We learned their language and deciphered their culture. We believed in contextualizing God's eternal message in ways the local people could understand. We sought harvest by planting numerous local churches. We refused to create Western institutions, trusting McGavran's perception that they would likely become Western enclaves of control and that overseeing them would preempt direct evangelism and church planting. We set individual and group goals for planting new churches, nurturing these churches through various stages to maturity, and training leaders to serve in these churches. We were the children of Church Growth and measured ourselves according to growth standards.

A number of factors, however, mitigated an extremely pragmatic Church Growth approach. Our mission team rejected many of the sectarian excesses of the Restoration heritage. We upheld, however, its love for textual studies by focusing our ministry on gospel proclamation and biblical training of new Christians. We believed that God's work in the death, burial, and resurrection of his incarnate Son was the core of the gospel. We further held that for people to hear the gospel and grow to Christian maturity, this message should be conveyed narratively within the broad context of the biblical story. Once churches were planted through gospel proclamation, Christians were systematically nurtured through stages of maturity, which focused on teaching local leaders how to read the biblical text and theologically reflect on their cultural context.[3] This focus on biblical teaching continued in Sunday worship and midweek meetings, in congregation-based courses for church leaders, and in a Bible school overseen and managed by local church leaders. Throughout the years, Kipsigis Christians were acknowledged as "people of the Book" or as "textual teachers."

Our team publication, the *Kipsigis Kommunique*, which engaged the issues of communicating the gospel in this specific contemporary context, was read by many. As a team, we also began the journal *Missionary Anthropology*, patterned after the old *Practical Anthropology*, and renamed the *Journal of Applied*

Missiology, edited by Dr. Ed Mathews, when two of our team taught and ministered at Abilene Christian University.

Over the years, however, I grew increasingly skeptical of Church Growth perspectives. Anthropology was given more consideration than theology. The emphasis was on conversion rather than on making disciples. Therefore, missions was primarily evaluated by the number of converts and churches established rather than by the developing maturity of the body of Christ. I have come to agree with Steuernagel's statement, made at the Iguassu Missiological Consultation, that "we need to reposition ourselves and to work once again on the agenda."[4]

This repositioning, however, must be done with love and respect. In studying manuscripts for this chapter, I was surprised and perturbed by the reciprocal distrust of Church Growth proponents, who tended to be practitioners, and Church Growth detractors, who typically were theologians. At times, the detractors unmercifully indict the proponents' theological naïveté without fully understanding the historical contexts in which the movement was conceived. The detractors may not have read the primary sources of Church Growth literature. They may at times drastically overstate the case. For example, one missiologist describes Church Growth as "a conscience-smoothing Jesus, with an unscandalous cross, an other worldly kingdom, a private, inwardly limited spirit, a pocket God, a spiritualized Bible, and an escapist church. Its goal is a happy, comfortable, and successful life, obtainable through the forgiveness of an abstract sinfulness by faith in an unhistorical Christ."[5]

Too frequently this skepticism toward Church Growth has led to the negation of missiology as a discipline. Missiology, according to these critics, is merely a study of tactics and strategy, not a discipline rooted in theological reflection.

Church Growth proponents, on the other hand, feel that a traditional seminary education provides foundations for Christian ministry but does not offer "assistance with such daily challenges as winning people to Christ, assimilating newcomers, dealing with power families, initiating change, and a host of other matters." According to this perspective, "Church growth theory and theology, rightly understood, still provide the best answer to growing a faithful church—even in the twenty-first century."[6]

Church Growth proponents believe that many detractors have little experience in Christian ministry. Few of the detractors have experienced the feelings of the poor who are intimidated by the rich or the feelings of ethnic groups who have a heritage of distrust for one another. If those who oppose Church Growth had had these experiences, they would understand the need to proclaim the gospel to each specific ethnic group in a way that these particular people might clearly hear its message. As McGavran has said, people *do* come to Christ, almost without exception, without crossing social or cultural boundaries. Unbelievers cannot fully understand that "there is neither Jew nor Greek, slave nor free, male nor female, for [we] are all one in Christ Jesus" (Gal. 3:28) before they become Christians, but they discover this truth in the church as they grow in Christ. Without "people group" thinking, there is little evangelism.

Detractors and proponents, however, agree on one thing: Church Growth "both infuriates and inspires," but discussion of it "has never been boring!"[7]

This chapter enumerates both strengths and limitations of the Church Growth model and then calls for a new integrated missional model that supersedes the Church Growth and theological paradigms of the past.

STRENGTHS OF THE CHURCH GROWTH PARADIGM

Although I have some reservations about Church Growth perspectives, I recognize some significant strengths of the Church Growth paradigm.

A Focus on Personal Ministry

McGavran's Church Growth perspectives were formed while ministering from 1923 to 1955 in India, where colonial missionaries felt the need not only to Christianize but also to civilize. Mission compounds were established as enclaves of the new civilization. Replicating the Western culture with which they were familiar and developing Christian ministries in these Western enclaves provided a sense of security for missionaries with little preparation for significant cultural adaptation. The new convert, however, was separated from his or her family and friends, acculturated within the new "Christian" culture, and Westernized in the process. "The effect of this policy," according to Newbigin, was "two-fold. On the one hand the convert, having been transplanted into an alien culture, [was] no longer in a position to influence non-Christian relatives and neighbors; on the other hand the energies of the mission [were] exhausted in the effort to bring the converts, or more often their children, into conformity with the standards supposed by the missionaries to be required by the gospel."[8] From McGavran's perspective, both the acculturation of local people in a Western compound and the focus on perfecting rather than discipling "have the effect of stopping the growth of the church. Schools, colleges, hospitals, and programs for social action multiply, but the church does not."[9]

Within this context, McGavran challenged the missions community to shift from maintenance to ministry. He believed that the missions stations should be given to national church leaders to control and maintain. Missionaries should focus on evangelizing the lost and incorporating them into local churches. These missionaries (and the national leaders they train) should view themselves as identificational, incarnational ministers. The end result of this thinking was a massive repositioning of personnel and resources into personalized forms of direct evangelism and church planting.

McGavran's call to change from maintenance to ministry has had a significant impact on both domestic ministers and cross-cultural missionaries. Christian evangelists were challenged to minister personally rather than indirectly through institutions. They were encouraged to humbly follow the example of the divine One of God who became flesh and dwelt among us (John 1:14), touching the untouchable, loving the unloved, redirecting stray sheep. McGavran rightly challenged God's servants to empathetically enter into culture and minister directly with the people.

The Missionary Nature of the Church

In his distinctively strident way, McGavran placed the mission of the church on the theological agenda. Even before the word *Christendom* was coined, he spoke against the model, rooted in a Constantinian heritage, which was not repudiated by early Protestantism. Under Christendom, all people were considered Christians from birth, negating missions in the life of the church for many centuries. McGavran has been a catalyst in the Christian movement, helping the church realize that to be faithful, it must participate in world mission.

In his class Theology for Missions Today, McGavran assigned his students the task of analyzing the creedal foundations of their denominations and describing the content according to Scripture's missionary mandate. The introduction to the assignment reads as follows:

> Let me sum up very briefly what I shall be saying for several days in many different ways and what you will be working on, each in his own way, for several days. I set before you four propositions.
>
> 1. Most of the current creeds, both written and unwritten, were framed during the centuries when the Protestant churches were sealed off from the non-Christian world and were almost completely non-missionary.
> 2. Most doctrines are deficient in the missionary dimension. They were formulated for existing Christians against the errors and mistakes of other Christians. They were not formulated under the impulsion of the Great Commission. This has greatly hindered the spread of the Gospel.
> 3. Since the Great Commission is an integral part of the Bible and is a central strand in God's revelation and Christ's atoning death, this also means that many doctrines are not as biblical as they might be.
> 4. Christians (theologians, missionaries, ministers and others) do well when they seek to make each doctrine biblically more true and missionarily more adequate. Each doctrine should drive Christians and churches out to the evangelization of the three billion.[10]

The students were then given the rigorous task of analyzing the particular creeds of their denominations and making them "biblically more true and missionarily more adequate." The exercise was quite revealing. His students soon discovered that a missional identity was absent from most of their heritages.

McGavran asserted that the priority of the church is not to care for itself but to become God's ministers to the *ethne* of the world. Churches become selfish and self-satisfied, preoccupied with themselves rather than with reaching the lost with the gospel. This "introverted churchism" was a theme running throughout McGavran's writings and lectures.[11]

Emphasis on Pioneer Evangelism

As we have already discussed, the Church Growth movement helped the church and the missionary movement focus on pioneer evangelism and prioritize the needs of unevangelized sectors of the world. This emphasis was reflected in two movements, one centered around McGavran's perspective of receptivity and the other around Ralph Winter's view on unreached peoples.

To McGavran, the world was not static, but dynamic. He therefore perceived that people's receptivity to the gospel message is always changing. Sometimes the hearing of the gospel creates no response. It appears that people feel no need for the gospel. At other times the message hits home in a society crying over problems and overwhelmed by fears. Often in such situations, a large number of people joyfully seek the Lord in baptism, organize vibrant fellowships, and revitalize their society around the message of Jesus Christ. McGavran specifically describes examples of varying receptivity, factors causing fluctuation of receptivity, and the practical ramification of this principle for mission policy.[12] He felt that the ultimate source of receptivity is the mighty acts of God working through the Holy Spirit to convict the world of sin. Fields not bearing fruit should be held lightly until signs of a possible harvest are evident. When such signs become evident, concentrated numbers of workers should be called in to reap the harvest.[13]

Ralph Winter, sometimes called the father of frontier missions, inspired the evangelical missionary movement to prioritize the unreached people of the world. Unreached people, according to the Lausanne Committee for World Evangelization, do not have an "indigenous community of believing Christians with adequate numbers and resources to evangelize this people group without requiring outside assistance."[14] In recent years, the focus has shifted from receptive to unreached people, especially those of the 10/40 Window, a slice of the world stretching from North Africa through the Middle East to China and Japan.

Although the perspectives on receptivity and unreached peoples have been and still are debated, one fact is undeniable:

the discussions have led mission leaders, agencies, and local churches to focus on pioneer evangelism.

Incisive Evaluation

An important element of Church Growth, borrowed from the Enlightenment, is incisive critique. As William Abraham suggests, within the Church Growth movement, there is an "aggressive, iconoclastic spirit that is determined to get at the facts." He rightly states that "we surely need to know not only where the church is growing and declining but why it is doing so."[15] Leslie Newbigin, while acknowledging that "the [biblical] emphasis falls upon the faithfulness of the disciples rather than their numbers,"[16] also writes, "McGavran is ... right to press upon us the question, Why is there not more concern for the multiplication of believers and more evidence of its happening?"[17]

Those studying the church should not be frightened by the use of the social sciences but only by its misuse. Truth can be discovered in many forms and in many disciplines. In a very real sense, missionaries should be primarily practical theologians but also anthropologists. They should exegete not only the text but also the context.

Church Growth analysts, although vastly overstating the value of numbering, have, through comparative evaluation, led to wide-ranging discussions of modern missionary strategy.

LIMITATIONS OF THE CHURCH GROWTH PARADIGM

Church Growth thinking has significant strengths and benefits, but its limitations must also be acknowledged.

In the July 1989 issue of *Missiology*, McGavran spoke of a lion that was devouring the evangelical missionary movement. He identified this lion as the social gospel, "the idea that mission [missiology] is primarily helping those great groupings of humankind who are less fortunate than we are."[18] I would, however, propose that an even greater lion threatens the missionary movement. That lion is pragmatism—segmented from biblical theology—which drives the agenda of the church. This pragmatism is described in the following sections.

Anthropocentric Focus

Unintentionally, Church Growth practitioners developed a missionary model vulnerable to the spirit of their age. Assuming they could chart their way to success by their ingenuity and creativity, they focused on what humans do in missions rather than on what God is doing. Their beginning point was humanity rather than divinity. They saw the missional task as merely setting goals, developing appropriate methodologies, and evaluating what does or does not work rather than as seeking God's will based on biblical and theological reflection. Although they advocated faithfulness to God, the system they proposed was based on human intelligence and ingenuity, with little reference to God and the nature of the gospel. McGavran and his protégés (myself included) are thus children of modernity.

For example, McGavran's *Understanding Church Growth*, described as Church Growth's statement of "maturity and reflection,"[19] is a wonderfully pragmatic book. This epochal treatise, however, does not present an integrative theology to form its beginning presuppositions, except that God desires the church to grow (which we will discuss later in this section). Scripture is occasionally used, but only to give validity to some methodology or anthropological construct. Harvest theology, for example, illustrates the need to focus on receptive people.

In multicultural contexts, the competition for members and the drive for numerical success have resulted in a consumer mentality. Missionaries and ministers have sought to market the gospel like any other product and present it in a culturally appealing way. In this way, a Western consumer mentality, rather than biblical theology, has set the agenda of the missional endeavor.

Analyzing Church Growth in view of epistemological sources—how knowledge is framed within the human mind—reveals an interesting cognitive mix. Of the two traditional internal sources of knowledge, logic and intuition, Church Growth focuses on human logic. Of the two external sources, observation and authority, Church Growth paradoxically focuses more on observation. Church Growth, like modernism, is based primarily on the use of human logic and observation. Paradoxically, the Bible, the Christian source of authority, is secondary. *How we consciously and unconsciously prioritize and systematize our sources of knowledge at the most basic level will ultimately form our Christian message and the nature of missions and evangelism.*

This emphasis on logic and observation can be illustrated by the nature of Church Growth research. The methodology of social research seeks to pattern the observation of respondents and systemize these observations in logically coherent ways. This research helps the Church Growth practitioner determine what people desire from a church, how people hear the gospel, and who is receptive. The research focuses almost exclusively on the social context.

Social research, while beneficial in understanding human culture, is not the foundation of missiology. All missiological decisions must be rooted, either implicitly or explicitly, in theology so that they mirror the purposes and mind of God. Too frequently missions practitioners take the theological foundation of missions for granted. Paul Hiebert writes, "Too often we choose a few themes and from there build a simplistic theology rather than look at the profound theological motifs that flow through the whole of Scripture. Equally disturbing to the foundations of mission is the dangerous potential of shifting from God and his work to the emphasis of what we can do for God by our own knowledge and efforts. We become captive to a modern secular worldview in which human control and technique replace divine leading and human obedience as the basis of mission."[20]

David Hesselgrave's analysis of the thematic content of book reviews and articles published in major missions journals (*Missiology, International Review of Missions,* and *Evangelical Missions Quarterly*) confirmed this absence of theological foundations in contemporary missiology. Concluding that missiology gives more attention to the social sciences and history than to theology, he asks, "Of what lasting significance is the evangelical commitment to the authority of the Bible if biblical teachings do not explicitly inform our missiology?"[21] Without theological foundations, missions quickly becomes merely another human endeavor.

The Segmentation of Theology and Praxis

An anthropocentric approach is by its very nature *pragmatic.* The pragmatist asks functional questions concerning success or goal fulfillment, such as Does this work? or Will this help the church to grow? Such questions, void of theological reflection, create a dichotomy between strategy and theology. The role of theology is to provide the message of mission; strategy supplies the method by which the message is conveyed to the people. This pragmatic thinking "de-emphasizes theological problems, takes for granted the existence of adequate content, and consequently majors in method."[22]

Methodologies and strategies, never theologically neutral, should be shaped by the gospel itself. Darrell Guder writes:

> Christianity has . . . consistently reduced or distorted the gospel. Many of the problems with which non-Western churches struggle have to do with the versions of the gospel that the missionary evangelists brought them, and much of the spiritual health of those churches may be attributed to their willingness to struggle afresh with the basic challenge of the gospel. We simply may not assume that our formulations of the gospel, as familiar and time-tested as they may be, exhaust the fullness and the scope of God's great good news, culminating in the life, death, resurrection, and mission of Jesus Christ. *Every judgment we will make about the methodologies of evangelism will depend upon our answer to the questions: What is the gospel? What is the fullness of the apostolic message? What is salvation? What does the church's gospel mission intend? What is the missio Dei ("mission of God") that defines the identity, purpose, and the way of life of the church?* [Italics added][23]

The dichotomy between strategy and theology has become increasingly evident in recent years. Thom Rainer writes, "Since 1988 most of the literature identified with church growth has been concerned with methodology; methodology of worship; methodology of marketing; methodology of leadership; methodology of evangelism; etc. It is easy to understand why critics are screaming that a new idolatry is being promoted by the Church Growth Movement. Methodology, once subservient to and a tool of theology, would now appear to be an end instead of a means."[24]

Missions reduced to methodology is as empty as spiritual gifts without love—like a "resounding gong or a clanging cymbal" (1 Cor. 13:1). Methodologies and strategies must be a servant, never a master, to the mission of God. In every aspect of ministry, therefore, the practitioner must begin with a study of biblical theology. Strategy formation will then be based on biblical and theological insights.

For example, the church planters' first step should never be conducting a survey to analyze the culture or determine searchers' felt needs. Neither should they develop the organizational structure for the future church by studying the structures of various growing churches. These studies can be beneficial, but without first developing a biblically rooted ecclesiology, the questions asked and the understandings received are superficial. Scripture reflecting on the nature of the church, like 1 Peter and Ephesians, should shape a biblical understanding of the church. For example, in Ephesians 2:19–22, Paul uses multiple metaphors to describe the nature of the church. The church is a *new nation;* newly converted Christians are "no longer foreigners and aliens" but "fellow citizens" in a community of faith (2:19). The church is a *family,* "God's household" (2:19). The church is a *holy temple,* well constructed, with each part joined together and built around Jesus Christ, the cornerstone. These perspectives are based on God's mighty acts in conversion; those dead in sin (Eph. 2:1–3) have been made alive with Christ (2:4–7) by God's grace (2:8–10). Paul stacks metaphors one on another to illustrate a redeemed fellowship "brought together under ... Christ" (Eph. 1:3–11) and existing "for the praise of his glory" (1:12).

Because they provide an inspired picture of God's divine community, these biblical perspectives form the foundation of strategy. They are snapshots of what God expects the newly planted church to be.

Priority must therefore be given to theological formation. Cultural analyses and strategy formation should be developed through the grid of these biblical and theological perspectives. Samuel Escobar writes, "Theology, history, and the social sciences are useful as tools for a better understanding of God's Word and of contemporary missionary action, but only the Word is inspired and always fertile to renew the church in mission." For example, in 2 Corinthians, Paul, reflecting on his own missionary practice, points "to the Old Testament teachings as well as the living revelation of God in Jesus Christ through the Spirit. The Spirit-inspired missionary acts of Jesus, Paul, and the apostles, as well as their Spirit-inspired reflection on their practice, are authoritative for us in a way in which no other post-apostolic missionary practice or reflection is authoritative."[25]

Escobar disparagingly critiques Church Growth as "managerial missiology."[26] There are both accuracies and distortions in these allegations. On the one hand, Church Growth tends to emphasize evangelistic activities that can be easily tabulated and statistically analyzed: how many people have replied in writing to radio or television broadcasts, responded to the invitation at a crusade, been baptized during a particular year, or become part of new churches being planted. Meeting these goals demonstrates the effectiveness of marketing the message of Jesus or the church. The problem with these goals is not merely ascribing success to numerical goals but reducing the gospel to what is measurable. Escobar rightly comments that sometimes "the slow process of development of a contextual theology for a young church tends to be considered inefficient and costly, and it is easy to substitute prepackaged theologies translated from English."[27] In addition, the church should never present itself as a vendor of Christian services to fulfill the felt needs of consumers. When "gaining the loyalty of members and retaining that loyalty"[28] becomes the driving force of the church, members have difficulty speaking of the sovereign reign of God, the foolishness of the cross, and holy living. In these matters, I concur with Escobar's critique.

On the other hand, Escobar writes that in managerial missiology, "missionary action is reduced to a linear task that is translated into logical steps to be followed in a process of management by objectives, in the same way in which the evangelistic task is reduced to a process that can be carried on following marketing principles."[29] This negation of linear processes for sequentially doing missions seems naïve if the processes are developed through the grid of God's kingdom rule. Escobar's sweeping negation seems to exclude processes of teaching new converts the story line of the Bible, of training new Christians to become leaders, and of developing missionaries who move from being learners to ministers to mentors to guests as they phase out of the work of an established church. Mature Christian churches tend to have mature processes, even linear modules, of understanding Christian growth and development. In this sense, I believe that we cannot negate management from missiology.

By way of summary, a pragmatic model of ministry develops form and function of ministry without establishing the theological rationale for Christian living and ministry. The central question, What is the gospel we proclaim? does not permeate the fabric of missionary life and activity but is merely assumed as its foundation.

Theological Level of Inquiry

Church Growth did not begin as a theologically integrated discipline. Arthur Glasser admits that "Dr. McGavran's theological method [did] not involve the orderly unfolding of a system based on inner-evolved principles."[30]

The focus of the movement has been primarily methodological, and its theology developed in the heat of controversy when its methodological postulates were disputed.[31] When challenged, Church Growth proponents sought to theologically defend the centrality of evangelism in the life of the church, its rationale for numerical growth, the need for the church to reach receptive peoples, and why missionaries should work to develop homogeneous communities of believers. Church Growth methodologies, developed through social understandings, subsequently needed theological justification. The theological posture, therefore, was apologetic, not formative.

Steuernagel urges us to "reposition ourselves and to work once again on the agenda."[32] This is best done by laying the broad theological foundations of missiology and then progressing to discussions of methodologies and strategies. With theology at the vortex of missiology, the church and its missionaries will begin to minister in new and different ways. Stuart Murray, in *Church Planting: Laying Foundations*, provides an example of this process. He writes: "All church planters operate within theological frameworks, but often these are assumed rather than articulated and adopted uncritically rather than as the result of reflection. Theological principles may influence strategy and practice less than unexamined tradition or innovative methodology. . . . An inadequate theological basis will not necessarily hinder short-term growth, or result in widespread heresy among newly planted churches. But it will limit the long-term impact of church planting, and may result in dangerous distortions in the way in which the mission of the church is understood."[33]

Murray then provides formative theologies to lay the foundations for church planting and describes the nature and character of church planting in terms of these models. A formative theology is the *missio Dei*, or mission of God, the perspective that mission is not a human invention or a program of human ingenuity but is an extension of the activity of God who sends and saves. This perspective is theocentric rather than anthropocentric; by extension, it is Trinitarian: "God is the Missionary, who sent his Son and sends his Spirit into the world. . . . Mission is defined, directed, energized, and accomplished by God."[34] The church, then, is a "body of people sent on a mission" rather than a "vendor of religious goods and services."[35] *Missio Dei* influences one's understanding of the nature of the church: "Participating in the *missio Dei* will involve shifting the emphasis from a focus on the life of the local church . . . to a concern for the world in its need, joys, and struggles."[36] It will broaden the scope of mission to include not only evangelism and church planting but also other purposes of God, including social justice and environmental concerns. God's concern for the world, then, becomes the concern of the church involved in God's mission. *Missio Dei* infers spiritual formation; God's attributes and purposes become incarnate in his people. Finally, Murray says, "Church planting presents an opportunity to express something of the nature of our missionary God . . . consciously engag[ing] in church planting as fellow workers with God and with others." God's creativity, community, and teamwork become models for ministry.[37] Murray also discusses the theological models of incarnation and the kingdom of God and their application to church planting. The practice of church planting is thus placed within theological, rather than mere pragmatic, frameworks.

Missiology is a multifaceted discipline. The *social sciences* (anthropology, sociology, psychology) enable missionaries to exegete another culture, interpret emic (insider) meanings, understand how people live together in groups, compare one culture to another, and perceive psyches of various people within cultures. *History of missions* reflects on past paradigms of mission theology and practice. Understandings of *contextualized ministry* (evangelism, church planting and development, leadership training) help missionaries develop theologically focused, yet contextually appropriate, strategies. These strategies guide missionaries to teach unbelievers, incorporate new Christians into communities of faith, nurture them to maturity, and train developing leaders to minister within the maturing movement of God. Other disciplines (linguistics; Islamic, Hindu, and Buddhist studies; folk religion; etc.)

provide tools for the missionary task and heighten understandings regarding Christian approaches to non-Christian peoples.

What, then, is the role of theology in missiology? None of these disciplines of missiology can function individually on its own criteria. Therefore, *mission theology* functions to prioritize and clarify the functions of these disciplines in relationship to the purposes of God.

The social sciences, for instance, developed during the modern age and are rooted in secular presuppositions. Church Growth practitioners have too frequently felt that anthropology is merely "a toolbox" containing instruments "which are not intrinsically related to one another." The practitioner, oblivious to the "theoretical assumptions on which the tool is based" and the set of presuppositions "which it forms, can merely pick and choose whatever tools work."[38] Church Growth has generally opted into a structural-functional model of anthropology, which "is based upon a static view of the world."[39] According to C. R. Taber, "'Cultural givens' take on permanence and rigidity; it suggests that whatever is endures. This cannot help but undermine the hope of transformation which is central to the gospel."[40] Consequently, missionaries must not view anthropology as a neutral discipline. Rather, they must develop a theology of culture through which to evaluate anthropological approaches and their resulting insights. Biblical theology provides foundational presuppositions that guide the Christian anthropologist in cultural analysis.

Focus on Numerical Growth

For many theologians, the most perturbing and controversial issue of the Church Growth paradigm is its emphasis on numerical growth. McGavran writes: "Mission is a divine finding, vast and continuous. The chief and irreplaceable purpose of mission is church growth."[41] He also says, "Winning many to the Christian life must be the dominant concern of all Christians."[42] McGavran's words are not merely passing statements, reflecting one of many emphases. They represent the foundational presupposition of Church Growth. Glasser, in summarizing McGavran's theological position, describes this focus on growth: "God wills the growth of His church. A chief and irreplaceable element in her ministry is the proclamation of the Gospel to all mankind and incorporation of those who believe into her communal life. Only through the deliberate multiplication of vast numbers of new congregations all over the world will the church be able to evangelize this generation. When she ceases to perform this mission, something fundamental is lost in her very essence as the people of God in the midst of the nations. The church that does not grow is out of the will of God."[43]

As part of the interaction with this core perspective, I will survey the research of two Restoration scholars.

Carl Holladay writes that people become hostage to the metaphors they employ. *Church Growth* has become one such metaphor. Thus, seeking to understand causes of growth, places where growth is possible, and qualities of leaders of church growth becomes the lens through which Scripture is interpreted. This metaphor is "both provocative and evocative in the ways it shapes our assessment of ourselves and our mission." Furthermore, Holladay writes, numerical growth was not a "pervasive concern of Jesus and the New Testament writers." Only Luke, "with his fondness for statistics,... documents the numerical growth of the early Christian Church." Luke's primary purpose, however, was not to document church growth and development but to authenticate the Gentile mission.[44]

John Mark Hicks, on the other hand, writes that the biblical scholar should not be "disconcerted" about "the issue of numerical growth." Luke's use of statistics is based on a theology of covenant restoration rooted in the Old Testament. "Just as Israel multiplied and increased in number in the Old Testament, so restored Israel would multiply and increase in the Messianic age. Numerical growth is a covenant blessing." This "restoration-fulfillment" theme is reflected in Luke's writing of Acts. The use of words like *auxano*, an agricultural term meaning "to grow" or "to increase," and *pleroo*, which means "to multiply," infer numerical growth. The language of Acts is "theologically significant because it is the combination of terms used by the LXX [the Septuagint] in Jeremiah to describe the blessedness of the messianic community, of restored Israel." The prophetic expectation was that Israel and Judah would be reunited, that the nations would gather at Jerusalem to honor God, and that their numbers would greatly increase in the land (Jer. 3:16–18). In other contexts, Jeremiah writes about the remnant of Judah, whom God will gather from among the nations and bring back to their land, "where they will be fruitful and increase in number" (Jer. 23:3–5). A descendant of David, "a righteous Branch," will reign as king over this growing community (Jer. 23:5). These same terminologies are used in the Creation scene when God tells the people he created to "be fruitful and increase in number" (Gen. 1:22, 28; 8:17; 9:1, 7). This emphasis is also reflected in a few places in Pauline literature. Although Paul's primary emphasis in the epistles was to equip young missionaries and churches to deal with specific problems, in Colossians 1:6, for example, he "uses *auxano* to describe the spread of the gospel into the whole world." This growth in the church is a blessing from God in the same way that children are a blessing from the Lord (Ps. 127:3) and "the increase of Abraham's descendants" was a blessing (Gen. 12:2; 13:14–16).[45]

How, then, should we understand these differing perspectives of growth in Scripture? Surely, reading Scripture through the narrow lens of Church Growth, as Holladay suggests, accentuates the success and truncates the struggles of the church to become a community reflecting the kingdom of God. Ministry strategies are frequently developed as a type of triumphalism, promoting human egos or agendas. Promotion then guides decision making rather than the biblical theologies of the mission of God and the inbreaking of God's kingdom. The motivation for use of statistics becomes self-aggrandizing and self-promoting. Christian ministry must not be done out of "selfish ambition or vain conceit" but patterned after the incarnation of Christ, who humbled himself, took the nature of a servant, and became obedient to death (Phil. 2:3–8).

It is also apparent from Scripture that God does desire the growth of his church. God, who said, "Be fruitful and increase in number," at Creation and who prophesied through Jeremiah that the remnant would "be fruitful and increase in number," is the God who blessed the early Christian church (Acts 6:7; 9:31; 12:24; 16:5; 19:20; 2 Thess. 3:1). This growth is rooted not in human initiative or ability but in God who causes things to grow (1 Cor. 3:5–9). Evangelism, moreover, is concerned not only about initial proclamation or baptism but also about "that set of intentional activities which is governed by the goal of initiating people into the kingdom of God for the first time."[46]

The use of statistics and the numbering of Christians should be motivated by compassion for the flock, finding those who have wandered away (Luke 15:3–6). Caution is necessary that counting be done specifically and humbly, motivated not by human ego but by care for the church. The value of church growth studies is that they typically reveal unperceived weaknesses. This is likely due to the fact that when people come to Christ, there is public celebration, but those who leave go unnoticed.

While ministering in Africa, our missions team did a major church growth study every two years. This study measured not only the number of churches and adult Christians but also the levels of literacy and types of leaders officially ordained within local churches. The 1982 study, which reflected a lower growth rate than anticipated, led us to new methodologies of work. First, our team realized that because we frequently took national church leaders to help open other areas to the gospel, their home areas were neglected. We resolved to encourage ministers to develop a vision for their own areas and concentrate their work close to home. Over a period of years, clusters of churches developed as churches planted other churches within walking distance of their church. Today these clusters of churches have their own organization of evangelists, elders, and servants, and all churches in the cluster meet as one community during the first Sunday of every month. Second, our team decided that *revival* should be redefined. Originally, *revival* meant encouraging unfaithful members to return to the church, by ministering in their homes and in meetings within the community of the church. Reflection on the church growth study revealed that churches with a high attrition rate also had theological and spiritual problems. *Revival* then began to address spiritual issues by helping core members to reflect theologically on these problems. Church growth studies thus enable the missionary to theologically and methodologically critique a missions ministry, and out of this reflection, new emphases of ministry emerge. An authentic church growth study will always reveal weaknesses of the church, which will then provide understandings for theological and methodological reflection.

Brazilian missiologist Alex Araujo acknowledges that numbers are useful descriptors for planning certain types of activities. He warns, however, that "number-thinking has become a distorting factor in the way certain people or cultures think about reality. . . . [This] *numerological thinking* . . . has trouble assessing value without comparing numbers. . . . [It] equates quality with larger numbers and lack of quality with lower numbers.... The problem is not with the use of numbers where they are helpful, but with a numerological way of interpreting reality."[47]

One continuing paradox is the theologians' aversion to counting converts while having high sensitivity to the number and quality of new students coming into their seminaries. Requirements from the Association of Theological Schools direct our institutions to develop strategic initiatives with well-defined plans, including numerical goals. Can we develop such strategies and goals for our institutions while suggesting such practices are wrong in our churches?

THE MISSIONAL PARADIGM

The four limitations of Church Growth that we have discussed—anthropocentric focus, pragmatics and the segmentation of theology and praxis, theological level of inquiry, and focus on growth—suggest the need for a new model of missions. This new paradigm would maintain the strengths of the Church Growth model—a focus on identificational ministry, belief in the missionary nature of the church, and incisive evaluation—while broadening its theological horizons. The model, termed *missional*, is rooted in an understanding that a missionary theology should permeate both theology and missiology. Andrew Kirk writes:

> All true theology is, by definition, missionary theology, for it has as its object the study of the ways of a God who is by nature missionary and a foundational text written by and for missionaries. Mission as a discipline is not, then, the roof of a building that completes the whole structure, already constructed by blocks that stand on their own, but both the foundation and the mortar in the joints, which cements together everything else. Theology should not be pursued as a set of isolated disciplines. It assumes a model of cross-cultural communication, for its subject matter both stands over against culture and relates closely to it. Therefore, it must be interdisciplinary and interactive.[48]

The *missional helix* visualizes such an "interdisciplinary and interactive" approach to the practice of ministry and provides a corrective to traditional Church Growth perspectives.[49]

The Missional Helix

In ministry formation, neither theology nor strategy stands by itself as a self-contained discipline; they are two strands of an ongoing process involving various elements. Ministry formation can be seen as a spiral. The coils turn round and round, passing the same landmarks, but always at a slightly different level. This spiral, a helix, is descriptive of the process of effective ministry formation.

The spiral begins with *theologies*, such as the *missio Dei*, the kingdom of God, incarnation, and crucifixion, which focus and form our perspectives of culture and the practice of ministry. *Cultural analysis* forms the second element of the helix. Cultural awareness enables missionaries and ministers to define types of peoples within a cultural context, to understand the social construction of their reality, to perceive how they are socially related to one another, and to explain how the Christian message intersects with every aspect of their culture (birth rites, coming-of-age rituals, weddings, funerals, and so on). The spiral proceeds to consider what has occurred historically in the missional context. *Historical perspective* narrates how things got to be as they are, based on the interrelated stories of the particular nation, tribe, the church, and God's mission. Finally the spiral considers the *strategy*, or practice of ministry, within the missions environment.

The missional helix is a spiral because the missionary returns time and time again to reflect theologically, culturally, historically, and strategically in order to develop ministry models appropriate to the local context. Theology, social understandings, history of missions, and strategy all work together and interpenetrate each other. Thus, praxis impacts theology, which in turn shapes the practice of ministry. In figure 1, the broken line between the four elements of strategy formation demonstrates how each interacts with the others.

The diagram is a helix because theology, history, culture, and the practice of ministry *build on one another* as the community of faith collectively develops understandings and a vision of God's will within their cultural context. Like a spring, the spiral grows to new heights as ministry understandings and experiences develop (figure 2).

Each of these four elements (theology, history, culture, and strategy) is essential in reflecting on and planning for all types of Christian ministry.

The Relationship between the Four Elements of Ministry Formation

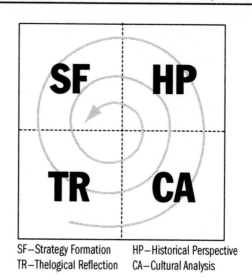

SF—Strategy Formation   HP—Historical Perspective
TR—Thelogical Reflection   CA—Cultural Analysis

Figure 1

Functions of the Missional Helix

The missional helix is useful in at least two ways. First and foremost, it provides a model of decision making for the Christian practitioner that must become both intentional and instinctive. In other words, the missionary or minister should seek theological understandings, cultural analysis, historical perspective, and strategy formation in the process of developing patterns for ministry. Second, the missional helix could be used as a model for theological education. Equipping for ministry should not put high emphasis on some elements and give little consideration to others. Rather, it should provide an intentional, integrated model of ministry formation.

CONCLUSION

I embrace Steuernagel's belief: "As we move into a new century, I share the conviction that we need to reposition ourselves and to work once again on the agenda." The Church Growth model is inadequate. By beginning with anthropology rather than theology and by segmenting theology and practice, it assumes that its model for missions reflects the nature of God. In other words, Church Growth determines effective practice and then seeks to validate this practice by the use of Scripture. The movement emphasizes growth rather than faithful proclamation of the gospel and faithful living of the gospel.

A missional model, on the other hand, begins with theological reflection, while taking seriously cultural analysis and strategy formation.

The Missional Helix

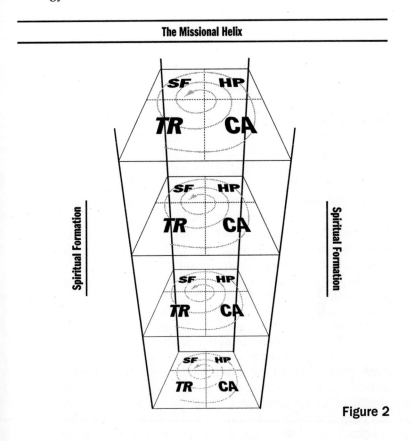

Figure 2

A CENTRIST RESPONSE
Charles Van Engen

Over the years, I have found Gailyn Van Rheenen's writing always stimulating, focused on the primary issues, constructive, and creative. Having grown up and ministered among the Mayan peoples of southern Mexico, I have resonated with his publications dealing with missiological issues in animistic contexts, finding them informative and helpful. I am impressed with Van Rheenen's work that seeks to create a multidisciplinary, spiraling methodological process in missiology that is highly integrative, bringing together theology, culture, history, and strategy in mission practice. I am intrigued by the "missional helix" idea that Van Rheenen outlined at the end of his chapter and would encourage the reader to read about it further on Van Rheenen's website and in his e-mail communications.

People often ask me to summarize the essential components, the center, of Church Growth theory. I now have something I can give them to read, for Van Rheenen has given us an excellent overview of the strengths of the Church Growth paradigm. I believe Gailyn is accurate in his assessment of those strengths when he says, "Church Growth analysts, although vastly overstating the value of numbering, have, through comparative evaluation, led to wide-ranging discussions of modern missionary strategy." I appreciate Van Rheenen's concern for missionary strategy and mission practice. And with this emphasis, he has captured one of the deepest convictions of McGavran. From the time when he first began asking about mission practice in India and throughout his entire career, McGavran's passion was the evaluation of effective mission strategy and practice. In terms of such evaluation, I consider Donald McGavran the greatest missiologist of the twentieth century. No one else stimulated the reexamination and reevaluation of mission practice throughout the entire mission world (ecumenical, evangelical, Roman Catholic, and Pentecostal/charismatic) like McGavran did.

Of course, such questioning was not always appreciated and created the climate of polemics that often seemed to surround people's reaction to McGavran's ideas. Van Rheenen is right in quoting Darrell Guder that "Church Growth 'both infuriates and inspires' but discussion of it 'has never been boring!'" I think Van Rheenen is also on target when he says later in the chapter, "An authentic church growth study will always reveal weaknesses of the church, which will then provide understandings for theological and methodological reflection." Over the past thirty years of my association with Church Growth, I have begun to understand more fully McGavran's contention that too often the detractors of Church Growth seem to prefer to examine the speck in the eye of Church Growth theory than to look carefully at the beam in their own eye of mission practice. For this reason, I appreciate Van Rheenen's focus on mission practice in his balanced critique of the Church Growth paradigm.

Van Rheenen has highlighted four major weaknesses of Church Growth theory: anthropocentric focus, pragmatics, theological level of inquiry, and focus on numerical growth. I think he has selected the four most glaring weaknesses of the movement, and I believe his critique of these four is fair, balanced, and well-stated. My discomfort with Gailyn's critique comes at the point of seeking alternatives to these weaknesses. I agree with him, for example, that "social research, while beneficial in understanding human culture, is not the foundation of missiology. All missiological decisions must be rooted, either implicitly or explicitly, in theology so that they mirror the purposes and mind of God." And yet, as one who has worked extensively in the area of contextualization, I would hasten to ask how one can do contextually appropriate theology apart from a profound immersion in the culture in which one is theologizing. Far too much Western theology has been blind to its own syncretism and has too often imposed on non-Western cultural contexts Western cultural viewpoints as if they were the gospel. And far too much Western theology has been so abstracted from reality as to have little or no impact on personal or social life. I know this is not where Van Rheenen would be located, because in the last section of his chapter, he brings these together in what he has called the "missional helix." However, in critiquing Church Growth's strong dependence on anthropology and cultural analysis, I believe we must avoid divorcing the social, psychological, cultural, and human situation from something we call "theology."

Van Rheenen's critique of pragmatism is well taken and echoes many other voices that especially spoke out against Peter Wagner's writings that made the concern for results (measured primarily in terms of numerical church growth) a nearly essential component of Church Growth theory. This is the emphasis to which Samuel Escobar referred pejoratively as being "managerial missiology." I agree with Van Rheenen's fair and pointed critique of Escobar at this point.

Van Rheenen is rightly concerned about determining one's missiology solely on the basis of the numerical growth it may produce. In Church Growth theory, the ends are too easily used to justify the means. It is not necessary for me to document this weakness in Church Growth theory since it is well known.

This being the case, however, I believe it is important to consider the possibility that this aspect was not an original characteristic of Church Growth theory. As I read *Bridges of God*, for example, I do not find a result-oriented pragmatism—that numerical growth is the exclusive basis on which mission practice should be evaluated—to be very strong in McGavran's thinking. In *How Churches Grow* and in *Church Growth and Christian Mission*, issues like indigeneity, spiritual maturity, and the church's impact on its context are included as matters to be evaluated. In my reading of McGavran's early works, I believe he considered numerical analysis as a tool, a "thermometer" (a word McGavran himself used on several occasions), that demonstrated where there was need for reevaluation and for a change in mission strategy to bring renewed focus and health to the mission enterprise. Wagner's "seven vital signs" of a healthy church also place numerical growth in a subordinate position alongside many other concerns about the life, health, and mission of the church. It appears to me that numerical growth as a pragmatic goal that overshadows other issues became a greater weakness in Church Growth theory after about 1980. For example, if one compares the three editions of McGavran's *Understanding Church Growth* (1970, 1980, and 1990), one will notice that the pragmatic language tends to increase with each edition. And it may be that in North America, the continual emphasis on studying and reporting about large churches and the celebration of decadal percentages of growth increased the significance of this weakness in North American Church Growth.

Van Rheenen is right in his assessment of the low level of theological inquiry evident in Church Growth theory. Yet I would suggest that there may be more theological reflection threading its way through Church Growth theory than is normally understood. It depends, of course, on what one means by "theology." If by "theology" one means (and I know Van Rheenen does not), for example, propositional, syllogistic, Western, systematic theology, then Church Growth appears to have little of it. This is a work waiting to be written. However, if one means by "theology" a contextual reflection on what God is doing and wants to do in mission, an endeavor patterned after the theological reflection of the early church in Acts 15, then one could make a case that Church Growth theory is replete with much solid and insightful theology. In fact, I would suggest that Van Rheenen's missional helix is theologizing at its best and that the entire helix is theological. In that sense, McGavran's life commitment, as I have paraphrased it, that it is God's will that women and men become disciples of Jesus Christ and responsible members of Christ's church, constitutes one of the most profound theological statements made in missiology. I believe it is just as biblical and theological as, if not more biblical and theological than, Henry Venn and Rufus Anderson's "three-self formula," which dominated Protestant missions for nearly a century. I consider it just as biblical and theological as, if not more than, John R. Mott's watchword associated with the World Missionary Conference of Edinburgh, 1910: "The evangelization of the world in this generation." I think it is just as biblical and theological as, if not more than, the World Council's language in the 1960s of "reading the signs of the times." And I would consider it just as biblical and theological as, if not more than, liberation theology's "the preferential option for the poor." As Van Rheenen has stated so clearly in his chapter, we need to rethink the agenda of mission in this new century, and this calls us also to reconsider our methodologies both in missiology and in the task of doing theology of mission.

I commend Van Rheenen for his balanced and insightful critique of Church Growth emphases. I resonate with the concluding remarks at the end of his chapter. It is an essential and imperative part of missiology to question and evaluate mission strategy and practice—including the question of whether the results of the missionary activity are consistent with the stated philosophy and goals. Effectiveness is important. Results do matter. The issue, however, is to be biblically clear and theologically appropriate in terms of the basis on which such evaluation is carried out and the methodology to be followed in doing so.

The Church Growth movement itself must revisit Donald McGavran's missiological priorities, which recognized that numerical growth is not the goal of mission; it is a desired by-product. As McGavran would say it, "It is God's will that men and women become disciples of Jesus Christ." In McGavran's missiology, conversion was always primary. May we all together seek new and increasingly effective means whereby women and men so loved by God may be introduced to our living Savior Jesus Christ through the ministry of the Holy Spirit. Donald McGavran would want us all to remember that there are 4.5 billion people speaking thousands of languages and representing multitudes of cultural mosaics who yet do not know Jesus Christ. This is our agenda for the twenty-first century.

A RENEWAL RESPONSE

Howard Snyder

Van Rheenen's chapter is a very helpful contribution to the theology and practice of Christian mission. He details some of the abiding contributions of Church Growth thinking while noting several limitations. His missional helix model is healthily interdisciplinary, integrating (as he says) "theology, history, culture, and the practice of ministry." I am not sure I would call it a "new paradigm" (it is essentially the model we follow at the E. Stanley Jones School of World Mission and Evangelism, Asbury Theological Seminary), but here it is nicely conceptualized and presented. Any biblically sound theology of the growth of the church must, as Van Rheenen says, interactively integrate the four components he identifies: theological reflection, cultural analysis, historical perspective, and strategy formation.

This model is indeed a timely corrective to most Church Growth thinking. While Van Rheenen does not go into much depth in elaborating the model, I see it as practically useful. Three key areas that would need to be more fully discussed are biblical hermeneutics, a missiological understanding of culture, and the interface between these two—that is, the challenge of contextualization without syncretism. Van Rheenen gives some useful hints, reminding us that Scripture itself is fundamentally and inherently missional and pointing to Hiebert's "critical contextualization" model. Much more work needs to be done in this area in order to take both Scripture and culture seriously in ways that are faithful to the gospel of Jesus Christ. But Van Rheenen is moving in the right direction.

Van Rheenen's summary critique of dominant Church Growth thinking is well stated: "By beginning with anthropology rather than theology and by segmenting theology and practice, it [Church Growth] assumes that its model for missions reflects the nature of God. In other words, Church Growth determines effective practices and then seeks to validate this practice by the use of Scripture." I understand Van Rheenen to be saying that the valid, and valuable, insights and learnings from Church Growth studies need to be integrated into a more biblically and theologically adequate missiology—a full-orbed *missio Dei* that takes seriously the missionary nature of the Trinity, a biblical theology of culture and of the kingdom of God, and a sound ecclesiology consistent with these key themes.[50] I agree.

Van Rheenen emphasizes, "How we consciously and unconsciously prioritize and systematize our sources of knowledge at the most basic level will ultimately form our Christian message and the nature of missions and evangelism." Yes; this is essentially the point I attempt to make in my response to Van Engen's chapter.

I question, however, the following statement, which Van Rheenen quotes approvingly: "Participating in the *missio Dei* will involve shifting the emphasis from a focus on the life of the local church ... to a concern for the world in its need, joys, and struggles." This, however, is misleading, implying a false dichotomy and a misunderstanding of the biblical (missional) nature of the church. What do we find in the New Testament? Precisely a focus on local church life and comparatively little on the "need, joys, and struggles" of the world. The reason seems obvious: churches have a tendency to go wrong, to become divided, corrupted, lukewarm, or self-serving—in other words, to cease to be faithful and missional. A vital, faithful missiology will indeed focus on the life of the church, not in a narcissistic way, but in ways that help the church be what it is called to be: the presence of Jesus Christ in the world for the sake of the salvation of the lost and the full manifestation of God's reign.

I second Van Rheenen's call for "a biblically rooted ecclesiology" that draws upon the rich variety of ecclesial metaphors found in Scripture. It is a positive sign that missional ecclesiology has been receiving increased attention in recent years. I see the pressing need to develop ecclesiology missionally in several interrelated directions if our churches are to be fully biblical and faithful to the *missio Dei*. Churches that grow in a healthy, holistic way will be marked by these dynamics:

1. Trinitarian insights—the church as a "reflection" (Miroslav Volf) or "echo" (Colin Gunton) of the Trinity.[51]
2. The church as the community of God's reign: God's people corporately, visibly, and authentically, even if imperfectly, "signing forth" the reality and promise of the kingdom of God. Churches that know they are in the kingdom business, not just church business.
3. Churches of the Spirit—not only created by, but continuing to live in, the power of the Holy Spirit—growing in the fruit of the Spirit and living and ministering through the multi-colored grace of Spirit-given gifts (1 Peter 4:10).
4. Churches that exist as social movements of the Spirit, learning that missional churches are movement churches. Here we can learn from emerging social movement theory, while keeping grounded biblically.
5. Churches that visibly embody the reconciliation across racial, caste, tribal, gender, ethnic, and socioeconomic lines that is promised in the gospel of Jesus Christ. Churches that demonstrate (as more and more local churches are beginning to show) that multiethnic, socioeconomically diverse congregations, faithful discipleship, and ongoing significant numerical growth are not mutually exclusive.
6. Above all, churches that are incarnational; that is, Christian communities that give ecclesiological shape and meaning to Jesus' statement, "As the Father has sent me, I am sending you" (John 20:21). These will be churches that, like Jesus, are fully in the world but not of the world; churches for which the designation "body of Christ" has rich missional and discipleship meaning.

As the empirical church of Jesus Christ today becomes increasingly ethnically and culturally diverse, I see hope (through the Spirit) for such a full-orbed missional ecclesiology, one that is inherently dynamic and reproductive. Most ecclesiology has been too indebted to traditional categories and the four classic marks of the church: one, holy, catholic, and apostolic. As I have suggested elsewhere, a dynamic and biblically faithful ecclesiology will understand the church not only as one, holy, catholic, and apostolic, but also as many, charismatic, local/contextual, and prophetic. This is a fuller and more biblically grounded understanding of the church's genetic endowment.[52]

AN EFFECTIVE EVANGELISM RESPONSE

Elmer Towns

Gailyn Van Rheenen has presented a very interesting theory of Church Growth based on a missional helix that has four premises. A person's theology, as well as his Church Growth strategy, is not a self-contained discipline but a dynamic, ongoing process that is seen in the four phases of this helix. First, a person must begin with *theologies*, such as *missio Dei*, that focus on both culture and ministry. Second, *cultural analysis* says the missionary/minister must understand and apply to evangelism the social and cultural context. Third, he gives *historical perspective* to understand how things got to be as they are, and fourth, he gives *strategies* which become the practice of ministry. These four phases interact with each other and influence each other to develop a holistic strategy.

Van Rheenen says there are four limitations, or weaknesses, in the present Church Growth paradigm that demand change. First, he says Church Growth is anthropocentric, focusing on what humans do in missions rather than on what God is doing. He says traditional Church Growth begins with humanity rather than deity. However, what classical Church Growth calls for is a balance between God and man working together. Jesus commanded his disciples to go preach, baptize, make disciples, and teach. That is human responsibility, and Jesus promised that he would be with them as they carry out the Great Commission (Matt. 28:19–20; Mark 16:15; Luke 24:46–48; Acts 1:8). If Van Rheenen is accurate, why does not Jesus say, "The Holy Spirit is doing the work of missions, so go find out where he is working and get involved in that work"?

The second weakness Van Rheenen cites is that Church Growth is pragmatic and produces segmentation between theology and praxis. He claims that Church Growth asks questions such as "Does this work?" or "Will this help the church to grow?" He goes on to say that pragmatic thinking de-emphasizes the theological, takes for granted the existence of adequate content, and majors on methods. I do not think this is so. Technically, is not pragmatism that function of thought that guides actions, and a belief that truth is preeminently tested by practical consequences? Pragmatism is not the true nature of biblical evangelism or Church Growth, because they are grounded on the Word of God. Church Growth believes that all individuals are lost, that Christ died for all, and that the church has been given a commission to reach all and to assimilate them into a Christian church. Truth is not open to pragmatic exploration. When the church is not doing or accomplishing what it has been commanded, then we need to ask such questions as Why are we not carrying out the Great Commission? and Why is our evangelism not effective? We must be grounded on the truth of Scripture, the objective nature of the Great Commission, and the eternal unchanging content of the gospel.

A traditional Church Growth approach believes that truth is eternal and cannot change. It believes that eternal principles are transcultural and transtemporal. However, methods must be applied, or changed, from generation to generation and from culture to culture. We ask questions to determine which method is best to carry out the commission of reaching all people. Van Rheenen is right when he says, "Methodologies and strategies must be a servant, never a master, to the mission of God."

The third weakness Van Rheenen points out deals with the theological level of inquiry. He suggests Church Growth was "apologetic," answering questions and responding to problems rather than being originally motivated by an "orderly unfolding of a [theological] system based on inner-evolved principles." (He quotes Glasser.) Van Rheenen wants us to be more thoughtful, analytical, and systematic. He suggests that traditional Church Growth has *defended* the centrality of evangelism in the life of the church, *defended* numerical growth, and *defended* its need to reach receptive people and work among homogeneous communities of believers. Our defense makes Church Growth apologetic, and not proactive, in forming our theology. Yes, we have defended our movement against these charges, but we do not think we're defending ourselves; rather, we believe we are teaching a mandate given to us from the Word of God. Much of the church has not been evangelistic in focus, so we have to correct a lack or a misdirection. Hence, we appear apologetic. So, yes, we were not born in theological inquiry. Jesus challenged us to "go . . . work . . . disciple . . . and teach." He did not challenge us to understand theology or formulate theology. Jesus calls to us, "Follow Me, and I will make you fishers of men" He did not call us to discuss or to analyze the issues.

The fourth weakness Van Rheenen mentions is that the traditional Church Growth movement focused on growth and/or numbers. I think Van Rheenen is unfair to accuse McGavran of being unduly influenced by his Restoration roots. If anything, McGavran was influenced more by his shift from a liberal theological position to a commitment to biblical Christianity. Van Rheenen quotes Carl Holladay's criticism of numbers. When he says, "Only Luke" had a fondness for statistics, or fondness for documents of numerical growth, he strains at a point to say that the documentation of numerical growth in Acts was not used to validate Church Growth doctrine but rather was seen as an authentication of the Gentile mission. To Van Rheenen's credit, he gives a broader perspective of numerical growth, to include both Old and New Testaments, both spiritual and numerical growth.

Van Rheenen suggests traditional Church Growth has a "narrow lens" in viewing numerical growth in the Word of God, resulting in a type of "triumphalism" or promoting human egos or agendas, resulting in motivation that becomes self-aggrandizing and self-promotion. However, when true Church Growth is a partnership of God and the human instrument, how can it be guilty of those abuses for which it is attacked?

So, according to Van Rheenen, these four limitations suggest to him the need for a new model for missions that would strengthen Church Growth. To his credit, he would have all theology defined by missional theology, so that missions is not just a "roof" that is added after the whole theological building has been completed, but rather missions is included in the foundation, mortar, joints, and everything else. If this is in fact the truth, let it be.

A GOSPEL AND OUR CULTURE RESPONSE
Craig Van Gelder

This is a most interesting chapter. Here is someone who sought to fully indwell and live out the missiological theory of Church Growth as formulated by Donald McGavran. Here is someone who continues to have appreciation for this movement, who has come through a significant transformation of reframing Church Growth both theoretically and theologically. I found myself informed and instructed by the author's argument.

He clearly identifies many of the issues and most of the problems associated with the Church Growth movement, both as conceived by McGavran and as developed by numerous disciples of the movement. And he interestingly notes the tendency for proponents of Church Growth to be practitioners and for detractors to be theologians. This insight probably explains why so little of what is often proposed by the practitioners is appreciated by the theologians and why so little of the critique of the theologians is taken seriously by the practitioners. As one who has sought to found strategic action (mission and ministry) in theological foundations that are informed by the theoretical perspectives of the social sciences, I find this continued disconnect between practitioners and theologians to be troubling. Practitioners need to be pushed to think theologically about strategic action, and theologians need to be pushed to think strategically about theological foundations in relation to theoretical perspectives.

It appears to me that this disconnect reflects the deep chasm woven into Enlightenment thinking and modernity in the divide between theory and practice, a divide that theological education has had a very difficult time overcoming ever since Schliermacher.

Collapsing this divide needs to be high on the agenda of those seeking to be biblically faithful and strategically relevant. It is my impression that in the past few decades, significant literature has begun to emerge that is seeking to do just this. It is my conviction that, in general, both theological educators and ministry practitioners would be served by engaging this conversation and that, in particular, the conversation about Church Growth would be helpfully informed by engaging this conversation.

I found Van Rheenen's discussion of McGavran's context particularly helpful, even though I have read similar accounts of this in the past. What struck me in the author's treatment was the extent to which Donald McGavran was a product of Enlightenment thinking and the extent to which his choices were shaped by the ideology embedded in this worldview. This shows up in his use of the research methods of the social sciences to substantiate both his missiology and his ecclesiology. And this results in the unfortunate tendency for his theology to become highly action-oriented and pragmatic. In reality, McGavran was using one strain of Enlightenment ideology— factual, objective, researched facts—to correct what had become the problem in much of church life. This problem was the product of another strain of Enlightenment ideology embedded in mission practice—the transfer of the institutions of Western civilization to the rest of world as if these were somehow universal expressions of Christian civilized life. Both ideological commitments are misdirected from a biblical and theological perspective.

The author makes this point clear in his review and critique of Church Growth. While he appreciates a number of themes that were introduced into the missiological discussion by McGavran's work and his numerous followers, Van Rheenen provides an incisive naming of the elephants that are embedded in the theology, theory, and practices of the Church Growth movement. His unmasking of the movement's pragmatism as the real issue to be addressed is helpful. He does so by noting how starting with anthropology results in a bias toward human agency, which allows for a quick one-step move to obedience to the Great Commission as the primary theological motif. This issue has continued to plague the theological method of the Church Growth movement throughout its history. In many ways, the Church Growth movement is one major twentieth-century extension of the classic nineteenth century mission movement at this key point of what represents the center of mission. The same understanding is present in both movements that the fulfillment of the Great Commission is to be understood primarily in terms of our obedience being the chief theological center point for framing our understanding of God, the world, the church, and our involvement.

The debate about the motive and method for mission has been around for sometime. The 1892 work of Gustav Warneck, who was serving as the newly appointed professor of mission at Halle, is important to note along these lines. Warnack's basic thesis is that the Reformers did not have a theology or practice of mission and that it was not until the work of the Pietists in the eighteenth century and the evangelicals in the nineteenth century that missions came into the life of the Protestant church. This reentry of missions was founded primarily on the notion that the Great Commission is still valid and that our obedience to it is still necessary (see, for example, William Carey's *Inquiry*). The theology of McGavran and the Church Growth movement follows in this line of thought, and as such, it has failed to interact sufficiently with the extensive developments in recent decades regarding mission theology that are related to the *missio Dei* and the redemptive reign of God in Christ, announced by Jesus as the kingdom of God.

The author uses this theological understanding of mission to offer his critique of Church Growth, which I found insightful and helpful at numerous points. At the end of the chapter, the author constructs his own approach to the development of a missional paradigm, which he calls the "missional helix." This model incorporates the four dimensions of theology, cultural analysis, historical perspective, and strategy and places them within a dynamic spiral framework for understanding an approach to mission and ministry. I found the missional helix to be intriguing, but its placement at the end of the chapter and its introduction in a rather summary way does not provide enough substance for using this model to develop a fuller missiology and ecclesiology. Perhaps this was not the author's intent, but nevertheless, this conversation and his contribution to it would probably have been strengthened by a more substantive development of his proposed model.

Chapter 4 Notes: Reformist View

[1]The Restoration movement, frequently called the Stone-Campbell movement, developed on the American frontier and is inclusive of three different streams: Churches of Christ, Christian Church (Churches of Christ), and the Disciples of Christ. McGavran was an evangelically oriented Disciple of Christ.

[2]Donald A. MacGavran to Gailyn Van Rheenen, 29 January 1985.

[3]This process of church maturation is described in more detail in Gailyn Van Rheenen, *Missions: Biblical Foundations and Contemporary Strategies* (Grand Rapids: Zondervan, 1996), 155–59. Decisions relating to the intersection of gospel and culture (For example, how do young men and women become adults and marry?) were made by local leaders based on a process of cultural analysis, biblical reflection, and custom formation. Paul Hiebert's model of "critical contextualization" was very important to us.

[4]Valdir Steuernagel, "Learning from Escobar . . . and Beyond," in *Global Missiology from the Twenty-first Century—The Iguassu Dialogue,* ed. William D. Taylor (Grand Rapids: Baker, 2000), 127.

[5]Orlando E. Costas, *Christ Outside the Gate: Missions Beyond Christendom* (Maryknoll, NY: Orbis, 1982), 80.

[6]Gary L. McIntosh, "Biblical Church Growth: Growing Faithful Churches in the Third Millennium," *Journal of Evangelism and Missions* 1 (Spring 2002): 59.

[7]Darrell L. Guder, "Evangelism and the Debate over Church Growth," *Interpretation* 47 (April 1994): 147.

[8]Lesslie Newbigin, *The Open Secret: Sketches for a Missionary Theology* (Grand Rapids: Eerdmans, 1978), 122.

[9]Ibid., 122.

[10]Arthur F. Glasser, "An Introduction to the Church Growth Perspectives of Donald Anderson McGavran," in *Theological Perspectives on Church Growth,* ed. Harvie Conn (Nutley, NJ: Presbyterian and Reformed Publishing, 1976), 24.

[11]Ibid., 24–25.

[12]Donald A. McGavran, *Understanding Church Growth* (Grand Rapids: Eerdmans, 1970), 216–32.

[13]Ibid., 230.

[14]Damian Efta, "What Are the Unreached?" *Evangelical Missions Quarterly* 30 (January 1994): 28.

[15]William J. Abraham, *The Logic of Evangelism* (Grand Rapids: Eerdmans, 1989), 75.

[16]Lesslie Newbigin, *The Open Secret: An Introduction to the Theology of Mission* (Grand Rapids: Eerdmans, 1995), 125. This is a revised edition of *The Open Secret: Sketches for a Missionary Theology* (1978).

[17]Newbigin, *The Open Secret* (1978), 142; cf. Guder, "Evangelism and the Debate over Church Growth," 147.

[18]Donald McGavran, "Missiology Faces the Lion," *Missiology* 17 (July 1989): 339.

[19]Thom S. Rainer, "Celebration of Criticism," *Global Church Growth* 30 (July–September 1993): 5.

[20]Paul Hiebert, "De-theologizing Missiology: A Response," *Trinity World Forum* 19 (Fall 1993): 4.

[21]David Hesselgrave, *Today's Choices for Tomorrow's Mission* (Grand Rapids: Zondervan, 1988), 139–44.

[22]Samuel Escobar, "Evangelical Missiology: Peering into the Future at the Turn of the Century," in *Global Missiology for the Twenty-first Century,* ed. William. D. Taylor (Grand Rapids: Baker Academic, 2000), 110.

[23]Guder, "Evangelism and the Debate over Church Growth," 148.

[24]Rainer, "Celebration of Criticism," 6.

[25]Escobar, "Evangelical Missiology," 102.

[26]Ibid., 109–12.

[27]Ibid., 110–11.

[28]George Hunsberger, "Missional Vocation: Called and Sent to Represent the Reign of God," in *Missional Church,* Darrell L. Guder (Grand Rapids, MI: Eerdmans, 1998).

[29]Escobar, "Evangelical Missiology," 109.

[30]Glasser, "An Introduction," 26.

[31]Charles Van Engen, *The Growth of the True Church* (Amsterdam: Rodopi, 1981), 16, 324.

[32]Steuernagel, "Learning from Escobar," 127.

[33]Stuart Murray, *Church Planting: Laying Foundations* (Scottsdale, PA: Herald, 2001), 39.

[34]Ibid.

[35]George R. Hunsberger, "Sizing Up the Shape of the Church," in *The Church Between Gospel and Culture,* ed. George Hunsberger and Craig Van Gelder (Grand Rapids: Eerdmans, 1996), 333–46.

[36]Murray, *Church Planting,* 40.

[37]Ibid., 41–42.

[38]Robert L. Ramseyer, "Anthropological Perspectives of Church Growth Theory," in *The Challenge of Church Growth,* ed. Wilbert R. Shenk (Scottdale, PA: Herald, 1973), 66.

[39]Escobar, "Evangelical Missiology," 111.

[40]C. R. Taber, "Contextualization," in *Exploring Church Growth,* ed. Wilbert R. Shenk (Grand Rapids: Eerdmans, 1983), 119.

[41]Donald A. McGavran, *Understanding Church Growth,* 3d ed. (Grand Rapids: Eerdmans, 1990, revised by C. Peter Wagner), 22.

[42]McGavran, "Missiology Faces the Lion," 340.

[43]Glasser, "An Introduction," 30–31; cf. Alan R. Tippett, *God, Man, and Church Growth: A Festschrift in Honor of Donald Anderson McGavran* (Grand Rapids: Eerdmans, 1973).

[44]Carl R. Holladay, "Church Growth in the New Testament," *Restoration Quarterly* 26 (2nd quarter, 1983): 83–102.

[45]John Mark Hicks, "Numerical Growth in the Theology of Acts," *Journal of the American Society for Church Growth* 8 (Spring 1997): 17–34.

[46]Abraham, *The Logic of Evangelism,* 95.

[47]Alex Araujo, "Right Use of Statistics, II," internet discussion board posting, June 13, 2001, share-knowledge@strategicnetwork.org.

[48]Andrew Kirk, *The Mission of Theology and Theology as Mission* (Harrisburg, PA: Trinity Press International, 1997), 50.

[49]The missional helix is presented in Gailyn Van Rheenen, "From Theology to Practice: The Helix Metaphor," *Monthly Missiological Reflection*, no. 25 (2002).

[50]Good work along this line has been done by a number of people, notably Lesslie Newbigin, E. Stanley Jones, John Livingston Nevius, Orlando Costas, Vinay Samuel, Chris Sugden, Miriam Adeney, Wilbert Shenk, George Hunsberger, Samuel Escobar, René Padilla, Ron Sider, Ruth Tucker. I would certainly not characterize Costas's criticism of North American Church Growth thinking as Van Rheenen does. Costas's work was constructive, and it is interesting that Van Engen in his chapter specifically endorses Costas's "integral and holistic" understanding of growth.

[51]See Howard A. Snyder with Daniel V. Runyon, "Church, Trinity, and Mission," chap. 3 in *Decoding the Church: Mapping the DNA of Christ's Body* (Grand Rapids: Baker, 2002).

[52]Howard A. Snyder with Daniel V. Runyon, "Do Churches Have DNA?" chap. 1 in *Decoding the Church.*

Chapter Five

RENEWAL VIEW

RENEWAL VIEW

*Church Growth must be based on
a biblical vision of the church as the vital
community of the kingdom of God*

Howard Snyder

When I was a pastor in Detroit in the 1960s, in São Paulo, Brazil, in the 1970s, and in Chicago in the 1980s, I kept careful track of attendance and membership statistics. I wanted to know just where we were as a church, and where we were headed, in reaching more people. I was always gratified if the stats showed some growth over the previous year's averages and at least a little concerned if they did not.

In the beginning, when I was right out of seminary, my understanding of the church and church growth dynamics were pretty unformed. Yet even then I knew that statistics were nothing more than indicators of more important things. They were possibly vital signs but were mere symptoms compared with the deeper spiritual, social, and personal dynamics that had to do with our identity as (hopefully) a faithful part of the body of Christ. I have always known intuitively—but perhaps also in part from my church background—that church growth was secondary to more basic realities and that church growth can happen for positive or less than positive reasons.

Through forty years of varied experiences and historical and theological studies, I have not found reason to change that intuition. As the various Church Growth debates have swirled during the past decades, I have always felt myself to be both an advocate and a critic of Church Growth. Churches *should* grow. If they do not, we should know why. But we should also know that church growth is not, never was, and never will be the primary concern of people who are deeply seeking first God's kingdom and his righteousness and justice. Genuine church growth is primarily a matter of how God's Holy Spirit forms, judges, renews, and *again* renews, the body of Christ.

In this chapter, I will present my deepest convictions about church growth, partly in concept and partly through reflection on personal experience. In the first section, I will discuss five theses concerning the church and its growth and the reasons for them. In the second section, I will trace my own journey, showing how the understanding of renewal and growth presented here is grounded in personal history. Finally, I will suggest how insights from church renewal can yield a practical strategy for both life and growth in the body of Christ.

FIVE THESES ON CHURCH RENEWAL AND GROWTH

A renewal perspective on church growth can be summarized through several theses or presuppositions. These seem to me to be valid, based on Scripture, church history, and what we know of the church as the social-spiritual body of Christ. They are starting points for a perspective on church growth from the standpoint of God's renewing work in the church in the past and in the present. If these are true, then several practical lessons about the life and growth of the body of Christ follow in consequence.

1. Under God, the Bible is the supreme and final authority concerning the church's life and growth, "so that whatsoever is not read therein, nor may be proved thereby, is not to be required [of anyone] that it should be believed or thought requisite or necessary" not only to salvation but also to the church's life and growth.[1] Or to put it more positively, God has given us the Bible not only so that we may know the way to heaven but also so that we may know how to live *corporately* on earth as the body of Christ.

All Church Growth thinking must be critically examined by the written Word of God and by the life and teachings of Jesus Christ, the incarnate Word, applied to us by the Holy Spirit. This means that all theories and techniques for the growth of the church must be carefully tested for biblical compatibility, just as new computer software must be compatible with the computer's operating system. If it is not, serious glitches will occur that will be evident in the long run, if not immediately.

The Bible is fundamentally a book about the church—what it is, how it is to function faithfully in the world, what its destiny is. More accurately, the Bible is a revelation about Jesus Christ, Head and body. The most important things we need to know about the life and growth of the body of Christ are all found in Scripture. The problem is that the church often does not really mine biblical truth in its search for faithfulness, effectiveness, or "success," except perhaps as this relates to *individual* salvation and *individual* discipleship.

Look at history. Renewal movements through the centuries have more often than not been ignited by a rediscovery of some key truth of God's Word that the church had buried or forgotten. Biblical truth flamed forth by the Spirit and reignited the church, whether that neglected truth was the gospel to the poor, salvation by faith, the certainty of Jesus' return, or the deeper work and gifts of the Spirit. This phenomenon is a clue to the power of God's Word. But the ongoing task, in times of flame or in times of famine, is constantly, faithfully to "study the Scriptures" because they reveal what it means to know Jesus and to be the Jesus community (John 5:39).

Frankly, I have been surprised through the years with the superficial way the Scriptures have been dealt with in some Church Growth texts—the misapplication or misappropriation of biblical metaphors or other biblical material in the interest of views of Church Growth that have little or no real scriptural basis.

Granted, the Bible is not a church growth textbook. But that is precisely the point. The primary focus of the New Testament is not on church growth but on the nature and life of the Christian community, the kind of *being* of the church that almost inevitably produces growth if the church remains open to the Spirit.

2. *It is God's will not only to plant, grow, and perfect the church but also to renew it.* Most Church Growth theory has focused on the planting and growing of the church, with perhaps some attention given also to "perfecting" or "discipling." But this misses a rich, vital stream of biblical truth.

The Holy Spirit is both the creating Spirit and the renewing Spirit. "In the beginning," at Creation, "was the Word ... through ₗwhom] all things were made" (John 1:1–3), and the Word still brings "times of refreshing" (Acts 3:19) when God's people turn to him.

The Bible, in both Testaments, is full of the language of renewal and new life. Evangelicals tend to apply this primarily, or exclusively, to the new birth or to the birth of the church. But exegesis of the renewal theme in Scripture shows that often the principal reference is to the renewal of God's people—Israel (primarily) in the Old Testament and the interethnic, multicultural, international church in the New Testament.

Many instances of this rich renewal stream in Scripture could be cited. One example is the turn/return theme prominent especially in Isaiah, Jeremiah, and Ezekiel. A study of terms such as *revive, restore, renew,* and *return* introduces one to large blocks of biblical material that reveal the Bible's renewal perspective. What we discover in studying such passages is God's concern to restore *both* his people and his whole creation, to "renew the face of the earth" (Ps. 104:30).

Christians in the Reformation tradition have tended to see the biblical promises of restoration and renewal almost exclusively in two ways: as the renewal of Israel in the new covenant in Christ and the birth of the church, and in an ultimate eschatological sense, at the end of history. The biblical picture is more *continuous* than this, however. God is *always* at work to renew his church and his creation if we are open to this renewing work. A renewal perspective on church growth expects God to work *now,* in any context where people seek him, to bring new life and vitality to the church.

Down through history, some Christians have of course stressed the present renewing, reviving work of the Spirit. For Protestants, this has usually taken the form of a focus on revival. A huge amount of literature is available on revival. Church history has witnessed great controversies about the theological appropriateness of revivalist theology and "measures," whether those of George Whitefield, Charles Finney, D. L. Moody, or Aimee Semple McPherson. A renewal perspective, however, focuses beyond revival phenomena and asks about the renewing work of the Spirit in the church as an ongoing principle of life and growth-producing vitality.[2]

God is in the church renewal business. If we miss this renewal perspective, we too easily become impatient with stagnant, nongrowing churches and put all the emphasis on starting new churches or "replanting" old ones. Whole denominations have at times adopted this as strategy, with mixed results. It is said (sometimes explicitly, sometimes less so), "Growth occurs in new churches, so let's put all our attention there and let stagnant or declining churches fend for themselves." Planting many new churches is a shortcut to supercharging overall growth. But there is something wrong with this strategy, both practically and theologically. God wants to renew the church—*every* church—that will pay the price.[3] And simply as a matter of strategy, effective church renewal can contribute at least as much to overall growth as can a focus on new church planting.

3. The church is essentially a living, dynamic spiritual, physical, and social organism, so its growth must be understood in similar fashion. Much Church Growth (and other) thinking about the church fails to appreciate the organic *complexity* of the church, reducing it to organizational or mechanical models that easily violate the church's essential genius as body of Christ.[4]

Even advocates of Church Growth will admit that much Church Growth strategy has produced little or no significant growth and ongoing vitality in the church over time. Why is this? Diagnoses will vary, of course. In my view, two primary causes are that often the complex organic spiritual-social nature of the church has been misunderstood or underestimated and that (consequently) too much stress has been placed on the *growth* of the church and not enough on the renewal and vitality of the Jesus community.

By what models and metaphors do we most truly and helpfully understand the church? It seems to me that if we are to inhabit the worldview of Scripture (as Lesslie Newbigin suggested), we will make the principal biblical models and metaphors of the church primary in all times and cultural contexts. These, of course, are the church as body of Christ, people and family of God, bride of Christ, and branches of the true Vine—all living, organic, relational images that work in any culture. If we take such images seriously, we are naturally led (biblically and practically) to a renewal perspective.

This leads to the next affirmation:

4. The nature of living things is to grow and reproduce themselves. Therefore, the growth of the church is always to be expected, though growth can occur for healthy or unhealthy reasons.

Healthy church growth is therefore to be affirmed. Pastors, and in fact all Christians, should expect their churches to grow. Lack of growth is in most cases a symptom of a problem that needs to be addressed.

The fact that the nature of the church is to grow is the most important biblical and theological principle of church growth. I say *biblical and theological,* rather than *natural* or *pragmatic* because this fact is more than a mere observation from nature. It is assumed throughout Scripture. God's creatures are to be fruitful and multiply. Israel is a vine planted by God, intended to grow and be faithful. Many of Jesus' parables make sense only because of the vital principle of growth and reproduction built into God's world—the germination of seeds, the growth of plants, the expectation that fig trees will produce fruit, even the leavening power of yeast. Images of growth and reproduction can be used of evil and judgment, as well as of righteousness: "Thrust in thy sharp sickle, and gather the clusters of the vine of the earth; for her grapes are fully ripe" (Rev. 14:18 KJV). From Genesis to Revelation, the Bible is full of images from life, with the clear lesson that all physical life comes from spiritual life, from God himself.

The fact that the church has life within it is thus a theological principle. It is grounded in who God is and in the work of the Spirit in creating the church as the body of Christ. God is the one who has placed within the church a principle of life. Thus, the main "secret" of church growth is not the discovery of methods or techniques to make the church grow but rather those biblical principles of church vitality that are so much the focus of the New Testament.

This is what Christian Schwarz neatly calls the "all-by-itself principle." "A man scatters seed on the ground. Night and day, whether he sleeps or gets up, the seed sprouts and grows, though he does not know how. All by itself the soil produces grain—first the stalk, then the head, then the full kernel in the head" (Mark 4:26–28). It is important to note that this parable refers not in the first instance to the church but to the kingdom of God. But the principle of life is the same. God has placed the power of life within living things, and "all by themselves" they grow and reproduce if the conditions are right.

Schwarz is correct in his book *Natural Church Development* that the church is a living thing and that its life is fundamentally organic, or "biotic" (the term he prefers).[5] Often Church Growth thinking has not paid enough attention to this organic, biotic nature of the church and its meaning for the nature of church life and reproduction.

This fact of a principle of life and reproduction within the church reminds us also that the key issue is not *growth* but *health*. The issue is not growing churches but healthy churches. Healthy churches grow under normal circumstances; planning for growth is not required if the proper environment exists. Growth takes care of itself, though of course it creates multiple challenges for leaders to nurture the growth and to turn growth into producing "much fruit" (John 15:5, 8). If the primary focus is on growth rather than health, however, an inversion of values and priorities easily takes place. Growth can occur at the expense of health. Doctors know this is true physically and watch for a whole range of pathologies in which growth is a sign of disease, from hormone imbalances to cancer. We can spot parallels in the life of the church. Doctors worry not only about disease but also about substances that artificially speed up growth, such as certain kinds of steroids, at the expense of overall health. Alien factors can be introduced into the body of Christ that greatly increase growth but perniciously undermine health and spiritual wholeness.

A focus on church health has its own pitfalls, however. Two in particular: First, "health" can be understood too humanistically, too psychologically or therapeutically. It then becomes a damper on genuine spiritual vitality, undercutting genuine worship and faithful witness. Second, church health can focus too narrowly on the church and miss the fact that the church exists not for itself but for God's mission in the world. A church may look vital and healthy—it may be growing and reproducing itself, nurturing its own children, teaching the Word, helping people live upright lives—but if it is not bearing effective witness within its cultural context to God's kingdom, its conception of health is far too narrow. It would be like a family that is safe and healthy within its own home but that is doing nothing to overcome the disease and pollution that surrounds it in the larger community. Healthy churches take seriously Jesus' petition that God's "will be done on earth as it is in heaven" (Matt. 6:10). They make the Lord's Prayer not only their petition but also their plan of action.

Biblically (as well as pragmatically) understood, the church has life within it. As I say, this is a theological point, not just a pragmatic or strategic one. It has to do with the essential nature of the church. Too much church growth strategizing is like exhorting a plant to grow, or giving it artificial and possibly toxic nutrients, or placing it into an artificial environment, or worse, manipulating and artificially shaping its growth or conjuring up a grotesque hybrid form of the church—rather than letting the church grow into the vine God intends, subject to the nurturing and pruning that God brings.

I can hear the protest, however: Yes, it's all very well to talk about the church having life within it. That may be true for some churches. But what about dead ones? Isn't it true that some churches have no life? In that case, how can we expect renewal or growth? Wouldn't starting a new church make more sense?

Fair enough. Churches can die, in the sense that they lose the spark of God within them or are so self-centered or sinful or divided that God's Spirit can hardly be expected to produce life and growth. Are such churches really candidates for renewal?

Yes! The amazing, mystifying thing about church renewal through the ages has been precisely this phenomenon of renewal happening when the church seemed totally dead. Willem Visser 't Hooft asked hopefully in *The Renewal of the Church,* "What is it that makes for the rebirth of the Church when everything . . . would seem to point to its approaching death? Why is it that the great attempts to suppress it have so often led to its renewal?"[6] The very questions suggest hope for renewal.

Dry bones can live again. How does this happen? Through the prayer and fasting of a remnant, and most often through a key prophetic figure whom God uses to bring about a renewal or revival that starts out looking more like a resurrection. God works through a Luther, a Spener, a Wesley, a Francis, or a Clare to spark a renewal. Somehow the dry deadness of the church turns into tinder for a fresh conflagration. Often such renewal comes also, in part, in response to need or crises or tensions in the larger society, what anthropologist Anthony F. C. Wallace called "cultural distortion."

People who long for church growth should never lose hope for church renewal. And just as there are insights and principles we can learn to foster church growth, so there are insights we can gain about how to cooperate with God's Spirit in becoming catalysts for renewal in the church.

This perspective is relevant for church planting and for evangelism in new areas or among unreached people, as well. The church cannot be renewed, of course, if it does not yet exist. But new initiatives in missions and church planting have often sprung from the heart of renewal movements. To take one example: the amazing missionary outreach of the early Moravians that so inspired William Carey sprang directly from the great Pentecostal renewal of the Moravian Brethren in Herrnhut, Germany, in 1727. Dozens of similar examples could be cited, from early monasticism to Azusa Street in 1906–09. Often pioneer evangelists and church planters are ignited or forged in the fires of renewal.

This leads to the fifth and final thesis:

5. *Since the historical record shows that God has in fact repeatedly renewed the church, the history of renewal movements is instructive for understanding the dynamics of church growth.* A significant body of literature on the history of renewal movements can profitably be mined for insights into church growth as well as renewal.

As hinted above, such study includes investigating the great revivals of history, but it includes much more. Typically, when evangelical Protestants think of church renewal, they think of either the great revivals and awakenings of the past or the mid-twentieth-century renewal that came about through small groups and "body life," or perhaps the twentieth-century charismatic renewal. We can learn much from these revivals. But the horizon for the historical study of renewal is much broader.

The historical study of renewal begins with the recognition that the New Testament church, though on one level a "new thing" and a new creation, was in a wider perspective a renewal of God's work recorded in the Old Testament. The church born in Jesus' ministry and at Pentecost gave initial fulfillment of the prophetic promise that God would renew his people. The history of renewal then proceeds with the awareness that church history is the story of repeated renewals.

Within a century of the close of the apostolic period, many Christians were thirsting for fresh renewal. Some felt there was need for "new prophecy" and a fresh outpouring of the Holy Spirit, giving rise to the New Prophecy movement (often called Montanism). About the same time, monasticism began as a movement of renewal. The long history of monasticism, continuing to the present, is really the history of repeated waves of renewal, often sparked by common, initially unrecognized, unordained simple Christians who allowed the Spirit to use them. Looking back now, we call them saints (or perhaps heretics, depending on whether or not they ran afoul of the church hierarchy).

Typically, Protestants begin their recounting of revival and renewal with the sixteenth-century Reformation, or perhaps somewhat earlier with the Waldensians or the Czech Reformation.[7] But this is a foreshortened view. There has never been an extended period in time or a place on earth where the church has been present, it seems, that some form of renewal was not stirring or threatening to stir. And usually the stirring starts at the periphery, the margins, among the poor or the masses, as we should expect, given biblical themes of God's particular concern for the poor, the alien, the widow, and the orphan and given what we now know about the sociology and anthropology of social movements.

I would argue, then, for a renewal-movement perspective on church history that yields rich insights for church growth. A renewal-movement perspective bridges the two ways church history has generally been studied. The dominant way is to study church history primarily in terms of the church's doctrines and institutions, tracing particularly whatever ecclesiastical lineage one finds oneself in. A second, "deviant" approach is to trace what might be called "the secret history of the faithful remnant." This view is still common today among some underground churches and house churches and among some people who see revivals of a particular sort to be the key to understanding church history.

A renewal-movement perspective, however, combines these two approaches. It sees church history as a sort of oscillation between these two poles. On the one hand, the church always drifts over time towards institutionalism, valuing uniformity, stability, predictability, and authority. On the other hand, there is frequently a "charismatic" counterpull in the direction of renewal, newness, experimentation, openness to the Spirit, and the involvement of all believers (not just a clergy elite) in leadership and ministry. The renewal-movement perspective can acknowledge that God works *both* in the "institutional" church, even when it appears like a dry root (cf. Isa. 11:1–10), *and* in troublesome new movements that do not fit accepted categories. One can learn from this double perspective, gaining insights from new movements without feeling required either to endorse them *en toto* or to condemn them.

Renewal movements can be studied in several ways. One is to trace the history of such movements and note common characteristics. Even while giving due allowance to the uniqueness of each movement, one can learn from the things they have in common. Because we are talking about the church as a living organism, it is possible to make practical transferences from what we learn of renewal movements to the dynamics of renewal in local congregations and in broader networks of churches (such as denominations) today.

In investigating a range of renewal movements in church history, I have observed eight characteristics that seem in varying degrees to be common to all such movements. These are:

1. A rediscovery of the heart of the gospel experience of Jesus Christ or of the Holy Spirit. This often constitutes a sort of experiential and conceptual paradigm shift in which the experience of God becomes central rather than secondary or absent. Often connected with this is a vision for the recovery of the dynamic of the New Testament church.

2. An inevitable tension with the church's institutional forms or traditions.

3. One or more key catalytic leaders who are available to God.

4. A rediscovered sense of community and new forms of community.

5. A life of active discipleship as the norm for all members; a new emphasis on discipleship and personal responsibility.

6. The practice of the priesthood of believers and spiritual gifts. This often appears in the form of itinerant ministry or preaching and often includes the public ministry of women and of "unschooled, ordinary" Christians (Acts 4:13). Some renewal movements explicitly teach such universal ministry and gifts; others simply have the practice without the theory.

7. Preaching the gospel to the poor or the marginalized, reaching the masses the traditional church has neglected.

8. Renewal movements generally exhibit the *energy* and rapid growth of a genuine social movement. They manifest social movement dynamics and often have significant social impact if appropriate patterns and forms are found and effective leadership is present.[8]

Renewal movements have much to teach the church today about the dynamics of church life and growth. They also provide key insights regarding church structure.[9] These are conclusions I have come to over the past several decades, through the course of a personal journey in ministry and research. A review of that journey will help clarify the above points and also show why I believe renewal insights have practical relevance for Church Growth today.

A PERSONAL JOURNEY

My understanding of church growth is of course grounded in my own story. My parents had been Free Methodist missionaries in the Dominican Republic, where I was born, and I grew up with a strong sense that the church was to be missionary and evangelistic, as well as committed to worship and the living of devout and holy lives. My parents returned to the United States in 1940, when I was less than a year old, and my father pastored a small Free Methodist church in Fairchance, Pennsylvania, located in a soft-coal mining region of the Appalachians south of Pittsburgh, near the West Virginia border.

My father became a professor at Spring Arbor Junior College and High School in 1944, so my growing-up years were spent in the context of a small southern Michigan town where the communities of church, college, and village pretty thoroughly overlapped and intermingled. The Free Methodist Church (the only one in town for most of my time there) was of course the college church, and the pastor was the college pastor. Checking the statistics now, I find that the church grew in total membership from 188 in 1944, to 244 in 1952, and then to 312 in 1959, the year before I left to complete my college work at Greenville College. This was modest growth that pretty well paralleled the postwar growth of the college and was not much due to evangelism in the surrounding area. During the same period, the Sunday school more than tripled, growing from an average attendance of 151 in 1944 to 471 in 1959. Since the denomination had a fairly strict membership covenant, worship attendance typically averaged about twice the official total membership, running in the same range as Sunday school attendance. During these sixteen years, the congregation birthed only one small congregation in a nearby town (actually started, I believe, by college students), though it tried rather halfheartedly to do so on a couple of other occasions. Much of the mission of the church was understandably focused on the residential college and high school students.

The church and college, typical of the denomination, had a strong emphasis on foreign missions. For three years, my pastor was James Hudson Taylor of the famous Hudson Taylor family. He and his wife, Alice, a very effective preacher and teacher, were with us for a brief period after having to leave China and before they could begin mission work in Taiwan (Formosa at the time).

I grew up, then, with the expectation that the church should be committed to personal holiness, that it should grow, and that it was part of a worldwide missionary enterprise. To me, there seemed to be much spiritual vitality in the church, especially in the worship services, though in fact the church was not particularly effective evangelistically. From time to time, there were stirring, sometimes overwhelming, revivals in which nearly everyone sensed the very near presence of God's Spirit.

Overall, this experience of the church, buttressed by our own Christian family life, was positive, though some of my friends and family experienced it negatively, as too confining or too focused on specific behavioral expectations.[10] Reflecting back after nearly half a century, I believe that the main things I gained from that formative church experience were a deep sense of the reality of God, a devotion to Jesus Christ and his cause, a conviction that the call to holiness touched every area of life, and an awareness that the church had a global mission. I see now that the church culture had little sense of social justice (other than perhaps the Prohibition cause, which in fact was not taken very seriously as a political force) and was quite conservative politically. It would be only a slight exaggeration to say that our congregation was the Republican Party at prayer. The culture was also in a measure implicitly, if not overtly, racist.

Still, most of the Christians I knew were devout, loving, and holy people, and my own commitment to and faith in Christ was solidified during these growing-up years. Most importantly, I saw

God work in people's lives and in the life of the church, steadily and at times dramatically. My upbringing gave me an appreciation, I think, of the reality and the possibilities of the church.

Seminary was a broadening experience, in a number of dimensions. I came to see that the church of Jesus Christ was much broader than the particular tradition I had known. Theologically and in terms of the church's mission, probably the greatest impact came through knowing and taking classes with Dr. Gilbert James, a sociologist (sort of a Tony Campolo figure) of my own denomination who had earlier been engaged in sometimes risky interracial evangelism in the South. The main things I gained from him were the fact of the church as a social (and sociological) reality, the church's call to social justice, and God's passion for the poor and the city. Gilbert James came to Asbury during the time I was a student there, as the first professor of the church in society; some only half-jokingly called him the "professor of worldliness." I still remember his inaugural lecture as professor: "The Church in Society: The Wesleyan Way."

I graduated from seminary in 1966, and my wife and I were delighted to be able to spend two years in northwest Detroit, in the Redford community, even though this was the height of what was then billed as "the urban crisis." The notorious Detroit riot broke out on July 23, 1967, just a week before our daughter's birth, in a poor neighborhood near downtown Detroit where our denomination once had a church. The church I pastored, which had been relatively strong during the Sunday School days of the 1950s, had declined steadily for the previous seven years. We had 101 members. In two years of ministry, we were able to reverse the slide and to convince the church to remain in the city (where it still is), which meant it would have to confront "the racial issue."

Our two years in Detroit convinced me, however, that I really had no *ecclesiology*, no thought-through theology of the church. So I began reading and studying Scripture. How to integrate my own past formation and my seminary learnings into a coherent theology of the church, including its structure and mission? I had collected a number of the new books just then coming out on Church Growth, church renewal, and urban ministry. During our first couple of years in Brazil, particularly during the months we were in language school, I read a number of these books; dug into issues of the church, the poor, and justice in my

Bible study; and had long conversations with people from other traditions. A colleague in language school, Simon Wolfert, introduced me to the Dutch Reformed tradition and the work of such figures as Kuyper, Dooyeweerd, and Berkouwer. These discussions helped me clarify my own thinking about the church in relation to culture.

This period I would now describe as my second conversion. Earlier I had been converted to Jesus Christ; now I was converted to the church—that is, to a deep sense that the gospel was not just "me and Jesus" but Jesus Christ, Head and body. The church was a social organism for the sake of God's mission, with a particular calling to Jesus' mission to the poor. Brazil was a very good context in which to make that discovery, although at the time, I was only vaguely aware of the beginnings of Latin American liberation theology. I came to my own form of liberation theology by another route, but one that gave me both sympathy with and some critical distance from the liberation theology of the 1970s and 1980s.

In reading the Church Growth literature of the time (particularly McGavran, Winter, and Wagner), I found myself constantly saying, "Yes, but . . ." I learned a lot and still feel that McGavran's *Bridges of God* is a classic. In our mission work, I saw some churches grow (and others decline or stagnate), and I learned more about the power of the gospel to transform lives and form vital communities of faith. I began to reflect on these matters in my writing. My learnings were crystallized in my book *The Problem of Wineskins: Church Structure in a Technological Age* (InterVarsity, 1975).

Opportunities for denominational service in the United States and for doctoral studies at Notre Dame University brought us back to North America in 1975. Notre Dame was at the time an ideal place to pursue questions of the church and its mission from a historical and theological standpoint, for there I had contact with Roman Catholic professors (some of whom had been involved in the birth of the Catholic charismatic renewal), Methodist professors such as Stanley Hauerwas, and most importantly, the Mennonite scholar John Howard Yoder (who directed my dissertation). My area was historical theology, but my focus in every course was ecclesiology. How did Augustine, or Aquinas, or Barth understand the church? What positive things could I learn from medieval Catholicism, and from the

Radical Reformation? I became increasingly fascinated with renewal movements in church history (in some measure, no doubt, because of my roots in the Wesleyan revival in England) and accordingly became convinced that the key question for faithful gospel witness today is not so much church growth as church renewal. After conversations with Yoder, I decided to focus my dissertation research on German Pietism, the Moravians, and early Methodism as renewal movements. I had already done a paper for Yoder on John Wesley (the genesis of my book *The Radical Wesley and Patterns for Church Renewal*), and that fed naturally into my dissertation research, which was the principal basis for my later book *Signs of the Spirit: How God Reshapes the Church.*

I would now describe these years as the time of my third conversion: conversion to the kingdom of God. I became convinced that the key question was not the growth or even the vitality of the church *in itself* but the question of the church's faithfulness as witness to the promise and intention of God's reign. This was the point of my 1977 book, *The Community of the King,* and later of *Liberating the Church: The Ecology of Church and Kingdom* (InterVarsity, 1983).

From 1980 to 1988, my family and I had the opportunity to live in Chicago and to serve in the Irving Park Free Methodist Church (as well as to engage in other ministries). As pastoral coordinator of this church from 1982 to 1988, I had the opportunity to practice what I preached. It was a very confirming experience, particularly as I worked with a pastoral team of young men and women.[11] It was especially gratifying to see excitement grow as a diverse congregation became infected with a vision not just of the church but of God's reign. It was infectious and motivating to discover that we were in the kingdom business, not just the church business. Material that later appeared in some of my books, particularly *A Kingdom Manifesto* (InterVarsity, 1985), became practically useful to us as we worked together in a small but significantly growing church in an older urban neighborhood. My writings from this period owe much to the sisters and brothers with whom we co-labored in building a vital congregation that sought in multiple ways to show signs of the kingdom.[12]

As a result of these experiences, I continue to be convinced that (1) a key issue is the fundamental nature of the church as body of Christ; (2) the way to healthy, sustained church growth is through church renewal and ongoing vitality; and (3) the church is called to live for God's mission and God's kingdom, not for itself. Its "success" is to be measured by its contribution to God's kingdom.

The result of my personal journey and my continuing learnings and reflections on the church as outlined in the first section of this chapter come to focus in several practical ways as we reflect on church life and growth today.

A RENEWAL STRATEGY FOR CHURCH GROWTH

Is there a church growth *strategy* from the perspective of church renewal? What can we learn from a renewal perspective that will help the church to grow faithfully and sustainably?

We should take note first of all of the dramatic growth that is now happening around the world. Philip Jenkins points out in his book *The Next Christendom* that the common North American perception of Christianity's decline is a myth. The Christian faith is being reborn and renewed in all kinds of ways in all kinds of places. Globally, "Christianity is flourishing wonderfully among the poor and persecuted," Jenkins notes, "while it atrophies among the rich and secure." If we take a historical overview, we note "the number of times that the faith seemed on the verge of destruction" but then burst forth with new vigor. "And whether we look backward or forward in history [in the light of current trends], we can see that time and again, Christianity demonstrates a breathtaking ability to transform weakness into strength."[13] Jenkins documents the many places the church is growing worldwide, not only in new independent churches but also in the renewal of older traditions.

If we look at actual church growth, both historically and in the contemporary world, we see that the most dramatic, culture-changing examples of growth have come about not from the discovery and conscious application of Church Growth principles and strategies but from renewal movements. We may argue, of course, that such movements intuitively applied Church Growth principles, and that no doubt is correct.[14] Still, what does it say about Church Growth theory and practice that the most dramatic growth often occurs where such theory and practice is unknown or unrecognized?

At the other end of the historical spectrum, we learn something similar from Rodney Stark's book *The Rise of Christianity: A Sociologist Reconsiders History*. Stark demonstrates that the spread and influence of the Christian faith in the first three centuries was due less to intentional strategies of evangelism and church growth than to the social impact of Christian virtue and morality, the dynamic of Christian countercultural community, the faith's ability to answer ultimate questions, and the evangelistic impact of Christian compassion, particularly in times of calamity such as plagues and wars.[15]

Thus, the key to church growth is understanding the dynamics of the Christian faith as a movement and the implications of renewal movements for church life and growth today in varied contexts.[16] A major part of such an approach, necessarily, is an ongoing dialogue with Scripture and openness to the Holy Spirit to do "new things" in birthing and rebirthing the church in diverse cultures and societies.

If it is true, as I believe it is, that learnings from renewal movements can be transferred to the lives of local churches or networks of churches, then it is possible to delineate practical renewal approaches to church growth, vitality, and reproduction. Though many other things might be said, the following points distill some vital growth-and-renewal insights from the church's long history of rebirth and renewal. The goal is to build healthy, vital congregations that are marked by wholehearted love for God, warmhearted love for all people, and a passion for God's kingdom purposes. Nothing less deserves to be called "renewal."

Pastors or other leaders seeking to nurture healthy, growing churches should consider the following course of action:

1. Begin with life. Renewal begins with recognizing the sparks of life already present in the church and then fanning those sparks into flame. The principle is basic and self-evident: life begets life.

This means identifying the life and vitality already present in both people and structures. Who are the persons in the congregation that demonstrate in their lives that they truly know God (or hunger to know him) and are ready to put Jesus and his body first? Here is a key starting point for renewal, as it was for Jesus and his disciples and has been at the beginning of every great revival and renewal movement.

But this is also a structural issue. What *structures* are life giving or life sustaining? Is there any functioning life-support system in the congregation? It may show up in surprising places. It may be an ad hoc group of members who meet and support each other spiritually. It may be a family network or some other social configuration. A renewal strategy begins with recognizing, affirming, and building on such structures, if they exist. Renewal often begins by testing the wind, discerning where God's Spirit is already blowing or breathing, and cooperating with the Spirit.

2. *Let dead or dysfunctional structures and patterns lie* for the time being, rather than seeking to dismantle or change them. Better to bypass unhelpful patterns and structures than to provoke controversy and opposition by attacking them. Attacking entrenched patterns usually raises defenses instead of furthering renewal.

This does not mean passivity or surrender. Where institutional barriers block renewal, these must be faced squarely and eventually changed. But by beginning with life rather than focusing on barriers, leaders foster a process that with time leads to less stressful opportunities for bringing structural renewal.

For many Christians, the church is a place of security in a troubled world, so any talk of change is threatening. A wise renewal strategy recognizes this. Rather than initially proposing major changes in tradition or structure and thus making enemies, wise leaders value patience while keeping an eye on the goal and working to rebuild the life of the church on a more organic model.

3. *Seek to nurture all the people.* Pastors, elders, or other leaders will normally be the key people in developing and implementing a renewal strategy, and they should understand that they must pastor and nurture all the people, not just those who seem open. Not everyone wants renewal; some may oppose it. But wise leaders can often change the whole climate and win over prickly opponents simply by being available to and pastoring all the people.

Church leaders bent on renewal face the temptation to in effect play favorites, focusing on those who are open to the renewal agenda and ignoring others. Careful strategy does require investing especially in those most open to renewal, as Jesus did. But it also means not neglecting anyone, and particularly not shutting anyone out.

4. *Build a balanced ecology of worship, community, and witness.* The church is a living organism, and the major elements of its

life are worship, community, and witness.[17] Healthy church growth is the fruit of a balanced vitality of God-centered worship; caring, accountable community; and witness in the world. Effective renewal strategizing asks, Are we providing believers with the opportunities and the structures for these key aspects of their life together?

5. *Develop an infrastructure of accountable, face-to-face community.* Neither excellent organization nor the internet will ever take the place of face-to-face nurturing community that continues over time. Some form of small group, cell group, or home fellowship seems to be required as a basic structure in vital churches. Though specific forms will vary, this principle is cross-culturally appropriate and valid.

A pragmatic renewal strategy will use some form of small group or subcommunity as a *basic structure* in congregational life, not as an optional add-on. Renewal movements have usually seen the practical value of meeting in homes as a more informal and "family" setting for experiencing Christian community, though this may not work in every culture.

6. *Affirm and facilitate the ministry of all believers.* This is absolutely key. One of the most remarkable and consistent marks of renewal movements is the way they motivate and enlist all members in some form of ministry that both cements their devotion to the movement and forwards its aims and dynamics. This is a sociological observation, but the theological principle is more fundamental: All believers are priests and workers in God's vineyard. All members of the body have a function within the body.

The key biblical affirmations here are the gifts of the Spirit, the priesthood of believers, and servanthood in following Jesus. All believers are called, and should be equipped and empowered, for ministry.

As part of a renewal strategy, this emphasis calls for several things: teaching on spiritual gifts and universal priesthood, modeling this in speech and structure, providing training and opportunities for leadership development, and affirming initial faltering steps at ministry or exercising gifts. The ministry of all believers needs to be demonstrated visibly in the three areas of worship, community, and witness. Perhaps most basically, this emphasis means conceiving of the pastoral role essentially as one of equipping believers for ministry (Eph. 4:11–12). This dovetails nicely with the use of small groups, which are essential discipling and equipping structure.

7. Develop some form of shared or team leadership. A natural corollary to the ministry of all believers is shared rather than solo pastoral leadership. It is striking how clear the New Testament is on spiritual leadership and yet how massively these biblical teachings are ignored in the church. Renewal becomes deeper and longer-lasting as a congregation increasingly implements biblical patterns of shared or team leadership. This therefore is a key issue of strategy.

In the New Testament, we see several key things about leadership in the body of Christ: authentic leadership is based on the Scriptural qualifications of character and giftedness; pastoral leadership is defined primarily as equipping the body for ministry; and team or plural leadership in each congregation is generally the norm.[18]

An effective renewal strategy understands that ministry grows out of community and that leadership grows out of discipleship. It seeks to demonstrate the servant leadership of Jesus Christ, not only in spirit but also in strategy and direction, following the example of Jesus with his disciples and of Paul with his coworkers.

This obviously means that pastors will need to begin by examining their own lives in the light of New Testament teachings about leadership, character, and servanthood. It means developing a core of spiritual leaders, disciples, and disciplers who demonstrate and model biblical leadership. The final result should be an effective pastoral leadership team in each congregation—regardless of what it is called, precisely how it is structured, or the denominational polity within which it functions.

8. Help the congregation discover its own identity as body of Christ and servant of God's reign. Implementing a renewal strategy based on these principles gives a congregation a strong sense of identity as body of Christ and as ministering community. It is important, however, that a congregation's identity be grounded in its own unique personality, culture, and range of gifts, not imposed by pastoral leadership. Each church is to be a sign and agent of the kingdom of God, but each will do this in a somewhat different way.

We learn in Scripture that pastors have the authority and the responsibility to lead. But the New Testament teaches that Jesus, and he alone, is Head of the church. Pastors are themselves fellow members of the body. The function of pastors, then, is to help the whole body "grow up into" Jesus Christ, the Head (Eph. 4:15), finding its identity and wholeness in him through the work of the Spirit. This means pastors are key catalysts in helping a congregation discover its own unique identity and mission within the framework of the biblical gospel of the kingdom. This is part of the discipling, equipping task.

Discovering self-identity is in part a natural by-product of the other elements discussed here. A congregation finds its kingdom identity as it ministers, grows, and flourishes through a range of spiritual gifts. This process can be made more intentional and self-conscious, however, through teaching and preaching, Bible studies in cells and home groups that explore the nature of the church, church retreats, seminars and classes, and similar experiences.

9. *Work to ensure that financial stewardship authentically reflects the church's mission and self-identity.* It is true, as is often said, that the use of money reveals one's *real* priorities. Finances may end up betraying the church's renewal and identity unless consciously brought under the lordship of Christ and into line with the church's stated mission and kingdom calling.

The whole area of finances should be seen in relation to the biblical image of the church and of New Testament discipleship. In the Sermon on the Mount, Jesus tells us where our priorities should lie. Matthew 6:33 applies as much to church finances as to personal priorities: we are to seek first God's kingdom and justice. If we do, other matters will take care of themselves.

In other words, kingdom priorities and pastoral goals should determine financial objectives and strategies. As the renewal and mission of the church increasingly become its central focus, this will be reflected in church finances. Often in this process some major redirection may be necessary, a shifting of priorities from property and program toward people and ministry.

10. *Help the church catch a kingdom vision.* This is ultimately the most important thing and reinforces all the above points. Each congregation needs a *vision* of God's reign—what God is doing and what he promises to do. This is a vision for community and worship, but it is also a vision for reconciling ministry in the world in which evangelism, discipling, and justice are inseparable strands in the fabric of ministry. Ongoing vitality is grounded in both the *vision* and the *practice* of consistent, continuous evangelism and compassionate, effective social trans-

formation. It is a beautiful thing when a congregation gets beyond the evangelism/justice hang-up and, at the practical level of ministry, does both, unconscious of the distinction. But reaching this point requires an overarching biblical vision of God's reign.

A kingdom vision gives life and focus to the church's worship, community, and witness. Worship becomes "reality therapy" in which the church affirms, against all visible signs to the contrary, God's present and ultimate victory in Jesus Christ. Kingdom vision makes worship the very center of the church's life.

A kingdom vision gives added meaning to the church as the community of the King, an outpost and foretaste of the age of shalom that is coming. And a kingdom vision gives impulse and coherence to the church's outward witness. It is the hope of Christ's kingdom that holds together the evangelistic and prophetic dimensions of the church's mission and keeps Christians laboring for that which as yet remains largely unseen.

Church renewal can turn inward; it can be understood and experienced in pretty subjective and narcissistic ways. A kingdom vision is an antidote to this danger. Church leaders concerned about balanced, long-lasting renewal will do well to develop and instill the vision of God's reign as a basic part of a renewal strategy.[19]

CONCLUSION

From a renewal perspective, the primary concern about church growth is that growth be understood in terms of the broader vision of God's kingdom and mission and that it be compatible with the nature of the church as the spiritual-social body of Christ. Sound, biblical church growth will be holistic and multidimensional, as Orlando Costas argued forcefully in *Christ Outside the Gate*. Speaking of the "multidimensional nature" of authentic growth of the church for the kingdom, Costas argued that numerical growth can be "a provisional goal of mission," but growth that focuses solely on numerical increase becomes a "mutilation of mission."[20]

This, it seems to me, is consistent with a renewal understanding of church growth—one that says the church exists not for itself but for the kingdom of God. The Holy Spirit of God continues to do new, renewing things. When he does, and when his people respond in faith and faithfulness, the church grows.

A CENTRIST RESPONSE

Charles Van Engen

For over twenty-five years now, I have made it a point of reading whatever Howard Snyder writes as soon as I can get my hands on it. Many of his books have been used as textbooks in my classes. So I consider it an honor and a joy to reflect on his chapter in this volume.

The five theses that Snyder offers in this chapter are right on. I wholeheartedly agree with all of them. Snyder is right that "it is God's will to renew the church." And he is equally correct that the American Church Growth movement has been relatively silent and seemingly unconcerned about church renewal. For years, J. Edwin Orr taught the history of revivals at Fuller's School of World Mission, and almost everyone studying in Church Growth in the 1970s and 1980s studied revivals with him there. For some reason, however, that did not translate into a concern for the renewal of the church, especially with relation to the church in the West.

I share Snyder's concern with "the superficial way the Scriptures have been dealt with in some Church Growth texts— the misapplication or misappropriation of biblical metaphors or other biblical material in the interest of views of Church Growth that have little or no real scriptural basis."

Snyder is also correct that it is the nature of things to grow. Howard's analysis of biblical principles of growth is excellent, and his analysis of the "pitfalls" to growth are on target. He is also correct, in my view, that the history of renewal movements is instructive for the life and growth of the church in the twenty-first century and that a major concern in this century must be focused on the renewal of the church: its pastoral leaders, its members, its organic life.

I appreciated Snyder's comment that the "lack of growth is in most cases a symptom of a problem that needs to be addressed." I share Snyder's concern over the love of technique that is seen in much Church Growth literature of late. I was intrigued and inspired by Snyder's eight characteristics of renewal movements throughout church history. As I have done with many of Snyder's statements, I'm sure I will cite many times in the years to come his statement: "The goal is to build healthy, vital congregations that are marked by wholehearted love for God, warmhearted love for all people, and a passion for God's kingdom purposes. Nothing less deserves to be called 'renewal.'"

Coupled with my enthusiasm for Snyder's renewal approach to church growth, I find myself uncomfortable at several points. First, throughout the chapter, the concept of growth that Snyder seems to associate with the Church Growth movement seems to be restricted to numerical growth. I feel this is an inaccurate representation. From the earliest articulations of Church Growth theory in Donald McGavran's *Bridges of God*, through his writing of *Understanding Church Growth,* to the later writings of Peter Wagner and others, "growth" in the Church Growth movement has always been viewed holistically and ecclesially. Although there have been a variety of differing emphases in the movement, one concept has been consistently offered: that numerical growth is only a thermometer, a symptom, an indicator, of other issues at work in the life of the church. Even in Peter Wagner's "seven vital signs," a description of church health and vitality that permeates Church Growth writing throughout twenty-five years of articulation of the theory, one will find the matter of numerical, statistical growth to be a minor point, a sign of health but not the ultimate goal.

Second, Snyder seems to create an artificial dichotomy between growth and renewal. I believe this may be the result of associating "growth" with numerical growth, as noted in the previous paragraph. So I find Snyder's comment confusing that "the primary focus of the New Testament is not on church growth but on the nature and life of the Christian community, the kind of *being* of the church that almost inevitably produces growth if the church remains open to the Spirit." Clearly the entire New Testament is concerned about the way the disciples of Jesus follow him; the way the members of the body participate in the life of the body; the way the church most clearly reflects, as in a mirror, the grace of Jesus Christ that transforms persons and social systems in the New Testament world. Yet the New Testament does not set up a dichotomy between a concern for the vitality of the church and its numerical growth. The book of Acts, for example, is concerned with all the facets of the nature, life, and growth of the church, including the numerical increase that Luke records at the outset of Acts with some regularity. But Luke never juxtaposes the numerical increase over against matters of the nature and development of the life of the church.

Moreover, Snyder's unnecessary dichotomy between growth and renewal misleads the reader in understanding how the founders of the Church Growth movement read history. Donald McGavran, Alan Tippett, Peter Wagner, and Ralph Winter were all readers and students of Kenneth Scott Latourette. In his one-volume work, *A History of Christianity*, and in his seven-volume *A History of the Expansion of Christianity*, Latourette's thesis is that Christian self-giving, agape love is the force that not only brought about the (numerical) growth and geographic expansion of the church but also brought down the Roman Empire.[21] So to call for a renewal-oriented reading of church history and give the impression that this has never happened would not be accurate. Stephen Neill's *A History of Christian Missions*[22] and Latourette's works have been basic history texts for anyone studying Church Growth. As Paul Pierson has been showing Church Growth students for many years at Fuller's School of World Mission, these texts demonstrate a deep concern for the renewal, revival, awakening, mission outreach, and vitality of the church in its dynamic interaction with its context, along with an interest in its numerical growth and geographic expansion. These texts are neither silent about renewal, nor do they create a large divide between renewal and growth, but rather they see them as facets of the same diamond. In my view, to juxtapose "Church Growth strategies" over against "renewal movements" is a false dichotomy and does not match my understanding of the Church Growth movement.

Third, I believe Snyder creates too wide a gulf between growth and health. "This fact of a principle of life and reproduction within the church," Snyder writes, "reminds us also that the key issue is not *growth* but *health*. The issue is not growing churches but healthy churches." I find this language confusing. From one perspective, the distinction makes little sense. Healthy plants and other organisms increase in size; they grow. In the 1974 film produced by Win Arn and Donald McGavran, *How Churches Grow*, McGavran concludes, "A healthy church grows. It is natural for the church to grow. In fact, when a church does not grow, you say there is something wrong." McGavran then goes on to emphasize conversion growth over against transfer and biological growth. It does not make sense to me to set one against the other.

On the other hand, to seek to emphasize health over against growth is also misleading. Here Snyder draws from Christian Schwartz's *Natural Church Development*. To stress what Schwartz calls a "biotic" approach to church health is unrealistic. The so-called biotic principle is drawn from the mechanistic world of science and the "laws of nature," which is not a biblical perspective of reality. Schwartz fails to take seriously the sinfulness of all humans who make up the church and the church's penchant throughout history to stray away from its Lord. Schwartz's eight essential qualities are impossible to create without the work of the Holy Spirit; they do not happen naturally. The church has a "natural" tendency to create structures, solidify processes, and petrify viewpoints to such an extent that it becomes as healthy as a tree with branches but no leaves because the roots have dried up and no sap will flow. This tendency toward the deformation and self-destruction of the church can also be borne out in history, and it is precisely why Snyder's call for renewal is right on target.

An overemphasis on health rather than growth will also tend to blind pastoral leaders to their context. Christian Schwartz's program for the church does not include any awareness of, listening to, or reaching out to those who yet do not know Jesus Christ. There is no contextual analysis in the eight essential qualities. The pastoral leaders of a congregation can foster all eight qualities in the life of a congregation and continue to be, or become even more, irrelevant to their surrounding context. In that case, I wonder what it means for that congregation to be healthy. Certainly it is not faithful to the call and mission of its Lord. To distance health from the holistic growth of the church is to move the church toward introversion and irrelevance, which can increase the illness of the church rather than its health.

I do not recognize the Church Growth movement in the caricatures that Howard Snyder draws when he writes, "Too much Church Growth strategizing is like exhorting a plant to grow, or giving it artificial and possibly toxic nutrients, or placing it into an artificial environment, or worse, manipulating and artificially shaping its growth or conjuring up a grotesque hybrid form of the church." There is no contact point in Church Growth theory for these analogies. In fact, one could demonstrate that the Church Growth movement has strongly been against all of these exaggerated ways to deform the church.

I am in full agreement with Snyder's emphasis on a three-part conversion, which he develops autobiographically: conversion to Jesus Christ as his Savior and Lord; conversion to the church, the body of Christ; and conversion to the kingdom of God. I think I would also like to hear of people being converted to becoming willing subjects of the King, called to transform the King's world. From reading his other works, I know Snyder's deep commitment to the transformation of the world. I miss a note about that here. I find it difficult to speak of the kingdom of God without in the next breath calling for a commitment to change the world, for whom Christ died.

A REFORMIST RESPONSE

Gailyn Van Rheenen

I have significantly learned from Howard Snyder's renewal perspectives of Church Growth. He rightly says, "The most dramatic, culture-changing examples of growth have come about not from the discovery and conscious application of Church Growth principles and strategies but from renewal movements." I appreciate his perspectives that God's creatures are to be "fruitful and multiply" and that metaphors of growth and expectation of growth are sprinkled throughout Scripture. His personal testimony of three conversions (to Jesus, to the church, to the kingdom of God) illustrates developing theological insights imperative to Christian ministry. Church leaders ministering in stagnant churches would do well to heed his practical pastoral hints for generating revival, such as "Begin with life" and "Let dead or dysfunctional structures and patterns lie for the time being." Above all, the renewal perspective does provide urgency, an acknowledgement that God is now working among his people, that "God's Holy Spirit forms, judges, renews, and *again* renews, the body of Christ."

Although I generally concur with the major thrust of Snyder's renewal perspective, I believe it also has a number of crucial limitations.

REDUCING CHURCH GROWTH TO NUMERICAL INCREASE

First, Snyder inadequately nuances the Church Growth perspective by reflecting on only the issue of numerical increase. I would have liked to read his perception of basic Church Growth perspectives (such as receptivity and the "people group" concept), Church Growth's anthropocentric beginning point for the development of ministry, and the use of a scientific, rational model for evaluating the church's growth. I assume that Snyder generally accepts these basic tenets and assumptions of Church Growth but believes that spiritual renewal should be at its core.

NEED FOR INTEGRATED THEOLOGY

The second and most significant critique has to do with the need for an integrated, rather than a piecemeal, theology.

I empathize with Snyder's testimony about his three conversions: to Christ, to the church, and finally to the kingdom of God. I have experienced a similar transformation in my life. I especially liked his statement that "the church is called to live for God's mission and God's kingdom, not for itself." These are theological affirmations of a pilgrimage of faith.

Often, however, theological foundations are assumed rather than integrated into the fabric of Snyder's writing. Snyder says that the Bible is "the supreme and final authority concerning the church's life and growth." His focus, however, is more on the *need* for spiritual renewal and its role in helping churches grow than on its *quality* and *nature*. Merely using a few theological statements does not put theology at the core of forming spiritual renewal.

For example, Snyder acknowledges the need to exegete "the renewal theme in Scripture" and the conversion motif of "turn/return." He even defines the New Testament church as a "renewal of God's work recorded in the Old Testament." Late in his chapter, he speaks of his conversion to the kingdom of God and says "the church is called to live for God's mission and God's kingdom, not for itself." These themes are significant, yet undeveloped. Generally, his reflection on renewal is more historical and pragmatic than theological.

The problem with promoting revival without adequate theological foundations is that its essence might be formulated more by popular evangelical culture or human felt needs than by biblical perspectives that reflect the purposes and mind of God. Thus, I fear revivals resulting from the discovery of some hidden, "neglected truth," which then reignites the church. Many of these revivals, rooted in popular culture, result in mere flare-ups rather than true fires of God. Others take root as institutional religious movements with a focus on their religious emphasis. Some "renewals" are syncretistic movements that either emphasize one or two aspects of the gospel or contort the essence of the gospel rather than focusing on the central themes that reflect the full glory of God. Any biblical theology of renewal must be rooted in such biblical motifs as the *missio Dei*, the kingdom of God, God's gospel, and God's giving in his incarnation and crucifixion. These are the themes of godly revivals.

Renewal is not the result of a strategy devised by human ingenuity. It is not a human plan. Revival is entering into the purposes of God and allowing God to form and guide us. It is rooted in humility, ascribing God to be God and allowing him to work in our lives. In the renewal process, disciples become transformed into the image of God (2 Cor. 3:18).

Snyder must therefore go beyond brief statements about theology to develop an integrative theology of renewal.

THE "ALL-BY-ITSELF" PRINCIPLE

Snyder borrows Christian Schwarz's "all-by-itself" principle and employs it to describe the development of a healthy church. The paradox, however, is that this phrase is rooted more in Enlightenment understandings of individualism and self-sufficiency than in the biblical perspectives of God's sovereign rule. The parable of the growing seed does say, "All by itself the soil produces grain—first the stalk, then the head, then the full kernel in the head," but the context is "the kingdom of God" (Mark 4:26–29). The theme of the parable is that God works in our lives over a period of time in ways that we cannot perceive or fathom. The transformation is without human ingenuity, thus "all by itself." However, God's hand is evident as he rules in our lives. This parable is an apt description of spiritual renewal.

GROWTH-HEALTH DIFFERENTIATION

Snyder affirms that church health is more important than church growth, maintaining that healthy churches, by their very nature, grow. This therapeutic analysis, however, does not significantly enhance his renewal perspective. Renewal is empowered more by looking to God and being transformed into his nature than by the church focusing on its own health. Both numerical growth and church health, while extremely important, are a result of God's work. Snyder compares and contrasts church growth and health despite his qualification that "church health can focus too narrowly on the church and miss the fact that the church exists not for itself but for God's mission in the world." Snyder's case for church renewal would be stronger if it were more fully founded on a biblical ecclesiology, with church growth and health understood as the results of renewal.

FROM THE PERSPECTIVE OF THE MISSIONAL HELIX

I have described in this book the missional helix, illustrating the intertwining, inseparable nature of theological reflection, cultural analysis, historical perspective, and strategy formation in preparation for the practice of ministry.

The missional helix model shows that Snyder's renewal perspective places strong emphasis on *strategy formation*. This area is also the greatest contribution of Snyder's chapter, as expressed in his section on "A Renewal Strategy for Church Growth." He also gives an adequate *historical perspective* to establish the significance of church renewal.

His renewal perspective, however, is lacking in the areas of *cultural analysis* and *theological reflection*. He does not consider the cultural contexts in which renewal occurs and how culture shapes renewal. Although he does express theological insights, these are not systemized into a theology of spiritual renewal. Developing an integrative theology of renewal would serve to both stimulate revival and help the people of God avoid syncretism.

WHAT IS THE SOURCE OF REVIVAL?

What, then, is the source of spiritual renewal? Renewal is not a human endeavor or the result of human strategy. In its authentic forms, spiritual renewal is the incarnating of God within our lives, based on theological formation. It is entering into the kingdom of God and allowing God to form and guide us.

I have appreciated Snyder's seminal chapter because it has provided a stimulus to my own devotion and direction.

AN EFFECTIVE EVANGELISM RESPONSE
Elmer Towns

Howard Snyder presents a view that is to the right of Church Growth, and I suggest that he is to the right for two reasons. A correct view of Church Growth is a balance between internal growth and external growth, and it might be pictured as a balance between organic growth and programmed growth. Some churches seem to grow from the inside out, just as in the natural world; plants and trees grow from the inside out. But at the same time, a farmer or a botanist produces growth, or faster growth, or more fruit from the outside in by creating the right conditions (sunlight, climate, water, fertilizer) and using the right soil (different nutrients in the soil produce greater growth in different types of vegetables, flowers, trees, etc.). Through external research, botanists have developed plants that are more beautiful, more hardy, or more healthy for us to eat. The point is it takes both external and internal factors to produce growth, in both agriculture and the church.

Howard Snyder emphasizes Church Growth from the internal factors—renewal and revival. I said he is on the right because if I were to err in one extreme, I would follow his example; I would err on the spiritual side of Church Growth—internal factors. But why err on one side or the other? Why not follow a balanced approach, applying both internal and external factors to carry out the Great Commission? Snyder is correct in his understanding of the church, he is correct in his understanding of Scripture, and he is correct in the need of supernatural help in all churches.

This chapter should be read and digested by all those who want to truly understand Church Growth. I cannot disagree with his five theses concerning the church and growth, and I recommend the application of his ten suggested principles of how to renew a church. What Snyder has said is good, but what he omits will leave the readers with a skewed view of Church Growth.

Snyder has said, "Genuine church growth is primarily a matter of how God's Holy Spirit forms, judges, renews, and *again* renews, the body of Christ." Yes, that is true, but look at the opposite side of that equation. Too many churches do not grow, and too many do not carry out the Great Commission. And these churches are not made up just of carnal believers or those who do not care. These are churches where people genuinely pray, work hard, work diligently in ministry, and want growth, renewal, and revival but receive only marginal results, if they receive any at all. You can plant a tomato sprout on the beach at the ocean, and as much as the tomato sprout has life and wants to grow, it cannot grow in the wrong environmental conditions, nor can it grow when it is planted in sand, which does not have nutrients that will produce growth. Snyder has not properly understood the cultural impact of the church. True, he says it is the nature of living things to grow and reproduce themselves. But he does not give proper attention to the influence of the social sciences—to the contribution that a study of culture, linguistics, and ethnic customs contributes to the planting, growth, and expansion of the church. When Snyder makes statements such as "Growth takes care of itself," this should be qualified by saying that growth takes care of itself when the proper sprout is planted in the correct soil, at the correct time of year, and nurtured in the correct way. What God does in growth is absolutely necessary, but the human worker also makes a vital contribution to the harvest.

I love Howard Snyder's emphasis on revival/renewal because this has been an emphasis of mine. I wrote two books on revivals, the first with Neil Anderson, titled *Rivers of Revival*, which was an analytical approach to describing what revival looks like.[23] I said that not all revivals have the same face, meaning they do not express themselves in the same way, nor are all revivals motivated by the same causes. The nine faces of revival presented in the book *Rivers of Revival* are:

1. The *repentance revival* emphasizes a moral cleansing of individual lives and of society as a whole.
2. The *evangelism revival* focuses on winning souls to Christ.

3. The *worship revival* centers on magnifying God.
4. The *deeper-life revival* emphasizes the experience of God's indwelling.
5. The *spiritual-warfare revival* devotes its energies to battling Satan and the other demons.
6. The *Holy Spirit revival* is characterized by extensive manifestations of the Spirit.
7. The *reconciliation revival* leads to the removal of barriers to racial and ethnic harmony.
8. The *liberation revival* focuses on gaining freedom from corporate and personal bondage.
9. The *prayer revival* displays considerable efforts at intercession and other forms of prayer.

If Snyder were to apply to the area of revival the research methods of both theology and the social sciences, he might note the different forms that revival takes and that the influence of a leader or church takes toward revival will determine somewhat the face that revival will have when God renews the church.

The second book I wrote on revivals, with Douglas Porter, is *The Ten Greatest Revivals Ever: From Pentecost to the Present*. In that book, we assembled a task force of seventeen scholars and Christian leaders to vote on the greatest revivals, placing them in order of their influence.[24] The ranking of these revivals followed several categories.

A revival was defined in this book as "an extraordinary work of God in which Christians repent of their sins as they become intensely aware of His presence in their midst, and they manifest a positive response to God in renewed obedience to the known will of God, resulting in both a deepening of their individual and corporate experience with God, and an increased concern to win others to Christ."[25]

Note that a revival is similar to a person fainting and then being brought back to consciousness. The idea of revival is to bring back to life, or to renew, one's zeal. I believe that when God sends revival to a church, denomination, or nation (including culture), the result is church growth, both internal and external growth.

Also, when a church is revived, a positive influence is exerted on society, or the surrounding culture. As a matter of fact, the "ten greatest revivals" were measured by their positive impact on the greater culture in which the churches were located.

Snyder tends to confuse revival and renewal. Whereas revival is a supernatural work of God, renewal may be brought about by a church's endeavors to bring itself back to life. As an illustration, when a church gets a renewed vision, a new program of outreach to the poor, or a new evangelistic outreach, the church is renewed. Renewal tends to be something that comes from within the church, while revival comes from God. A simple definition of revival is "God pouring his presence on his people." This definition comes from the Scripture "I will pour out My Spirit on all flesh" (Acts 2:17 NKJV). It is also found in the passage "times of refreshing may come from the presence of the Lord" (Acts 3:19 NKJV). I would not take exception with anything that Howard Snyder has said about renewal and revival; I would only add to his definition the obvious supernatural causes of revival that have been historical phenomena throughout history, which I believe can happen today; to a certain extent, it is happening in certain South American and African nations. Sadly, very little revival is seen in America, even though some churches are experiencing renewal of purpose, renewal of programs, or renewal of outreach into the community. Also, some American churches may experience *internal revival* that involves the individuals within the congregation but not *atmospheric revival* that is poured out on corporate churches that affect their neighborhood, city, and state.

One last observation about this matter of Church Growth and renewal. Snyder has said, "Examples of growth have come about not from the discovery and conscious application of Church Growth principles and strategies but from renewal movements." Again, he is on the right side of being right. The renewal movements of the Wesleys in the first Great Awakening were successful and expanded worldwide because they gave attention to methods—that is, Church Growth methods—resulting in their being called Methodists.[26]

Church Growth has not ignored the things that Snyder has brought to our attention. Peter Wagner has discussed modality versus sodality in Church Growth. *Sodality* comes from a word implying "brotherhood," "community," or "an organized society." Throughout the growth of the Roman Catholic Church, there have always been sodality organizations that call for reform, renewal, or revival, because the Roman Catholic Church had become corrupt or had lost its purpose. Dominicans, Franciscans,

Jesuits, and many other indigenous orders with narrow purposes attempted to bring renewal to the Roman Catholic Church. This is part of what Howard Snyder is describing. Modality is the larger church itself—the Roman Catholic Church that was tied to legacy, usual procedure, structure, predictability of action, or the political state. While Snyder does not use these terms in his text, they are mentioned in note 2 under the typology of Ralph Winter.

When Howard Snyder affiliates with the healthy-church movement, he indicates there are many alien factors that could be introduced into the body of Christ that will undermine health and scriptural wholeness. He is correct. He could have mentioned problems influencing American church health and growth, for example, sensationalism, nepotism, pastors' egos, worldly music attempting to produce spirituality, Madison Avenue–type techniques to produce growth, and unabashed marketing evangelism. I embrace the healthy-church movements of Rick Warren, Christian A. Schwarz, and Howard Snyder, because healthy churches grow. However, let us make sure that we do not become unbalanced and emphasize only the spiritual factors to the neglect of natural factors. Snyder has said, "The key issue is not *growth* but *health*." A balanced statement might be, "The key issue is both growth and health." Snyder makes a great appeal for an often-forgotten element in Church Growth: spiritual growth. However, let us not swing from one extreme to the other and forget the role of science in determining the biblical principles of Church Growth, because a balance of internal and external growth can cause churches to grow and carry out the Great Commission.

A GOSPEL AND OUR CULTURE RESPONSE
Craig Van Gelder

I find many things in this chapter helpful in furthering a constructive discussion about church growth. The author's own journey, which is summarized in a helpful way, makes it clear that he has spent many years thinking carefully and reflectively about the issues associated with church growth. However, his focus being on a renewal perspective of church growth in relation to this discussion represents a fundamental dilemma for interacting with some of the key assertions developed within the author's argument.

Clearly the author wants to place this discussion about church growth into a larger framework. This framework is summarized in his conclusion, where he makes the following point: "From a renewal perspective, the primary concern about church growth is that growth be understood in terms of the broader vision of God's kingdom and mission and that it be compatible with the nature of the church as the spiritual-social body of Christ." The primary intent appears to be a desire on the part of the author to think both missiologically, focusing on God's kingdom and mission, and ecclesiologically, focusing on the spiritual-social body of Christ. I find myself resonating with these perspectives as larger frameworks for thinking about church growth. In fact, I would suggest the author would be served in strengthening his argument to bring these two points into conversation with one another, in thinking about church growth from the perspective of a missiological ecclesiology. The author makes some moves in this direction within this chapter, but this larger framework is secondary to the author's primary lens of utilizing church renewal as a way of reflecting on church growth.

At this point, I encounter some difficulty with the author's presentation. The larger question is left somewhat unexplored, although its linkages are suggested on numerous occasions. The larger question is the relationship of church renewal to the *missio Dei*—the mission of the triune God in all creation and the formation of a people of God to participate fully in this mission. Clearly the author, as so amply illustrated through the recounting of his own journey and as also demonstrated in some of his books, has come to see the "vision of God's kingdom and mission" as a larger missiological framework for thinking about the church and the world. But this does not appear to as fully inform his understanding of church renewal as he would like to suggest, which in turn has implications for his critique of Church Growth from a renewal perspective.

The author frames his critique of Church Growth from a renewal perspective in three ways: (1) through offering five theses on church renewal and growth, (2) through summarizing his personal journey, and (3) by presenting a renewal strategy for church growth. In relation to the first of his five theses, I would agree with the importance of the Bible being authoritative concerning the church's life and growth. But I think the author would be served by bringing his view of the Holy Spirit into a deeper conversation with his view of God's self-disclosure within and through Scripture. The Spirit uses the Word to shape and form a community of God's people. Through addressing such an interrelationship, the dynamic character of the life and ministry of the church in relation to the mission of God can better be established and more fully understood. I would, however, concur with the author's point that Scripture has often been used in superficial ways within the Church Growth literature.

The second and fifth theses appear to complement each other. They are about the theme of the renewal of the church, both in the biblical story and throughout history. The author's point is that it is God's desire not only to plant, grow, and perfect the church but also to continue to renew it and that God has been at work doing this throughout the ages. While granting the importance of the biblical theme of renewal, it really seems to me that the primary point here, once again, is more about the author's understanding of the ministry of the Spirit than about the specific dynamics of church life per se. The point seems to be that God's Spirit brings life, both in creation and in re-creation. The ministry of the Spirit within Scripture, and the work of the Spirit in the life of the church throughout history are worth exploring in depth, but this seems to me to be a larger discussion of the person and work of the Spirit. Trying to frame it within a discussion of church renewal tends to end up turning a subtext into the text.

The third thesis stresses the importance of thinking about the growth of the church in holistic terms, while the fourth relates growth to the nature of the church. Here we are at the heart of the issues associated with ecclesiology. What is the church? The emphasis on the spiritual-social reality of the church is well placed and represents one of the keys to the author's effective critique of some of the deficiencies of Church Growth. But it seems to me the argument could be strengthened here by more thorough attention to the rich range of biblical metaphors used to describe the church. While a number of metaphors are listed as illustrative, the author has a tendency to use the body of Christ as the primary image or referent in other places in his chapter. In addition, the use of Schwarz to reference the point about the organic, biotic, growing nature of the church, while helpful on one level, fails to capture the deeper reality of the creation of the church by the Spirit. While coming close, the author fails to make the obvious point that the church as a spiritual-social community is missional by its very nature and therefore by its very nature cannot but experience holistic growth when the Spirit's presence is sought and relied on.

The final section of "A Renewal Strategy for Church Growth" is interesting. The author shifts the discussion from a church growth strategy to a church renewal strategy. The goal, as stated by the author, is "to build healthy, vital congregations that are marked by wholehearted love for God, warmhearted love for all people, and a passion for God's kingdom purposes." The ten principles that the author provides shape a renewal strategy for achieving this. While I find these principles instructive and agree with them relative to their usefulness in thinking about ministry in and through the church, a fundamental disconnect seems to be at work here. While the author wants to shape the discussion in terms of "the broader vision of God's kingdom and mission," this section ends up being more ecclesial-centered than kingdom-centered.

This is where the author's confessed missiology would serve better as the basis for framing his stated ecclesiology, rather than having it serve more as a helpful referent point. His principles 8 and 10 come closest to this. What if the whole discussion were framed within these two principles as the larger eschatological reality? What if the kingdom of God, the redemptive reign of God in Christ, framed our understanding of the church instead of the church "discover[ing] its own identity as body of Christ and servant of God's reign," where the "church catch[es] a kingdom vision"? If this were the case, then church renewal would be reframed within the mission of the triune God in all of creation and the church's participation within this mission, and we would find church renewal, as well as the emphasis on church growth, to be more helpfully reframed with our comprehending the deeper mystery of God's creation through the Spirit of the spiritual-social reality we know as the church.

Chapter 5 Notes: Renewal View

[1]*The Doctrines and Discipline of the Methodist Episcopal Church, 1856,* Article 5, "The Sufficiency of the Holy Scriptures for Salvation," (New York: Carlton and Porter, 1856), 16.

[2]There are large issues here of eschatology, history, pneumatology, and ecclesiology that are beyond the scope of this essay—for example, the ways Jonathan Edwards and Charles Finney understood revival within a larger theological and eschatological framework. For an overview, see Howard A. Snyder, *Signs of the Spirit: How God Reshapes the Church* (Grand Rapids: Zondervan, 1989; Eugene, OR: Wipf and Stock, 1997), where I summarize seven "interpretive frameworks" on church renewal and renewal movements: *ecclesiola in ecclesia,* sect/church typologies, believers' church approaches, revivalism theories, revitalization movements (an anthropological approach), the modality/sodality typology of Ralph Winter, and the catholic/anabaptist typology articulated by Michael Novak and others.

[3]Consider the implications of Revelation 2–3 in this regard.

[4]This is elaborated further in Howard A. Snyder with Daniel V. Runyon, "The Church: A Complex Organism," chap. 2 in *Decoding the Church: Mapping the DNA of Christ's Body* (Grand Rapids: Baker, 2002).

[5]Christian A. Schwarz, *Natural Church Development: A Guide to Eight Essential Qualities of Healthy Churches,* trans. Lynn McAdam, Lois Wollin, and Martin Wollin (Carol Stream, IL: ChurchSmart Resources, 1996).

[6]W. A. Visser 't Hooft, *The Renewal of the Church* (London: SCM, 1956), 68.

[7]See, for example, the work of J. Edwin Orr.

[8]A number of examples of these characteristics and related renewal movement dynamics are found in Snyder, *Signs of the Spirit.*

[9]See Snyder with Runyon, *Decoding the Church,* 80–82.

[10]Lyn Cryderman gives an engaging account of growing up in the same church and community, just a little later, in his book *Glory Land: A Memoir of a Lifetime in Church* (Grand Rapids: Zondervan, 1999), republished as *No Swimming on Sunday* (Grand Rapids: Zondervan, 2001).

[11]Described as a case study in Howard A. Snyder, "Pastoral Leadership and the Priesthood of All Believers," in *Servants of the Word: Ministry in the Believers' Church,* ed. David Eller (Elgin, IL: Brethren, 1990), 101–17.

[12]A member of our pastoral leadership team later wrote an account of some aspects of our church's experience. See Craig Scandrett-Leatherman, "Ritual and Resistance: Communal Connectivity in a Church Retreat," *Missiology* 27, no. 3 (July 1999): 311–31.

[13]Philip Jenkins, *The Next Christendom: The Coming of Global Christianity* (New York: Oxford University Press, 2002), 220.

[14]For instance, George G. Hunter III documents the ways the remarkable eighteenth-century evangelical revival in England embodied vital Church Growth principles, in Hunter, *To Spread the Power: Church Growth in the Wesleyan Spirit* (Nashville: Abingdon, 1987).

[15]Rodney Stark, *The Rise of Christianity: A Sociologist Reconsiders History* (Princeton, NJ: Princeton University Press, 1996).

[16]The growing body of literature on social movement theory may prove to be very important for Church Growth studies over the next decades. In addition to the work of Rodney Stark, for a preliminary study, see Gregory Leffel, "Churches in the Mode of Mission: Toward a Missional Model of the Church," chap. 5 in *Global Good News: Mission in a New Context*, ed. Howard A. Snyder (Nashville: Abingdon, 2001), and also Leffel's 2004 Ph.D. dissertation, "Faith Seeking Action: Missio-Ecclesiology, Social Movements, and the Church as a Movement of the People of God" (Asbury Theological Seminary).

[17]See in particular my *Radical Renewal: The Problem of Wineskins Today* (Houston: Touch, 1996), chap. 10, where a model based on these three aspects of church vitality is elaborated.

[18]Key passages that yield insights for renewed leadership today are Acts 6:1–4; 20:28; 1 Corinthians 12:1–28; Ephesians 4:7–16; 1 Timothy 3:1–13; 2 Timothy 2:2; Titus 1:5–9; Hebrews 13:17; James 5:13–13; and 1 Peter 5:1–3.

[19]These ten points are elaborated more fully in Snyder, *Signs of the Spirit*, 300–311.

[20]Orlando E. Costas, *Christ Outside the Gate: Mission Beyond Christendom* (Maryknoll, NY: Orbis, 1982), 44–54.

[21]Kenneth Scott Latourette, *A History of Christianity* (New York: Harper, 1953); Latourette, *A History of the Expansion of Christianity* (Grand Rapids: Zondervan, 1970).

[22]Stephen Neill, *A History of Christian Missions* (New York: Penguin, 1964).

[23]Neil T. Anderson and Elmer L. Towns, *Rivers of Revival* (Ventura, CA: Regal, 1997).

[24]Elmer L. Towns and Douglas Porter, *The Ten Greatest Revivals Ever* (Ann Arbor: Servant, 2000). Members of the task force were Bill Bright, Gerald Brooks, David Yonggi Cho, Robert Coleman, James O. Davis, Lewis Drummond, Dale Galloway, Eddie Gibbs, Jack Hayford, Charles Kelly, D. James Kennedy, Ron Phillips, Alvin Reid, Chuck Smith, Tommy Tenney, C. Peter Wagner, and Steve Wingfield.

[25]Ibid., 18–21. The Revival of 1904, the Great Awakening (1727–50), the second Great Awakening (1780–1810), the General Awakening (1830–40), the Layman's Prayer Revival (1857–61), the World War II Revival (1935–50), the Baby Boomer Revival (1965–71), the Pre-Reformation Revivals (1300–1500), the Protestant Reformation (1517), and Pentecost, the beginning of revival (A.D. 30).

[26]In the book *The Ten Greatest Revivals Ever*, the methods that were tied to each great revival were noted, along with observations of the sociological, spiritual, and political results that came from that revival.

Chapter Six

PASTORAL REFLECTIONS

REFLECTION 1
David C. Fisher

I wish this book had been available twenty-five years ago. I needed help back then thinking through the confusing maze of issues raised by the Church Growth movement and my own pastoral experience.

During my first year as a pastor, my congregation experienced a spontaneous movement of God's Spirit. It was precisely what Howard Snyder describes as "renewal." Lives changed, people were converted, and our church grew dramatically. An entire small town felt the impact of the gospel.

I experienced "church growth" first hand. And I knew from the start that I was neither the source nor the power of this renewal. Something far beyond myself or anyone else was at work.

Ironically, perhaps, I had just graduated from Trinity Evangelical School, where Elmer Towns was teaching at the time. I took two courses from him. He had just published *The Ten Largest Sunday Schools and What Makes Them Grow*. I recall him commending a cadre of Bible Baptist pastors whose vision was, as Towns put it, to "build a great church in this city."

I was vaguely suspicious of that early form of Church Growth but was unsure why. Now I think I understand. It was the sheer pragmatism and methodological certainty so aptly critiqued in this book by Craig Van Gelder, Gailyn Van Rheenen, and Howard Snyder. I especially appreciated Gailyn Van Rheenen's critique. He points out the anthropological base of Church Growth theory. That is, it seems to me, part of a larger and ominous trend among evangelicals toward a sociological base for most pastoral theology. The practice of ministry has become the theology of ministry. What works is what is true. The Bible becomes a source book used to find texts that support the methodology. Several authors in this book point out this "deductive" tendency in the Church Growth movement.

Moreover, at the level of pastoral ministry, where any practical theology or methodology is worked out, most of the conversations I hear are seldom about the expansion of the kingdom of God, evangelism, or renewal. Rather, the focus seems to be on how big someone's church happens to be. In both lay gatherings and clergy meetings, one of the first questions I am asked is, "How large is your church?" And, if my observation is correct, most church growth is not conversion to Christian faith but people moving from one church to another. Bigger is assumed to be better, so focus is placed on quantity, regardless of quality— biblical fidelity.

Years ago I observed two friends and colleagues in pastoral ministry sharing their church growth charts with each other. Their joy seemed to be in the numbers on the chart, not in the souls placed in their care, nor in the changed lives. Growth itself seemed to excite them. That seemed to me a wrongheaded vision of the church. Craig Van Gelder's and Howard Snyder's assertions that a proper ecclesiology needs to precede pastoral methodology would have helped me put words to my questions. I am quite sure a well-thought-out doctrine of the church clarifies the way pastors lead.

I am now thirty-plus years into my pastoral ministry in churches large and small. My reaction to this book naturally reflects the way I read it. I plan to keep the book at my side as I continue this wonderful journey leading Christ's church.

Craig Van Gelder's chapter resonated with my pastoral experience and my understanding of the role of the church. I have been deeply influenced by Lesslie Newbigin's work, though I was unaware of the Gospel and Our Culture movement. I do not recall exactly how I came to my own ecclesiology and pastoral theology back in the 1970s. I do know it was a struggle to think through these issues while leading a large and growing congregation.

I also know that it seemed to me then, and now, that the kind of theology and methodology represented by some Church Growth writers was superficial at best and dangerous at worst.

After all, if church growth can be engineered and managed by me, at the end of the day, how do I know if it is God's work or mine?

Van Gelder's work and the larger Gospel and Our Culture work would have been a wonderful resource to help me negotiate through the many mission and ministry issues I confronted early on in my ministry. I thank God that seminary education, at least in some seminaries, now includes a strong and biblical theology of mission and the church. I do not recall that conversation in my seminary years. Ecclesiology then focused on polity, pastoral theology, and the duties of a pastor. The mission was off in a corner of the curriculum, in a short conversation about foreign missions.

But the best chapter in the book for me, a working pastor, was Howard Snyder's. I, too, experienced a God-sent renewal early in my ministry. I admit full pews and growing crowds make me feel good. But in my better moments, I am not satisfied with numerical church growth. It is not, as Snyder points out, a properly biblical goal. Churches can get bigger without getting any spiritual improvement. I have come to believe that numerical growth without powerful personal and corporate renewal accompanying it is vanity.

Van Gelder's chapter spoke powerfully to my understanding of church and mission; Synder made my heart sing. His longing for the church is mine.

As I write this response, the pastoral staff of the congregation I pastor is in long and difficult conversation about the health of our congregation. And we are trying to think about our health independently of any numerical growth payoff. In fact, we wonder if our congregation might be healthier with fewer people. We are talking about renewal and what that might cost us.

Would we be a healthier congregation if we were half our size? When people leave the church, is it a good or bad sign? If we attract people to the church, is it a sign of health or capitulation to a market-driven understanding of the church? If our congregation shows signs of ill health or spiritual dysfunction, what are the intended and unintended consequences of pastoral intervention?

We do not know the answers to these questions, but this book will help us discern God's will for our leadership of our congregation.

REFLECTION 2
Douglas Webster

We can be grateful to Dr. McGavran and his legacy for making American Christianity more sensitive to effective and holistic ways of communicating the gospel. He emphasized the importance of focusing on receptive people groups, witnessing through relational networks (family and friends), and using indigenous forms (native languages and culture) to express the gospel. McGavran's cardinal tenets of communicational effectiveness, theological contextualization, and cultural sensitivity are biblically sound and rooted in the experience of the early church. He exposed the ineffectiveness of institutionalized missions, artificial methods of evangelism, dead orthodoxy, and ethnocentrism. McGavran combined a passion for Christ, a keen sense of culture, and a deep love for the lost, with practical insights into the nature of communications, anthropology, and psychology. Inherent in his approach to missions and church growth was the dynamic interaction between the gospel and culture and the tension between accommodating the gospel to culture and contextualizing the gospel for culture.

Now almost fifty years after the release of Dr. McGavran's *The Bridges of God*, his groundbreaking work on church growth, missiologists, pastors, and theologians continue to debate the application of McGavran's theories to church growth in the twenty-first century. Today's heirs to McGavran's Church Growth movement are stretched across a wide spectrum of views, ranging from highly pragmatic approaches to church growth to indepth theological approaches. The tension remains between accommodating the gospel and contextualizing the gospel.

Elmer Towns comes closest to representing what most people think of when they consider the legacy of McGavran's Church Growth movement. He sees Bill Hybels, Rick Warren, Jerry Falwell, John McArthur, and Robert Schuller as direct descendants of McGavran. They have learned how to "package" their ministry through the "science" of Church Growth in order to engage in effective evangelism. Towns sees McGavran's emphasis on receptivity as consistent with today's concern to identify a church's target audience, and his homogeneous principle as compatible with today's seeker-sensitive strategy. He characterizes the proponents of the Church Growth movement as Bible-based and data-driven. They combine "eternal theological principles with insights from contemporary social and behavioral sciences."

The question, however, is how far we should go in shaping the gospel message to fit the expectations and thought forms of the culture. When does the "seeker" become a "consumer" and begin demanding from the church an accommodation that distorts the gospel? In other words, when does Church Growth pragmatism hit the fan of a biblical theology of the church? The expenditure of emotional energy, material resources, and personal commitment to meet the high expectations of affluent, self-focused people diverts the church's resources from global missions and social justice ministry and effectively jeopardizes obedience to the Great Commission. Is it possible to sacrifice the substance of the gospel for the sake of a strategy that caters to consumer-oriented felt needs rather than true spiritual needs? The relationship between strategy and substance is an important one. Is theology driving Church Growth strategy, or are the needs of the consumer dictating strategy? Has the church lost out when worshipers can choose six worship styles (edgy alternative, acoustic, contemplative, exuberant praise and worship, traditional, classical)? Are we becoming a church of diverse tastes united around a video presentation of our favorite Christian speaker? By catering to self-interests and felt needs, the church is held hostage by the tyranny of desire. American culture has great material and relational expectations but little commitment to anything beyond immediate personal pleasure. Instead of showing people "a road right out of the self,"[1] the market-driven

---

[1] C. S. Lewis, *Surprised by Joy* (Collins: Fontana Books, 1972), 176.

church is providing spiritual strokes. It is not surprising that in a consumer-oriented culture, the deep-seated spiritual longing to worship God is scaled back to a Starbucks-enhanced spiritual experience.

Elmer Towns uses the word *Babel* to describe the present stage of the Church Growth movement because "each Church Growth authority" is doing their own thing in order to make "the eternal principles of Church Growth" work in their particular cultural niche. It seems everyone has to have his or her own unique vision for effective evangelism. So instead of seeing McGavran's original vision of church growth unraveling, Towns sees this Babel stage as "the logical and mature next step for Church Growth." He places McGavran on the side of the more pragmatic heirs of the Church Growth movement, but the next four views presented in this book challenge that conclusion and seek to develop an in-depth look at the relationship of theology and culture.

Craig Van Gelder's missiological approach advocates a deeper theological awareness of the nature of the church, culture, and the kingdom of God. The Gospel and Our Culture movement, influenced by Lesslie Newbigin, sees the church as a "sign" of the coming redemptive reign of Christ, when every dimension of life will be brought under his rule.

Charles Van Engen calls for a Church Growth theology "in the integral and holistic sense of Orlando Costas," with the ultimate goal of mission the coming kingdom of God. The *missio Dei* formation of Church Growth theology seeks to do theology "with Church Growth eyes." Van Engen contends that McGavran envisioned converted women and men becoming "a force for transforming the reality of their context, for social, economic, and political reconstruction." It is God's will for lost women and men to be saved by the grace of Jesus Christ and to be transformed by the Holy Spirit into responsible members of the body of Christ.

Gailyn Van Rheenen offers a "new model" to counter the anthropocentric focus and pragmatics of the Church Growth movement. He bases this new paradigm on the missional helix, which he describes as the spiraling interaction of theological reflection, cultural analysis, strategy formation, and historical perspective. Van Rheenen focuses on the epistemological roots of church growth. In place of a simple, pragmatic, humanistic approach, Van Rheenen argues that a true missionary "returns

time and time again to reflect theologically, culturally, historically, and strategically in order to develop ministry models
appropriate to the local context."

Howard Snyder lays out an agenda for multidimensional
church growth through church renewal. He draws on renewal
movements throughout the history of the church to describe a
multifaceted renewal strategy that strengthens, expands,
extends, and deepens the church for the sake of the kingdom of
God. His tenfold strategy for renewal consists of identifying
those who are alive in Christ, bypassing "dead or dysfunctional"
structures rather than wasting your time and energy trying to
change them, and seeking to nurture all people in Christ. Moreover, healthy church growth involves "God-centered worship;
caring, accountable community; and witness in the world." This
in turn means some form of small-group structure to facilitate
face-to-face community, every-member ministry, and shared
leadership. The congregation must discover "its own identity as
body of Christ and servant of God's reign," with a kingdom
vision that is reflected in its stewardship of time, money, gifts,
and energy.

What would Donald McGavran say to us today? Would he
agree with the more pragmatic proponents of Church Growth,
or would he advocate a missiological and theological corrective
to the fixation of popular success at the expensive of radical
Christian discipleship? It is one thing to understand cultural
trends and attitudes in order to discover meaningful starting
points for penetrating a culture with the gospel. It is quite
another thing to frame the gospel to fit the expectations, aspira-
tions, and dreams of the consumer.

REFLECTION 3
Roberta Hestenes

I first became aware of the term *"church growth"* in the late 1960s while serving in the 4,000-member University Presbyterian Church in Seattle, Washington. Early responses to the then new Church Growth movement tended toward the cynical, the critical, and the dismissive. Some gave positive reports, however, after they attended Church Growth conferences or seminars, read Church Growth books, and studied at Fuller Theological Seminary.

By the late 1970s, "church growth" had become a new way of thinking for me and for thousands of other pastors in the United States. Church Growth thinking provided a new set of tools to think through and plan for how the church effectively fulfills its calling to obey the Great Commission. Surprisingly, because it now seems so obvious, many benefits came simply from the emphases on data gathering and research, intentionality in reaching lost people, the importance of demographics and target populations, and staying focused on reaching new people with the gospel and helping them become Christ's disciples.

After I joined the Fuller faculty in 1974, I began to understand the more serious debates swirling around the Church Growth movement. In 1975–76, I began teaching a doctor of ministry course titled Building Christian Community through Small Groups, which was usually taken after students had completed the Church Growth course (which I had also completed). The lack of serious biblical foundations or sustained theological reflection in the Church Growth course gave me cause for concern. Research results were not very rigorous. Most of the Bible was ignored, and an adequate theology of the church and its calling seemed absent. It also appeared that cultural engagement to challenge the sins, evils, and failures of the culture was ignored, while common American cultural assumptions, like the importance of success, bigger is better, and the primacy of authoritarian male leadership went unexamined. None of this was ever intentional, but it happened.

Still, the enthusiasm, energy, insights, and tools directed toward the goal of outreach and growth were helpful to church growth students. One day, for example, a young Korean pastor visited my Fuller office. He introduced himself as the pastor of a tiny fifty-member Methodist congregation. He had prayed and fasted for forty days, served his people for a year with no salary, and now was at Fuller to learn everything he could about church growth. After two years of study and prayer, he went back to Seoul and, with God's help, grew the largest Methodist church in the world, with 60,000-plus members. Thousands of positive stories, small and large, could be told.

My concerns grew over the years, however, as I listened to what many pastors were taking away from their studies and their efforts. From my standpoint, this pragmatic orientation often was shown in an overreliance on human techniques, a weak theology of the church, a failure to grasp the deeper forces at work within American culture, an absence of an understanding of the kingdom of God, and a trivialization in understanding repentance, conversion, and costly discipleship. Much of this cannot be laid solely, or even primarily, at the feet of the Church Growth movement. There are numerous causes, including the cultural changes which were impacting American congregational life. Still, numerical growth is not God's only goal for the church, and gradually the language has shifted from "growth" to "health." This is both a gain and a loss; a gain if "health" is described holistically in biblical terms; a loss if outreach is deemphasized and new people are not sought and won to Christ and his mission. The original definition of "making disciples" used in the Church Growth movement was definitely deficient in that its end point appeared to emphasize incorporation into a local church rather than incorporation into fullness of life as a committed disciple of Jesus Christ, becoming like Christ, and doing his will in the power of the Spirit. However, some critics of Church Growth theory and practice (outside of this volume) would be more credible if they had persuasive alternatives to offer. It is still true that God works to seek and save the lost and uses human beings in that effort.

Whatever the intentions of the teachers and writers, many, if not most, working pastors are pragmatists looking for answers and solutions to meet the present needs of their churches. They need help in thinking theologically and biblically as they consider and adopt methodologies appropriate to biblical goals and their specific contexts. Scholars and writers now are dealing in much more depth with these important issues, including in the present volume, which should be very helpful to future generations of pastors and missiologists.

Overall, however, I believe the contributions of the Church Growth movement, past and present, far outweigh its shortcomings. God has used it for much good and continues to use it today, although in less visible and more diverse ways. An inward-turned, self-absorbed American church still needs to hear the call to go out into the world with the word, works, signs, and power of the gospel to bring people to Christ and to lifelong discipleship as part of a committed community of Christians.

AFTERWORD

Gary L. McIntosh

The purpose of *Evaluating the Church Growth Movement* is to provide an overview of differing viewpoints on the influential Church Growth movement.

As I have edited this volume, the positions and responses of each contributor have stimulated a great deal of personal reflection. My hope is that the discussions within this book have also caused you, the reader, to give more thought to the growth of the church.

While this book is designed to allow the readers to come to their own conclusions regarding Church Growth, perhaps a few closing comments are in order. Clearly the authors agree on some basic issues and disagree on some very substantive ones.

Each of the contributors agrees that the Church Growth movement has been, and continues to be, extremely influential. No other movement in the last few decades has driven the agenda of the church and missions more than the Church Growth movement. Of course, some believe this influence is positive, while others see it as somewhat negative. But they all admit the Church Growth movement cannot be ignored.

There is also agreement that the missionary nature of God and his church results in an expectation that the church should grow. Whether this is expressed as "church growth" or "growth of the church," the very nature of God's kingdom assumes that it will expand.

Flowing from the missionary nature of the church is the agreement that the church (and churches) must focus on ministry rather than maintenance. The priority of the church is not itself, but the world. Christ died for the world, and as he is Head of the church, it is expected that the church will sacrificially give itself to the world also.

In addition, the contributors agree that the church needs to do research to remove the "fog" (McGavran's term) so that we may discover the facts of where the church is growing and declining, as well as why it is doing so. Thus, the social sciences are useful tools, when used wisely, to help us better understand and minister in God's world.

The contributors disagree on a great number of issues, but perhaps the major disagreement is about the mission of the church. Is the church's mission to proclaim the gospel of salvation to people and persuade them to become followers of Jesus Christ and responsible members of his church? Or is the church's mission to proclaim the gospel of the kingdom and form an eschatological community of faith to be a witness to the world? Or is the church's mission a combination of both? How one understands "mission" will determine to a great extent whether he or she accepts or rejects the Church Growth movement.

While all the contributors agree that the church should grow, they disagree about how much initiative believers should take to assist in such growth. Is it proper for church leaders to make bold, optimistic growth plans based on research? Or is it more appropriate for leaders to focus on a church's spiritual health, trusting that a healthy church will grow? Or perhaps a combination of both?

Similarly, there is disagreement as to the measurement of church growth. Are numbers an adequate assessment of church growth? Or are other measures more helpful, such as the church's assistance of the poor? In short, what makes a church healthy? Faithful? Biblical?

Finally, disagreement is apparent when it comes to an understanding of contextualization and culture. The basic question is how much can a church adapt contextually to its culture without accommodating to the culture? Where does a church draw the line between being "in" the world but not "of" it? To what extent should pragmatic decisions drive the agenda of the church as it seeks to communicate to people in the various cultures of the world? These are questions that create disagreement and misunderstanding about church growth.

Obviously, the few agreements and disagreements just mentioned do not cover the entire book, but these are themes that seem to keep rising to the surface in the overall discussion.

From my perspective, the Church Growth movement does need to reflect more intentionally on its theological, epistemological, and hermeneutical foundations. The fact that the proponents of Church Growth thought have primarily been practitioners, as opposed to theologians, no doubt has pushed the movement toward an emphasis on strategy rather than theology. Additionally, Donald McGavran did not want to develop a theology of Church Growth but instead hoped each theological tradition would develop its own. For the most part, this has left the Church Growth movement without a completely developed theological foundation. The Church Growth movement does need to be more theologically reflective. Perhaps this book will encourage the proponents of the Church Growth movement to be more theologically intentional in the future.

SELECTED BIBLIOGRAPHY

EFFECTIVE EVANGELISM VIEW

Evangelism and Church Growth-Reference Library. CD-ROM. Ventura, CA: Regal, 2000.

Gibbs, Eddie. *Quantum Changes in How We Do Ministry.* Downer's Grove, IL: InterVarsity Press, 2000.

McGavran, Donald A. *Understanding Church Growth.* Grand Rapids: Eerdmans, 1970.

McIntosh, Gary L. *Biblical Church Growth.* Grand Rapids: Baker, 2003.

Rainer, Thom S. *The Book of Church Growth: History, Theology, and Principles.* Nashville: Broadman and Holman, 1993.

Schwartz, Christian A., and Chrisoph Schalk. *Implementation Guide to Natural Church Development.* Carol Stream, IL: ChurchSmart Resources, 1998.

Stetzer, Ed. *Planting New Churches.* Nashville: Broadman and Holman, 2003.

Towns, Elmer L., C. Peter Wagner, and Thom S. Rainer. *The Everychurch Guide to Growth.* Nashville: Broadman and Holman, 1998.

Towns, Elmer L., and Warren Bird. *Into the Future: Turning Today's Church Trends into Tomorrow's Opportunities.* Grand Rapids: Baker, 2000.

Warren, Rick. *The Purpose Driven Church.* Grand Rapids: Zondervan, 1995.

GOSPEL AND OUR CULTURE VIEW

Bosch, David J. *Transforming Mission: Paradigm Shifts in Theology of Mission*. Maryknoll, NY: Orbis, 1991.

Guder, Darrell, ed. *Missional Church: A Vision for the Sending of the Church in North America*. Grand Rapids: Eerdmans, 1998.

_____. *The Continuing Conversion of the Church*. Grand Rapids: Eerdmans, 2000.

Hunsberger, George R., and Craig Van Gelder, eds. *The Church between Gospel and Cultures: The Emerging Mission in North America*. Grand Rapids: Eerdmans, 1996.

Newbigin, Lesslie. *The Open Secret: Sketches for a Missionary Theology*. Grand Rapids: Eerdmans, 1978.

_____. *The Gospel in a Pluralist Society*. Grand Rapids: Eerdmans, 1989.

Scherer, James A. *Gospel, Church and Kingdom: Comparative Studies in World Mission Theology*. Minneapolis: Augsburg, 1987.

Van Engen, Charles. *God's Missionary People: Rethinking the Purpose of the Local Church*. Grand Rapids: Baker, 1991.

Van Gelder, Craig. *Confident Witness—Changing World: Rediscovering the Gospel in North America*. Grand Rapids: Eerdmans, 1999.

_____. *The Essence of the Church: A Community Created by the Spirit*. Grand Rapids: Baker, 2000.

CENTRIST VIEW

Hoge, Dean, and David Roozen, eds. *Understanding Church Growth and Decline, 1950–1978*. New York: Pilgrim, 1979.

McGavran, Donald A. *The Bridges of God*. New York: Friendship; London: World Dominion, 1955.

_____. *Understanding Church Growth*. Grand Rapids: Eerdmans, 1970.

Peters, George. *A Theology of Church Growth*. Grand Rapids: Zondervan, 1981.

Van Engen, Charles. *The Growth of the True Church*. Amsterdam: Rodopi, 1996.

_____. *God's Missionary People: Rethinking the Purpose of the Local Church*. Grand Rapids: Baker, 1991.

_____. *Mission on the Way: Issues in Mission Theology.* Grand Rapids: Baker, 1996.

Wagner, C. Peter. *Your Church Can Be Healthy.* Nashville: Abingdon, 1979.

_____. *Your Church Can Grow.* Ventura, CA: Regal, 1984.

Woodberry, J. Dudley. *Reaching the Resistant: Barriers and Bridges for Mission.* Pasadena: William Carey Library, 1998.

REFORMIST VIEW

Abraham, William J. *The Logic of Evangelism.* Grand Rapids: Eerdmans, 1989.

Guder, Darrell L. "Evangelism and the Debate over Church Growth." *Interpretation* 47 (April 1994): 145–55.

_____. *Missional Church: A Vision for the Sending of the Church in North America.* Grand Rapids: Eerdmans, 1998.

Kirk, Andrew. *The Mission of Theology and Theology as Mission.* Harrisburg, PA: Trinity Press International, 1997.

McGavran, Donald A. *Understanding Church Growth.* Grand Rapids: Eerdmans, 1970.

Murray, Stuart. *Church Planting: Laying Foundations.* Scottsdale, PA: Herald, 2001.

Newbigin, Lesslie. *The Open Secret: An Introduction to the Theology of Mission.* Rev. ed. Grand Rapids: Eerdmans, 1995.

Taylor, William D. *Global Missiology for the Twenty-first Century: The Iguassu Dialogue.* Grand Rapids: Baker Academic, 2000.

Van Rheenen, Gailyn. *Missions: Biblical Foundations and Contemporary Strategies.* Grand Rapids: Zondervan, 1996.

_____. "From Theology to Practice: The Helix Metaphor," *Monthly Missiological Reflections,* no. 25 (2002), http://www.missiology.org/mmr/mmr25.htm.

_____. "The Missional Helix: Example of Church Planting," *Monthly Missiological Reflections,* no. 26 (2002), http://www.missiology.org/mmr/mmr26.htm.

RENEWAL VIEW

Cairns, Earle E. *An Endless Line of Splendor: Revivals and Their Leaders from the Great Awakening to the Present*. Wheaton, IL: Tyndale House, 1986.

Durnbaugh, Donald F. *The Believers' Church: The History and Character of Radical Protestantism*. New York: Macmillan, 1986.

Jenkins, Philip. *The Next Christendom: The Coming of Global Christianity*. New York: Oxford University Press, 2002.

Lovelace, Richard F. *Dynamics of Spiritual Life: An Evangelical Theology of Renewal*. Downers Grove, IL: InterVarsity Press, 1979.

McLoughlin, William G., Jr. *Revivals, Awakenings, and Reform*. Chicago: University of Chicago Press, 1978.

Orr, J. Edwin. *Campus Aflame: A History of Evangelical Awakenings in Collegiate Communities*. Wheaton, IL: International Awakenings, 1994.

Riss, Richard M. *A Survey of Twentieth-Century Revival Movements in North America*. Peabody, MA: Hendrickson, 1988.

Snyder, Howard A. *Signs of the Spirit: How God Reshapes the Church*. Grand Rapids: Zondervan, 1989; Eugene, OR: Wipf and Stock, 1997.

Stark, Rodney. *The Rise of Christianity: A Sociologist Reconsiders History*. Princeton, NJ: Princeton University Press, 1996.

Ward, W. R. *The Protestant Evangelical Awakening*. Cambridge: Cambridge University Press, 1992.

ABOUT THE CONTRIBUTORS

CONTRIBUTORS

David C. Fisher has served as a pastor for thirty-four years, most recently as senior pastor of the Colonial Church in Edina, Minnesota. He is an adjunct professor at Bethel Theological Seminary and is a frequent professor in the doctor of ministry programs in several theological schools focusing on cultural and ministry issues. David is the author of *The 21st Century Pastor* as well as numerous articles and published sermons.

Roberta Hestenes serves as an international minister with World Vision. The author of seven books and numerous articles, Roberta is well known in Church Growth circles for her groundbreaking work in the area of small group ministry. Most recently she served as senior pastor of the 2,000-member Solana Beach Presbyterian Church in Southern California. For ten years, she was president and professor of Christian Spirituality at Eastern University, near Philadelphia, Pennsylvania. Dr. Hestenes founded the Christian Formation and Discipleship program at Fuller Seminary and directed the program for twelve years.

Howard A. Snyder serves as professor of the History and Theology of Mission at Asbury Theological Seminary in Wilmore, Kentucky. Previously he taught at United Theological Seminary, Dayton, Ohio, and has pastored in Chicago and Detroit and served as a missionary with the Free Methodist Church in Brazil. He has been at Asbury Theological Seminary since 1996, where he teaches in the E. Stanley Jones School of World Mission and Evangelism. Howard has written a number of books, including *The Problem of Wineskins, The Community of the King,* and *The Radical Wesley.* His most recent books are *Decoding the Church: Mapping the DNA of Christ's Body* (with

Daniel Runyon) and *Global Good News: Mission in a New Context,* which he edited. Howard has spoken frequently at colleges, seminaries, and conferences, including the 1974 International Congress on World Evangelization in Lausanne, Switzerland, the 1991 Evangelism 2000 Conference in Hong Kong, and the Mission Korea 2000 Conference in Seoul. In 1993, Howard and his wife visited thirteen countries in Europe, Asia, Africa, and Latin America, studying the life and renewal of the church.

Elmer Towns is a college and seminary professor, an author of popular and scholarly works (the editor of two encyclopedias), a popular seminar lecturer, and the developer of over twenty resource packets for leadership education. He began teaching at Midwest Bible College, St. Louis, Missouri, and was not satisfied with his textbooks, so he began writing his own. He has published over seventy-five books, six of which are on the Christian Booksellers best-seller list; several of his books are accepted as college textbooks. He is also the 1995 recipient of the Christian Booksellers Association's coveted Gold Medallion Award for writing the Book of the Year, *The Names of the Holy Spirit.* He cofounded Liberty University with Jerry Falwell in 1971 and serves as the dean of the School of Religion as well as a vice president of the university.

Charles (Chuck) Van Engen is the Arthur F. Glasser Professor of Biblical Theology of Mission in the School of Intercultural Studies at Fuller Theological Seminary. His doctoral dissertation, done at the Free University of Amsterdam, was on the ecclesiology of the Church Growth movement and was titled "The Growth of the True Church." He is the author or editor of numerous books, including *God's Missionary People* and *Mission On the Way.* He has recently coauthored *Communicating God's Word in a Complex World* (with Dan Shaw) and *Announcing the Kingdom: The Story of God's Mission in the Bible* (with Arthur Glasser, Dean Gilliland, and Shawn Redford). From 1973 to 1985, Chuck was involved in Theological Education by Extension, for pastors in the National Presbyterian Church of Mexico.

Craig Van Gelder has served since 1998 as professor of Congregational Mission at Luther Seminary in St. Paul, Minnesota. He is an ordained minister in the Christian Reformed Church. His graduate work includes: Master of Divinity (1978) from Reformed Theological Seminary, Ph.D. in Mission (1982) from Southwestern Baptist Theological Seminary, and Ph.D. in

Administration in Urban Affairs (1985) from the University of Texas at Arlington. He is a member of the American Society of Missiology, the Gospel and Our Culture Network, the Society for the Scientific Study of Religion, and the Urban Affairs Association. Craig is the author of *The Essence of the Church: A Community Created by the Spirit* (2000); the editor of *Confident Witness—Changing World: Rediscovering the Gospel in North America* (1999); a contributing author to *Missional Church: A Vision for the Sending of the Church in North America* (1988); and the coeditor (with George Hunsberger) of *The Church between Gospel and Culture: The Emerging Mission in North America* (1996).

Gailyn Van Rheenen served as missionary to East Africa for fourteen years, taught missions and evangelism at Abilene Christian University for seventeen years, and is currently director of Missions Alive, an organization dedicated to training talented, motivated Christian leaders as evangelists and church planters in urban contexts. His books *Missions: Biblical Foundations and Contemporary Perspectives* (Zondervan, 1996), *Communicating Christ in Animistic Contexts* (William Carey Library, 1991), and *The Status of Missions: A Nationwide Survey of Churches of Christ* (ACU Press, 2002) are widely used by both students and practitioners of missions. His website (www.Missiology.org) provides "resources for missions education" for local church leaders, field missionaries, and teachers of missions. His passion in life is to be used by God to teach unbelievers, nurture them to Christian maturity, and equip them as Christian leaders. He views himself primarily as an evangelist and a church planter and secondarily as a scholar in missions equipping.

Douglas Webster has served as the senior pastor of the First Presbyterian Church of San Diego since 1993. He is an adjunct professor at Bethel Seminary in San Diego and at Tyndale Seminary in Toronto. He is the author of numerous publications, including *The Discipline of Surrender: Biblical Images of Discipleship* and *Soulcraft: How God Shapes Us through Relationships*. He and his wife, Virginia, are the parents of three children.

EDITORS

Gary L. McIntosh is professor of Christian Ministry and Leadership at Talbot School of Theology, Biola University, located in La Mirada, California. He served from 1983 to 1986 as Vice President of Consulting Services for Win Arn's influential Institute for American Church Growth. An internationally known author, speaker, and consultant, Gary has written extensively in the field of pastoral ministry and church growth; his books include *One Size Doesn't Fit All, Staff Your Church for Growth,* and *Biblical Church Growth.* As president of the Church Growth Network, a church consulting firm he founded in 1989 (www.churchgrowthnetwork.com), Dr. McIntosh has served over 500 churches in 55 denominations throughout the United States Canada, and Southeast Asia. He is the editor of the *Church Growth Network* newsletter and the *Journal of the American Society for Church Growth.*

Paul E. Engle, series editor for Counterpoints: Church Life, served for twenty-two years in pastoral ministry and has been an adjunct teacher in several seminaries, teaching homiletics and doctor of ministry classes. He is a graduate of Houghton College (B.A.), Wheaton Graduate School (M.Div.), and Westminster Theological Seminary (D.Min.). Paul is the author of eight books, including *Baker's Wedding Handbook, Baker's Funeral Handbook,* and *Baker's Worship Handbook.* He serves as Associate Publisher for Editorial Development and as Executive Editor at Zondervan.

DISCUSSION QUESTIONS

CHAPTER 1: EFFECTIVE EVANGELISM VIEW

1. How do you define "church growth"? In what ways does your definition match those presented in this chapter? In what ways does it differ?
2. Describe the historical development of the Church Growth movement. What insights did you gain from this overview of the movement's beginnings?
3. Make a short list of the core concepts of the Church Growth movement as described in this chapter. Which ones do you resonate with? Which ones cause you concern? Why?
4. What do you see as the future of the Church Growth movement? Do you agree or disagree with the author's perspective?
5. As described in this chapter, what biblical insights does the Church Growth movement highlight? What biblical perspectives does it miss?

CHAPTER 2: GOSPEL AND OUR CULTURE VIEW

1. In your opinion, why have the Church Growth movement and church growth continued to be so popular among many congregations and church leaders in the United States?
2. What aspects of how the Church Growth movement came into existence provide insight into the strengths and weaknesses of this movement today? How are these aspects manifest in the current expressions of Church Growth?
3. In what ways might a biblical case be made that God wants the church to grow? How is this case similar to

and different from the emphases found in the Church Growth movement and church growth?

4. Compare and contrast the mission theology of the Church Growth movement with that of the Gospel and Our Culture movement. How are they similar? How are they different? What implications do these differences have for the church's mission?

5. Compare and contrast the ecclesiology of the Church Growth movement with that of the Gospel and Our Culture movement. How are they similar? How are they different? What implications do these differences have for the church's mission?

CHAPTER 3: CENTRIST VIEW

1. Given the nature of the covenanting, loving, self revealing God of the Bible, should church growth be an option or an expectation? Does God want his church to grow? Why or why not?

2. In what ways does the sinful nature of people contribute to their resistance and receptivity toward God? How might one's cultural context aid or impede his or her openness toward God?

3. What is the mission of Christ? How has Christ's mission been transferred to his disciples? What implications does this have for the growth of the church?

4. Compare and contrast the need for strategy and the need for trusting the Holy Spirit in growing the church. How can these two aspects be balanced for faithful ministry?

5. How important is it that Christ's disciples become responsible members of a local church? In what ways does involvement in a community of faith relate to becoming a transforming presence in a hurting world?

CHAPTER 4: REFORMIST VIEW

1. In what ways does Church Growth reflect the thinking of the modern age in which it was birthed?

2. This chapter says: "How we consciously and unconsciously prioritize and systematize our sources of

knowledge at the most basic level will ultimately form our Christian message and the nature of missions and evangelism." What epistemological sources are employed in Church Growth research? Which sources tend to be neglected? How does this influence missions and evangelism?

3. How are theology and ministry frequently segmented by a pragmatic Church Growth approach?

4. Describe the four ministry and research components of the missional helix. How does this model provide a corrective to Church Growth thinking?

5. According to this chapter, why should conducting a survey to analyze a church or a culture or to determine felt needs *not* be the first step in developing the practice of missions?

CHAPTER 5: RENEWAL VIEW

1. Compare the Renewal view with the Church Growth perspective. How are these two perspectives compatible? What are the major differences?

2. Reflect back on the five theses of church renewal described in this chapter. Which ones do you agree with? On which points do you disagree? Why?

3. Are any of the eight characteristics of renewal movements found in the Church Growth movement? If so, which ones? Which ones appear to be neglected by the Church Growth movement?

4. The author's personal journal clearly affected his views of church renewal. Thinking back on your own journey, how has it affected your view of church growth and church renewal?

5. How do you think a Church Growth strategy would differ from the church renewal strategy presented by the author? What underlying suppositions are responsible for these differences?

INDEX

Page numbers followed by *f* refer to figures. Page numbers followed by *t* refer to tables.

We want to hear from you. Please send your comments about this book to us in care of zreview@zondervan.com. Thank you.

ZONDERVAN.com/
AUTHORTRACKER
follow your favorite authors